This book gets one of the most important aspects of mission right—God's revelation of Godself comes to all humans through the gift of language. Using numerous stories and examples, it offers the kind of theology we need in mission today as we seek to discern how to share the good news of Jesus Christ in the twenty-first century world. It will persuade you that Jesus meets people in their own languages. We call him Jesus even though his mother named him Yehoshua because local languages matter. The missionary work that promoted colonial languages and trampled upon other peoples' cultures ought to be a thing of the past. This book will show you the way forward. It comes with my utmost recommendation.

Dr Harvey Kwiyani
Executive Director, Missio Africanus
Director, The Centre for Global Witness and Human Migration

Language is central to the identity of God, the flourishing of humanity, and the nature of the church. As a biblical theologian with deep interests in both linguistics and the mission of God, I have found this collection of diverse but also unified essays to be both enlightening and energizing. Biblically, theologically, linguistically, and missionally perceptive, *Language in the Mission of God* is much needed and deserves a wide readership.

Michael J. Gorman
Raymond E. Brown Professor of Biblical and Theological Studies, St. Mary's Seminary & University, Baltimore, Maryland, USA

On the Day of Pentecost those from every nation under heaven gathered in the streets of Jerusalem heard the wondrous works of God declared in their own languages and went on from there to resound the mighty divine deeds to the ends of the earth. *Language in the Mission of God* lifts up the various linguistic facets of the missiological enterprise—theoretical, biblical, practical, etc.—to empower contemporary Christian witness through many tongues, signs (for Deaf communities and beyond), and communicative speech acts for many peoples, ethnicities, cultures, and nations.

Amos Yong
Fuller Theological Seminary, California, USA

What is the role of language in all that God is doing? This book purposes not only to understand, but also to clarify the theological and missiological role of language. Its merit lies in the contributors' capacity to disclose God's mechanisms in dealing with human beings. The book reveals human beings' struggles to fully capture and express God's holy will in their broken situation. I recommend this book to any Christian committed to participate in God's mission in this multicultural world. Theologians, theological educators, and church leaders will find this book a longtime awaited tool for their academic and ministerial engagements.

Fohle Lygunda li-M (*DMin, PhD*)
Theology & Network Engagement (TNE) Manager for Africa
TEARFUND Global Influencing and Programmes Group (GIPG)

Language in the Mission of God is a powerful and timely exploration of language as a central tool in advancing God's mission across diverse cultures and communities. With voices from Africa, Asia, Europe, and the Americas, this book highlights how language shapes personal and cultural identity, underscoring the importance of honoring each community's unique linguistic heritage. With a well-deserved focus on the foundational work of SIL, this book provides both theological insight and practical guidance, making it an invaluable resource for anyone seeking to engage in ministry across linguistic boundaries and within today's vibrant tapestry of global Christianity.

Michael Pasquale
Professor of Linguistics, Director of Logos Center, Cornerstone University, Grand Rapids, Michigan, USA

Language in the Mission of God explores the often-overlooked role of languages in Christian mission, addressing a significant gap in understanding. The book celebrates the beauty and significance of all languages and affirms their unique contributions. Particularly striking is the portrayal of language as both a divine gift and a vital element of human identity, central to God's mission and the global Church.

Helpfully bridging theory and practice, this book encourages readers to see language not just as a tool but as a reflection of God's image and a means of expressing the gospel in every cultural and linguistic context. It is an excellent resource to dip into for specific topics or contexts. Notable discussions include the theological implications of language diversity, the concept of linguistic justice, and the role of Bible translation. I warmly commend *Language in the Mission of God* to all who seek to deepen their understanding of theology, mission, and the flourishing of diverse communities.

James Poole
Executive Director, Wycliffe Bible Translators UK & Ireland

For too long, churches have sidelined the ministry of translation of the word of God into different languages. *Language in the Mission of God* challenges and redirects many church leaders, missiologists, linguists, and Christians at large to the importance of Bible translation in knowing and worshiping God truly; discovering and living out true and redeemed identity; valuing and celebrating language diversity; and establishing a just and inclusive mosaic community of human beings created in the image of God.

No language deserves to die. God wants it expressed before His throne in concert with the multitude of other languages. Each language makes a unique theological contribution for the enrichment and greater understanding of the unfathomable creative triune God. Bible translation is indeed core to God's mission. It restores justice to minority languages and invites them to participate in the building of the Kingdom of God.

This book is truly the cure for the ignorance of the importance of Bible translation ministry. It will help you understand the multilayered efforts in translation work, and the far-reaching impact on life and theology. I recommend it most highly.

Rev. Dr. John Balema Laba
Theological Educator
AFRICA Executive Director for Le Pont International A Christian NGO working in Human Development.

This thoughtful starter on exploring language as a source of identity and meaning-making in a world of multiple literacies (oral, technology-based, and text-based) has been long in coming. Building on SIL's breadth of experience in translation and literacy, we now have a collection of experience-based insights on how language actually serves as carrier and receiver of the Word. Language shapes our way of looking at the world and shapes our mental stock-in-trade.

We in the Majority World, and especially Americanized Filipinos, are faced with a challenge to negotiate the residues of being shaped by an alien language, take advantage of its influence for our own functional uses, and at the same time plumb the depths of who we are as embedded in our own languages.

From a literacy perspective, the Protestant Reformation brought with it the rise of communication tools that tend to be largely cognitive, with an overemphasis on abstract concepts and linear thinking. Today, however, we are back to tribal drums and visual imagery. The more immediate emotional resonance of story-telling is likely to create a more receptive community. Yet, the advent of a new medium does not necessarily make the previous ones obsolete. Words, in so far as they owe their power to the Word, will endure.

Dr Melba Padilla Maggay
Founder and President, Institute for Studies in Asian Church and Culture, Quezon City, Philippines

With the significant participation of missiologists, linguists, and theologians, *Language in the Mission of God* calls readers to reconsider the sacral significance of language as the divine gift and powerful means for the further development of God's Kingdom.

The volume effectively discusses how language signifies the *Imago Dei* and plays an important role in the *Missio Dei*, arguing that language difference is not a curse but God's creation. The authors demonstrate that language is the bridge that links humans with the divine and individuals with each other. The rationale that every language serves a special purpose in magnifying the excellency of God counters the prevalent prejudice that establishes an informal linguistic hierarchy, thereby encouraging the Church to accept the multicultural reality of the world.

Numerous discussions, ranging from revisiting Babel to the real-world issues of language policy as a determinant of education, are detailed in each chapter and supported by research and real-life situations.

Language in the Mission of God is not just another book but a theological declaration and an action plan calling on the Church to listen, learn, and love in the world's languages. It is a valuable tool for anyone wishing to serve God through faithful proclamation and application of the word in our postmodern, global, multilingual, multicultural context.

Dr John P.A. Walada
OneHope Africa Vice-President; Professor at West Africa Advanced School of Theology (WAAST), Lome, Togo.

With *Language in the Mission of God*, SIL has published an important well-written, well-edited volume that has the potential to be paradigm-shifting for those who have never considered the questions it addresses. Each chapter reflects SIL's commitment to Scripture, Bible translation, language development, and mission. The contributors are diverse, representing African, Asian, Latin and Western voices, though many contributors also had roles in Europe (including Russia), and in Oceania.

The volume seeks to fill a lacuna in mission scholarship examining the role of language in Christian participation with God's mission. Considering linguistic diversity as a resource should challenge the paradigms by which many approach Christian mission. In the first chapter, readers are told that "as with culture, no one language is capable of capturing and expressing all that God is" and are reminded in chapter 14 that "language conveys culture". These are not new ideas to those familiar with World Christianity perspectives but they will be new to many.

Throughout the volume, the contributors demonstrate the thesis that each language has something to offer to Christian faith, practice, and theologizing. This book should be required reading for theological and biblical students across the globe. Short term mission teams, mission practitioners, and vocational Bible translators would also benefit by a slow and careful read of its chapters. We highly commend this book to all. Tolle, lege 'take up and read!'

Dr Joshua Robert Barron and Dr David Tarus
Association for Christian Theological Education in Africa (ACTEA)

Christianity is an incarnational religion. To save mankind, Jesus took a human form and came in human flesh. He was born in a human culture and spoke a human language. Just as God calls every person by his name, he wants to speak to every person in his or her own language, without interpretation. The Word of God has its most powerful impact when spoken in the language of the listeners. Language is a powerful vehicle of communication, not only between human beings, but also between human beings and God. God's mission is best accomplished in the language of the recipients of God's Word. This is what this book is all about: languages as God's media to reveal himself to men and women of every nation, tribe, language, and people.

Rev. Dr Douti L. Flindja
Academic Dean, West Africa Advanced School of Theology, Lome, Togo

Language in the Mission of God is a helpful addition to the scholarship surrounding the interplay between language, the Bible, and mission. Section 1 ("Foundations") provides an excellent theological basis for the importance of language for mission. But it is section 2 ("The Bible") that truly caught my attention. Applying speech-act theory to the Aramaic words of Jesus recorded in Mark's Gospel is fascinating; interpreting the giving of languages in the Tower of Babel story, not as punishment, but as blessing is convincing; and the chapter describing the languages of the Bible is very informative, as are the chapters focusing on Jesus' languages and Koine Greek. The articles that include translation case studies also make for very interesting reading. Section 3 ("Language and flourishing life today") concludes the book with some practical applications (including justice, poverty, and education) that anyone involved in mission should seriously consider.

Ben Chenoweth
Author of The Ephesus Scroll, The Corinth Letters, *and* The Rome Gospel

Language in the Mission of God

**SIL Global
Publications in Scripture Engagement 2**

Publications in Scripture Engagement is a peer-reviewed series published by SIL. Using the languages that people understand and identify with can both strengthen the use and impact of the Bible, and help strengthen the use of local languages. While most volumes are authored by members of SIL, suitable works by others occasionally form part of the series.

Editorial Staff
Susan McQuay, Editor-in-Chief
Eugene C. Burnham, Content Editor
Eleanor J. McAlpine, Proofreader

Production Staff
Priscilla Higby, Production Manager
Judy Benjamin, Compositor
Nathan Peck, Graphic Designer

The Tower of Babel by Lubov Arbachakova (cover image)
© Wycliffe Russia, 2025. Used by permission.

Language in the Mission of God

General Editor
Michael Greed

Volume Editors
Evan Falk
Dawn Kruger
Abou Sama
Charles Sanders

Foreword
Allen Yeh

SIL Global
Dallas, Texas

© 2025 by SIL Global
Library of Congress Control Number: 2025934695
ISBN: 978-1-55671-580-8 (pkb)
ISBN: 978-1-55671-581-5 (ePub)
ISSN: 2994-7286

All rights reserved

No part of this publication may be reproduced, stored in a retrieval system, or transmitted in any form or by any means—electronic, mechanical, photocopy, recording, or otherwise—without the express permission of SIL Global. However, short passages, generally understood to be within the limits of fair use, may be quoted without permission.

Data and materials collected by researchers in an era before documentation of permission was standardized may be included in this publication. SIL makes diligent efforts to identify and acknowledge sources and to obtain appropriate permissions wherever possible, acting in good faith and on the best information available at the time of publication.

Copies of this and other publications of SIL Global may be obtained through distributors such as Amazon, Barnes & Noble, other worldwide distributors and, for select volumes, publications.sil.org:

SIL Global Publishing Services
7500 W Camp Wisdom Road
Dallas, TX 75236-5629 USA
publications@sil.org

All Scripture quotations, unless otherwise indicated, are taken from *THE HOLY BIBLE, NEW INTERNATIONAL VERSION*®, *NIV*® Copyright © 1973, 1978, 1984, 2011 by Biblica, Inc.® Used by permission. All rights reserved worldwide.

Other Scripture translations cited in the text are:

English Standard Version (ESV)
The *ESV*® Bible (*The Holy Bible, English Standard Version*®). *ESV*® Text Edition: 2016. Copyright © 2001 by Crossway, a publishing ministry of Good News Publishers. The *ESV*® text has been reproduced in cooperation with and by permission of Good News Publishers. Unauthorized reproduction of this publication is prohibited. All rights reserved.

King James Version (KJV)
USA: The *King James Version* is in the public domain.
UK: Rights to *The Authorized (King James) Version* are vested in the Crown. Reproduced by permission of the Crown's patentee, Cambridge University Press.

New American Standard Bible (NASB)
New American Standard Bible®, Copyright © 1960, 1971, 1977, 1995, 2020 by The Lockman Foundation. All rights reserved.

New King James Version (NKJV)
New King James Version®. Copyright © 1982 by Thomas Nelson. Used by permission. All rights reserved.

New Living Translation (NLT)
Holy Bible, New Living Translation, copyright © 1996, 2004, 2015 by Tyndale House Foundation. Used by permission of Tyndale House Publishers, Inc., Carol Stream, Illinois 60188. All rights reserved.

New Revised Standard Version Updated Edition (*NRSVUE*)
New Revised Standard Version Updated Edition. Copyright © 2021 National Council of Churches of Christ in the United States of America. Used by permission. All rights reserved worldwide.

Contents

Tables	ix
Figures	ix
Contributors	xi
Preface	xvii
Foreword	xix
Introduction	1

Part One: Foundations	5
1 The Glory of God Through the Peoples and Languages of the Earth *Paul Frank*	7
2 The Mission of God and the Question of Language *Michael Greed*	11
3 Flourishing and Language *Michel Kenmogne*	25
4 Language: The Gift of God's Presence *Dawn Kruger*	41
5 Oral Language and the Mission of God *Abou Sama, with Bronwen Cleaver*	53
6 Sign Languages in the Mission of God *Stuart Thiessen*	65
7 Language and the Wider Mission Movement *Michael Greed and Evan Falk*	81

Part Two: The Bible	**91**
8 Speech Acts in the Bible *Michael Greed*	95
9 Language Diversity: Curse or Blessing? The Story of the Tower of Babel *Gary Simons*	107
10 Language Diversity: A Greater Glory *Based on a paper by Stephen Watters and Zachary Watters*	121
11 Language Use in the Bible *Michael Greed, with Paul Frank and Mamy Raharimanantsoa*	131
12 The Languages of Jesus *Michael Greed*	145
13 Koine Greek and the Mission of God *Eddie Arthur*	155
14 The Way from Babel: The Role of Language and Translation in Advancing God's Mission *Paul Kimbi*	167
15 The Continuum Between Language and the Mission of God *Sung Chan Kwon*	175
16 Mission as Translation: A Case Study in Contextualization *Michael Greed, with Kividi Kikama*	181
Part Three: Language and Flourishing Life Today	**193**
17 Language, Justice, and Mission *Evan Falk*	195
18 Language and Poverty *M. Paul Lewis*	211
19 Education and Language Policy Development as Components of Holistic Ministry in Multilingual Contexts *Catherine M. B. Young*	221
20 A Biblical Reflection on Language Shift and Identity *Maik Gibson*	233
21 Linguistic Hospitality in the Mission of God *Based on papers by Grace Chou, John Ommani Luchivia, and J. Stephen Quakenbush*	245
22 Conclusion: SIL, Language, and God's Mission *Michel Kenmogne*	259
Afterword: People on the Margins of Language	**273**
Scripture Index	**277**
Authors Cited	**277**

Tables

Table 6.1. Consequence versus Creation — 75
Table 10.1. Animal classification in Magar Kham — 126
Table 13.1. Languages of Palestine — 158
Table 22.1. God's mission in marginalized language communities — 266

Figures

Figure 16.1. Bible translation progress. — 183
Figure 17.1. Representation of De Swaan's "global language system". — 198
Figure 18.1. Duncan's five faces of poverty. — 213
Figure 18.2. Six faces of poverty. — 216
Figure 21.1. Sign in front of a private home in Grand Rapids, Michigan. — 251

Contributors

Edwin ("Eddie") Arthur has a PhD in Theology from Leeds Trinity University, UK (2019), awarded for his study into the way in which the practices and publicity of a sample of mission agencies overlapped. He currently works as a theologian-researcher for Wycliffe UK but has previously occupied a number of training and leadership roles in Africa and Europe.

Grace Chou has a DMin (Bible Translation track) from Gordon-Conwell Theological Seminary, USA (2020). She worked as a linguist and Bible translation consultant in Southeast Asia, 1996–2020. She is currently in a PhD program at Asbury Theological Seminary studying intercultural studies with a concentration on transformative development. She was born and raised in Taiwan.

Bronwen Cleaver has a PhD in Theology from the University of the Free State, South Africa (2024). She worked with SIL for seven years before becoming Director of the Institute for Bible Translation in Russia and a translation consultant. She is British by birth but has lived in Russia for twenty-four years and has a Russian passport. Her particular research interests are orality, oral Bible translation, and performance. She is married to Colin and has two adult children.

Evan Falk has an MA in Contemporary Missiology from the University of Gloucestershire, UK (2022), with a particular focus on justice as it is described in Scripture and its intersection with mission. Originally from Canada, Evan has worked with SIL since 2012, serving in numerous capacities and geographical contexts. Evan is currently Head of External Engagement for SIL Eurasia, and lives in Spain with his wife, Bonnie.

Paul Frank has a PhD in Linguistics from the University of Pennsylvania, USA (1985). He has two roles within SIL: Director of Professional Service Engagement and Associate Director for External Partnerships for the Language Solutions Portfolio. He has worked with SIL since 1982, including seventeen years in Colombia as a field linguist, linguistic specialist, Director for Language Affairs, and Country Director. Since returning to the U.S. in 2000, he has served as the SIL Vice President for Academic Affairs, the Executive Director of SIL subsidiary SIL LEAD, Inc., and the Bloom Program Director. He is a citizen and resident of the United States. He is married and has two sons and four grandchildren.

Maik Gibson has a PhD in Linguistics from the University of Reading, UK (1999). He has been working with SIL since 1998 and is currently SIL's Sociolinguistics Coordinator. His publications focus on the application of sociolinguistics to language development contexts (e.g., language naming, school language policy, language vitality, and texting). He is English, married to Rhiannon, a Welsh woman, and lives in the UK. They have three adult children.

Michael Greed has an MA in Global Leadership in Intercultural Contexts from the University of Gloucestershire, UK (2017), which included a firm missiological foundation. He has been working with SIL in Eurasia since 1991 and is Director of Communications for SIL Eurasia. British by birth and Finnish by choice, he has two passports and lives in Finland with his wife, Teija. They have two adult children.

Michel Kenmogne holds a PhD in African Linguistics from the University of Buea, Cameroon (2001). He served as Executive Director of SIL, 2016–2025. Previously, Michel was leader of Cameroon Association for Bible Translation and Literacy (CABTAL) and Wycliffe Global Alliance in Francophone Africa. His passion is to see language expand the bounds of God's kingdom. Michel and his wife, Laure Angèle, are from Cameroon and live in Germany. They have five children.

Kividi Kikama has an MA in Missiology from Fuller Seminary, USA (1981) and a PhD in Intercultural Studies from Trinity International University, USA (2000). After serving as a local church and district pastor in Congo, he served in a variety of mission-related roles in the U.S., including planting a church in Chicago to reach the French-speaking immigrants there. He is married to Lusikia Bonga Kikama; they have five adult children and nine grandchildren. Both he and his wife are from the Democratic Republic of Congo but are now naturalized U.S. citizens.

Paul K. Kimbi has an MA in Translation Studies from Africa International University, Kenya (2005) and a PhD in Biblical Studies/Practical Theology from the South Africa Theological Seminary, South Africa (2015). He served as a translation consultant for Cameroon Association for Bible Translation and Literacy (CABTAL) before joining Wycliffe Africa Area as Translation Coordinator. He presently serves as Consultant for Bible Translation Programs for the Wycliffe Global Alliance from Yaoundé, Cameroon, his home country.

Dawn Kruger has an MA in Contemporary Missiology from the University of Gloucestershire, UK (2019) and an MA in English Rhetoric and Composition from the University of Central Florida, USA (2005). Her greatest joy in working happens at the intersection of those two disciplines. Though now retired, she most recently has worked as a senior editor and communications consultant on the Executive Communications team for SIL; prior to that she was Director of Communication for the Asia and Pacific Area for Wycliffe Global Alliance. She and her husband, Nate, reside in Virginia, USA. They have four grown children and ten grandchildren.

Sung Chan Kwon has a PhD in Missiology from the Oxford Centre for Mission Studies (OCMS), UK (2019). His research, *A Missional Reading of the Fourth Gospel: A Gospel-Driven Theology of Discipleship* (Regnum Studies in Mission) (Fortress Press, 2023), approaches the reading of John's Gospel as a whole unit from a missional point of view. He has been working with SIL and Wycliffe since 1992 as a translator, as Director of Global Bible Translators (GBT), and, later, as Wycliffe Asia-Pacific Area Director. Kwon is currently Executive Director of Global Missionary Fellowship (GMF), an umbrella organization for eleven mission agencies in Korea including GBT. Korean by birth and residing there today, he and his wife, Ja-Hwa, have two adult children.

M. Paul Lewis has a PhD in Linguistics from Georgetown University, USA (1994). He worked with SIL for thirty-five years in Central America, in international roles in SIL, and as a sociolinguistic consultant in Asia. He retired at the end of 2016 after serving as general editor of the *Ethnologue* and Senior Consultant in Sociolinguistics. He continues to volunteer as a sociolinguistic consultant. Born in the U.S., he still claims some affiliation to the UK, the birthplace of his parents. Widowed, he has four adult children and five grandsons.

John Ommani Luchivia has an MA in Translation from the Africa International University, Kenya (1994) and a DMiss in Intercultural Studies from Fuller Theological Seminary, USA (2013). He has been working with SIL and related organizations since 1992 and is currently Global Scripture Access Director, while also serving as Scripture Engagement Consultant in Africa. He is Kenyan by birth and, together with his wife, Janet, has three children and one grandchild. They live in Nairobi, Kenya, where they serve as part of a pastoral team of a large, vibrant, multinational church.

J. Stephen Quakenbush holds a PhD in Sociolinguistics from Georgetown University, USA (1986). He has held various roles in SIL, as instructor, linguist, translator, and administrator in the Philippines, Asia, and at the Global level. He is currently director of SIL's Spiritual Life Team.

Mamy Raharimanantsoa has a PhD in Old Testament Studies from the University of Upsala, Sweden (2006). He worked for many years in the Republic of Congo as lecturer, academic dean and president of the Protestant University of Brazzaville. Today he is a Bible translation consultant for SIL in Congo and Madagascar. Born in Madagascar, he also has a Swedish passport and lives in Wales with his wife, Ruth.

Olivia Mamisoa Razafinjatoniary holds an MA in Translation Studies from the University of Antananarivo, Madagascar (2000), an MA in Bible Translation from the Nairobi Evangelical Graduate School of Theology, Kenya (2006), and a DMin in Bible Translation from Gordon-Conwell Theological Seminary, USA (2018). She joined SIL in 2008 and served as a translation consultant in SIL Eastern Congo Group until 2015. Then she joined SIL Southern Africa with her husband. She is currently the lead consultant for SIL's work in Madagascar. She and her husband are from Madagascar and are based in Cape Town, South Africa.

Abou Sama holds a PhD in Linguistics from the University of Lomé, Togo (2018), an MA in Anthropology from the University of Lomé (2008), and BA in Theology from the West African Advanced School of Theology (2019). He served as a linguistic researcher working on Gur languages in Togo-Benin with SIL. He has also held the positions of Administrative Director for SIL Togo-Benin and Executive Director of Wycliffe Togo. Since 2019, he has been a member of SIL's Board of Directors. He is married to Cécile Sama; they have three children and live and serve from Lomé, Togo.

Charles ("Chip") Sanders completed the work for a DMin in Global Christianity and Development from Gordon-Conwell Theological Seminary, USA (2020). His dissertation is entitled "Embracing the Winds of Change: Recommendations for SIL in Further Moving through Missional Paradigms."

Currently he serves as a Global Leadership Consultant with SIL. Chip and his wife, Kathy, are American citizens and have two adult children.

Gary F. Simons holds a PhD in Linguistics from Cornell University (1979). He served as Chief Research Officer for SIL and as Director of the Pike Center for Integrative Scholarship until 2024 and is the Executive Editor of *Ethnologue*. Early in his career with SIL he did fieldwork in the Solomon Islands and Papua New Guinea.

Stuart Thiessen holds an MA in Linguistics from the University of North Dakota, USA (2011). He, being deaf himself, is a Translation and Linguistics Consultant with DOOR International, an organization that is seeking to bring God's word to the Deaf people of the world. Previously, he served with SIL and Deaf Bible Society and, before that, as a pastor. He and his wife, Linda, live in Minnesota, USA. They have two married sons and two granddaughters.

Stephen Watters holds an MA in Linguistics from the University of Texas at Arlington, USA (1996) and a PhD in Linguistics from Rice University, USA (2018). He is SIL's Chief Research Officer and Director of the Pike Center for Integrative Scholarship. He holds an occasional adjunct teaching position at Baylor University and is a Visiting Scholar at the Institute for Studies of Religion, Baylor University. He has done fieldwork throughout South Asia and the Himalaya with interest in many aspects of sociolinguistics, linguistics, and translation.

Catherine M. B. Young holds an MEd in Literacy from the University of Sheffield, UK (2001) and a PhD in Education from the University of Bangor, Wales (2011), with research focused on multilingual education among non-dominant language communities. She is Director of Global Language and Development Services and a senior consultant in literacy and education with SIL. She has worked with SIL in Asia—primarily the Philippines and Bangladesh—since 1990 before beginning a global role in 2015. She lives in Gloucester, UK.

Preface

If one were looking for an organization dedicated to engaging with the issues surrounding language as its *raison-d'être*, anyone involved in mission, development, or government circles would undoubtedly point to SIL. Indeed, over the past century, SIL has stood up and advocated for peoples' languages, created fonts, scripts, and orthographies to enable them to be written, and promoted them as valued means to share knowledge and extend the bounds of God's kingdom.

We in SIL refer to ourselves as "Partners in Language Development". We research and regularly document the state of the world's languages in the *Ethnologue*. We describe languages and publish grammars, dictionaries, and instructional materials, furthering inclusive education. We also enable the translation of the Bible and other valuable resources that promote the flourishing of the speakers of those languages.

While SIL has been active on those many fronts for decades, the rationale behind our commitment to language has not been consistently made explicit. This book aims to provide a comprehensive view of language and its relationship to the multiple expressions of God's mission. It seeks to provide a response to the "why?" question that undergirds the variety of SIL's engagements that are all anchored in language and its many expressions in our world.

The authors in this book are all practitioners involved in various ways in harnessing the potential of language to advance the plans and purposes of God for humanity. As such, they are not just making theoretical explorations in what they write. Rather, their contributions stem from a practice centered on the rich experiences gained in their respective fields and deserve the attention of all who are involved in God's mission. We trust that anybody involved in building the Church, or in the demonstration of the good news (all aspects of showing compassion and mercy), will find in this book something that adds to the effectiveness of their work.

Underlying this book is the conviction that language can be used to destroy or to build, to divide or to unite, to curse or to bless, to undermine or to lift up. It invites the reader to choose a positive use of language that contributes to the advent of a world that is hospitable to all, where nobody is left behind or excluded because of the language or languages with which they most identify.

In a world that is being reshaped by the seismic shifts resulting from globalization, migration, and multilingualism, which endanger the viability of many minority languages, this book is an invitation for all practitioners in God's mission to join in reflection about how we continue to work together towards the advent of "a great multitude that no one could count, from every nation, tribe, people and language, standing before the throne and before the Lamb ... [crying] out in a loud voice:

> 'Salvation belongs to our God,
> who sits on the throne,
> and to the Lamb.' " (Rev 7:9b–10)

Dr Michel Kenmogne
Executive Director SIL Global (2016–2025)

Foreword

Language unfortunately is one of the most misunderstood aspects of Christianity, even though it is one of the most powerful tools Christians have at our disposal. Two major reasons for the misunderstanding are bad theology and culture wars.

The bad theology often stems from an erroneous hermeneutic of the story of Babel. This is clearly explicated in chapter 9 (among others) so I will not spend too much time on it. But essentially, the popular understanding of the scattering after the building of the Tower of Babel as a punishment by God for humans' arrogance and pride for presuming they can reach heaven does not hold up. A closer reading links Babel with the Cultural Mandate, which is the first commandment that God gives humans after they were created. God commanded people to spread over the entire earth but they disobeyed. Diversity of language was not a punishment, but rather God getting his people to comply with his command, similar to how God sending a big fish to swallow Jonah to go to Nineveh was not a punishment for Jonah but rather to redirect him toward obeying God's command. Humans doing wrong are not always met with the Lord's hand of rebuke but can also be met with course correction.

Culture wars also play a part, especially the Fundamentalist-Modernist Controversy of the early twentieth century. On one extreme, some eschewed culture to the point of seeing most of it as evil. Hearkening back to the Cultural Mandate, God actually *commands* humans to make culture to image him, but when we reject culture, it has the opposite effect in pitting culture against Christ. We are seeing a resurgence of this rejection of culture in politics, education, and the like, where departments of Intercultural Studies are being shut down. Linguistic and ethnic diversity risk being labeled as "woke," and the dominance of English has become the trend of the day, as if being Anglophone is the height of civilization. We forget that, at one point, people were burned at the stake for using English in Christianity. As the once-minority has become the now-majority, we need to not forget our roots, and treat the marginalized (chapters 17 and 18 insightfully unpack the relationship of language and justice) as we would have liked to be treated. This is nothing less than the Golden Rule. God states this in no uncertain terms: "When a foreigner resides among you in your land, do not mistreat them. The foreigner residing among you must be treated as your native-born. Love them as yourself, for you were foreigners in Egypt. I am the LORD your God." (Lev 19:33–34; cf. Exod 22:21; Deut 24:17–22).

If there is anything that the history of the transmission of the Bible has taught us, it is that the concept of a single or even holy language is not within God's plan. The New Testament—being written in koine 'common' Greek (see chapter 13)—was a shocking concept to first-century Jews who could not fathom the holy Scriptures being written in anything other than Hebrew. The Protestant Reformation, likewise, had pushback when people could not fathom the Scriptures to be translated into anything other than the "holy" ecclesiastical language of Latin (no matter that the "Vulgate" also meant 'common'). There were lethal consequences as people were persecuted and killed for translating the Bible into the vernacular. But God does not shy away from the common, the lowly, the everyday, as even our Messiah came in such a form. The late Yale missiologist Lamin Sanneh made this case in his landmark book *Translating the Message*, observing that the hallmark of Christianity is translation (as referenced in chapters 12 and 15 of this book). This is what separates Christianity from the other Abrahamic faiths, and it is in the very nature of the Incarnation: that God would translate himself into a human so that we may understand him better.

Translation and linguistic diversity are Christianity's secret weapon. It is what has caused Christianity to become the biggest religion on earth. It is the main tool of mission. It is what was seen at the founding of the Church at Pentecost in Acts 2:4–8, "All of them were filled with the Holy Spirit and began to speak in other tongues as the Spirit enabled them ... each one heard their own language being spoken." And it is what we will see in heaven, as Rev 7:9 describes, "After this I looked, and there before me was a great multitude that no one could count, from every nation, tribe, people and language, standing before the throne and before the Lamb."

This book is a welcome and much-needed addition to the missiological conversation. Too often, people assume that multiethnicity is sufficient for diversity in the church. But many colors does not many cultures make.

Language is an essential part of culture. It is people's heart-language, and in that sense, irreplaceable. Singing, reading, or hearing something in one's mother tongue (what chapter 21 calls "linguistic hospitality"), does something that monolingualism can never accomplish.

We are in the recent wake of the conclusion of the fourth Lausanne Congress, which took place in Seoul/Incheon, South Korea, in September 2024. There was much to commend but also to improve about the Congress. Sadly, the linguistic monopoly was played out in the choice of almost exclusively English-language, Western-composed, worship songs. However, the theme was appropriately integral mission (as explained in chapter 19) as "Let the Church Declare and Display Christ Together." The holistic nature of *declare* (John 1:1 talks about Jesus being the Word, as referenced in chapters 2 and 4 of this book) and *display* (1 John 1:1—same author!) balances that out with "That which was from the beginning, which we have *heard*, which we have *seen* with our eyes, which we have *looked at* and our hands have *touched*—this we *proclaim* concerning the Word of life." (italics mine). It shows the interwoven nature of language with other forms of missional engagement. The debate about which should be prioritized is superfluous. All are important.

Therefore, *tolle lege* 'take up and read', and my prayer is that this book can minister to you linguistically and beyond.

Allen Yeh
Dean and Vice President of Academic Affairs at International Theological Seminary, West Covina, California

November 2024

The Tower of Babel, by Lubov Arbachakova. Dr Arbachakova is Shor, a people group living in the Kemerovo province of southern Siberia. The tower is placed in the taiga or Siberian forest and is surrounded by fir trees. The builders are using horses and traditional sledges to construct the tower.

"[God's] benevolent act of dispersing the people at the Tower of Babel [was] intended to fulfill his missional purpose of filling the earth with the knowledge of his glory." (Kruger, chapter 4, 44–45)

What if language is not just a rough instrument in the hands of clumsy people,
not just something useful and occasionally poetic,
but something that can be divine, sacred,
expressive of the very image of God,
and an aspect of the imago Dei (being made in the image of God)
that is also vital to the missio Dei (the mission of God)?

—Charles ("Chip") Sanders, SIL Global

Introduction

> *In the past God spoke to our ancestors through the prophets at many times and in various ways, but in these last days he has spoken to us by his Son, whom he appointed heir of all things, and through whom also he made the universe. The Son is the radiance of God's glory and the exact representation of his being, sustaining all things by his powerful word.* (Heb 1:1–3)

God spoke. God has spoken. God speaks. God is the fountainhead of language. Yet, as the missiologist Chip Sanders states in "Embracing the Winds of Change",

> The use of language by God, even before creating humans, has not been appreciated enough. We have only recently begun conversations about the place of language in the mission of God. And clearly this topic is a lacuna in almost all western treatments of theology. (Sanders 2020:104)

Beginning to address this lacuna, SIL hosted a God and Language Forum in 2020, where twenty-nine missiologists, linguists, and other practitioners presented papers on aspects of the role of language in the mission of God. In his contribution, Sanders elaborates on his "winds of change" statement.

> [Many] cultures, and I believe the Scriptures themselves, have a sacramental rather than an instrumental view of

> language. Language is sourced in the Godhead. Through language the world was created. Through the Word, the world was redeemed. What if language is not just a rough instrument in the hands of clumsy people, not just something useful and occasionally poetic, but something that can be divine, sacred, expressive of the very image of God, and an aspect of the *imago Dei* (being made in the image of God) that is also vital to the *missio Dei* (the mission of God)? (Sanders in Greed and Kruger 2022:157–158)

Most of these Forum papers were subsequently published under the title *God and Language: Exploring the Role of Language in the Mission of God*. Those papers and the interaction around them laid the foundation for this current work, which seeks to understand the theological and missiological role of language. Our desire is that, given the nature and scope of this book, *Language in the Mission of God*, will both find its place in and contribute to the wider conversation of language in the context of God's mission.

God and Language Forum, 2020

Those who took part in the 2020 Forum, and thereby helped lay the foundations for this book are (in alphabetical order): Eddie Arthur, Grace Chou, Bronwen Cleaver, Matthew Crosland, Danny DeLoach, Margaret Doll, Evan Falk, Paul Frank, Maik Gibson, Michael Greed, Brian Harmelink, Larry Hayashi, Michel Kenmogne, Kividi Kikama, Paul Kimbi, Dick Kroneman, Dawn Kruger, Sung Chan Kwon, Paul Lewis, John Ommani, Steve Quakenbush, Olivia Razafinjatoniary, Abou Sama, Chip Sanders, Gary Simons, Steve Watters, Zachary Watters, Eberhard Werner, and Catherine Young. Two further papers were commissioned after the Forum, written by Donna Toulmin and Yunana Malgwi (co-authors), and Mamy Raharimanantsoa.

One omission that was identified from the 2022 publication was sign languages. Olivia Razafinjatoniary discussed them briefly, but a more in-depth treatment was necessary. We are grateful to Stuart Thiessen for stepping in and writing a new, more comprehensive chapter to fill this need.

While this book draws heavily on the papers presented at the God and Language Forum in 2020, and the subsequent publication of most of those papers in 2022, it is not simply a rearrangement of that material. The 2022 publication was "exploring the role of language in the mission of God". In this book we are endeavouring to present the fruits of that exploration, and, as SIL, we are beginning to formulate what the role of language is in all that God is doing. Therefore some chapters in this book are similar to chapters in the 2022 publication; the names of those authors are given in the *Contents*. Other chapters are entirely new material. The remaining chapters build on earlier work and give harmony to the voice presenting the role of language in the mission of God; such chapters are credited as "with" or "based on" in the *Contents*. The narrative voice in all other parts of the book is that of myself, Michael Greed.

Language speakers

In this book we write of "speakers" of a language. "Speakers", as noted by Evan Falk (2021, 2022), is not an ideal term in that it does not reflect the reality of the many sign languages around the world. Furthermore, it reinforces the idea that language is only what we say to each other and not part of how we interpret and interact with the world within our own minds. For example, as I compose this sentence, I am trying out different formulations of it in my mind, and in so doing am using language without speaking, signing, or writing it. To "use" language is more inclusive of sign language but casts language even more as merely a tool we apply to a problem. A basic tenet of this book is that language is more than a tool of communication.

My adopted homeland is Finland. In Finnish I would not be a "Finnish speaker" or an "English speaker"; I would be *suomenkielinen*, that is "Finnish-languaged," or *englanninkielinen*, that is "English-languaged". This terminology gets us away from tying language to the idea of speech alone. It would be a significant contribution to the greater cause of linguistic justice (see chapter 17) if something similar could be introduced into the English language, so that English-languaged people and English-languaged books might have a better set of tools for engaging with these issues. When this book references "speakers" of a given language, think *-languaged*.

Acknowledgements

We extend our heartfelt thanks to all those who participated in the God and Language Forum in 2020. Without your contributions, this project would not be where it is today.

Also special thanks to the editorial and review team (Evan Falk, Dawn Kruger, Abou Sama, and Chip Sanders), to the team of peer reviewers, and to Sue McQuay and her team at SIL Global Publishing Services, for seeing this project through to completion.

Most special thanks to our Creator God who gave us the gift of language when he made us in his image, and who sustained us by his powerful word in this book project.

Michael Greed, General editor, 17th July 2024

References

Falk, Evan. 2021. Linguistic injustice as a disruption to human flourishing: A missiological exploration. In Stephen Watters and Johannes Merz (eds.), *Exploring language and human flourishing*, 90–113. Leanpub. https://leanpub.com/languageandhumanflourishing.

Falk, Evan. 2022. Language, justice, and mission. In Greed and Kruger, 415–427.

Greed, Michael, and Dawn Kruger, eds. 2022. *God and language: Exploring the role of language in the mission of God*. Dallas, TX: SIL International. Leanpub. https://leanpub.com/languageandthemissionofgod.

Sanders, Chip. 2020. Embracing the winds of change: Recommendations for SIL in further moving through missional paradigms. DMin dissertation. Gordon-Conwell Theological Seminary, Hamilton, MA. https://www.sil.org/resources/archives/84417.

Sanders, Chip. 2022. Judgment and language in the mission of God. In Greed and Kruger, 150–163.

Note: Because *God and Language* is referenced frequently throughout the text, the full bibliographic entry is only shown in this list of references. In other chapters, citations and references will refer to it as "Greed and Kruger".

Part One

Foundations

This book is divided into three parts: "Foundations", "The Bible", and "Language and flourishing life today".

The foundations laid in part one introduce the twin themes of language and the mission of God.

Chapter 1, beginning at the end of the story, gives a glimpse of the vast multitude standing before the throne of God and before the Lamb. Paul Frank notes that every language will be represented there and draws out the significance of that fact.

Chapter 2 looks at the mission of God through the lens of God making himself known, which in turn leads to flourishing, abundant life. It then introduces language as a concept and looks briefly at linguistics, the study of language. Michael Greed examines the relationship between language and God's self-revelation, in particular, the role of language in creation, while in **chapter 3** Michel Kenmogne examines the relationship between language and flourishing life.

Drawing from the Exodus narrative, a key word in **chapter 4** is "tabernacle", which describes God's active presence with his people. Dawn Kruger discovers how the Word made flesh still dwells with us in language.

As noted in the introduction, language is part of how we interpret and interact with the world, and may be spoken, written, or signed. In **chapter 5** Abou Sama examines spoken language and oral traditions, showing how God uses them in his mission. In **chapter 6** Stuart Thiessen, while sharing his experiences as a Deaf person, discusses what the Bible says about deaf people, and provides some pointers for the Church's work among sign language communities.

Michael Greed and Evan Falk round off the first part of this book in **chapter 7** with an overview of mission in church history, from Christendom to the modern missionary movement, the emergence of *missio Dei* theology, and the Lausanne Congresses—and note the absence of language in the discussion.

Aleph

*Blessed are those whose ways are blameless,
who walk according to the law of the LORD.
(Psalm 119:1)*

1

The Glory of God Through the Peoples and Languages of the Earth

Paul Frank

> After this I looked, and there before me was a great multitude that no one could count, from every nation, tribe, people and language, standing before the throne and before the Lamb. They were wearing white robes and were holding palm branches in their hands. And they cried out in a loud voice:
>
> "Salvation belongs to our God,
> who sits on the throne,
> and to the Lamb." (Rev 7:9–10)

What a scene that will be! So many people you can't count them—millions upon millions. The sheer size of the multitude magnifies the glory of God. God doesn't want anyone to perish but everyone to come to repentance.[1]

But there is something about this multitude that goes beyond numbers. Not every *person* will be in that gathering around the throne, but every *people*

---

[1] A previous version of this chapter was presented at the SIL/JAARS Computer Technical Conference, 2004.

will be. Do we believe the Scriptures? God tells us that "*every* nation, tribe, people and language" (emphasis added) will be represented in his kingdom. I don't know how this can be. But the Apostle John reports this twice in his Revelation. He records the twenty-four elders worshiping Jesus, saying:

> "With your blood you purchased for God persons from
> *every tribe and language and people and nation.*"
> (Rev 5:9b [emphasis added])

It is common to talk about language and culture as barriers to the work of the Church. Linguistic and cultural diversity are not barriers to God's purposes; they are crucial elements for achieving God's purposes. We may see linguistic diversity as a problem to be solved. God sees it as a foundation stone for building his glory.

Linguistic and cultural diversity are often assumed to be the curse of Babel. They were not a curse. Is God a God of the "second best"? Did stubborn people frustrate the true purposes of God on the plain of Shinar, forcing God to confuse their languages? There on that plain people *were* stubborn. They *did* stand against the purposes of God. God *did* confuse their languages. But we're mistaken if we conclude the diversity of languages and peoples that resulted was contrary to the eternal purposes of God. God is not a God of the "second best". The scene that the Apostle John saw around the throne of God was what God intended from before the creation of the world. Without the diversity of nations, tribes, peoples, and languages, God's purposes are hindered, not helped. It is a tragedy whenever any person fails to trust God because he or she could not hear the gospel in a language they could understand. It is also a tragedy when any person feels that they have to give up their linguistic and cultural identity in order to become a Christian.

The Apostle Paul affirmed this truth when he spoke to the people of Athens:

> "From one man he made all the nations, that they should
> inhabit the whole earth; and he marked out their appointed
> times in history and the boundaries of their lands. God did
> this so that they would seek him and perhaps reach out for
> him and find him, though he is not far from any one of us."
> (Acts 17:26–27)

God made all the nations. God set the times in which they would live, and the exact places they would call home. And he did this for a purpose—that people would seek him and find him. God created cultural and linguistic diversity and intends them for his glory.

At Pentecost God once again intervened in the world's linguistic scene. The miracle of Pentecost was not that people of many nations and languages understood the gospel despite linguistic barriers. The miracle of Pentecost was that people of many nations heard the gospel *in their own languages*.

> "Aren't all these who are speaking Galileans? Then how is it that each of us hears them in our native language?" (Acts 2:7b–8)

At Pentecost God affirmed his eternal plan: men and women of every nation, tribe, people, and language would someday be around his throne. When people come to know him within their own cultural and linguistic uniqueness, God's purposes are advanced.

Jesus taught us to pray: "Your will be done, on earth as it is in heaven" (Matt 6:10b). God has already revealed his will in heaven—a diversity of peoples and languages around his throne. We need to pray and work that his will might also be done on earth—a diversity of peoples and languages as part of his Church.

So what is so important in the Kingdom of God about a diversity of cultures? God designed cultural variety in the world just as he designed a variety of gifts within the body of Christ. The body would not be the body unless there were many parts, each with its own unique role. Though we are all created in the image of God, no one of us is capable of expressing all that God is.

So it is with culture. One culture places a high value on generosity. Another emphasizes a strong work ethic. Yet another people seem to specialize in exuberant celebration. One nation honors—and even reveres—a monarch. Another focuses on the freedom of the individual. One culture excels at analyzing the most minute structures of the physical creation. Another has a keen understanding of unseen spiritual realities. No one culture is capable of expressing all of God's character. It takes a bewildering range of cultures to display here on earth the varied facets of who God is. Each one of them captures and expresses one aspect of God, his ways, and how we should worship him. At the same time, no culture is above reproach, and even in the examples given, our cultural values may obscure the face of God by corrupting these values or taking them to extremes.

How does language fit into this picture? God has made us so that language is central to our identity. We may speak many languages, but the language or languages that we speak are an intrinsic part of who we are and what community we belong to. For the crowd in Jerusalem on the day of Pentecost, their languages were the essence of their identity as nations or peoples. That is just as true today as it was two thousand years ago.

Perhaps in some mysterious way, as with culture, no one language is capable of capturing and expressing all that God is. Though we affirm that the Scriptures can be communicated through any and every language, it may be that not everything that could be said about God can be said equally well through any one language. In some strange way, each language is necessary, both as a means for expressing a people's unique identity and as a means for saying things about the world and about God that cannot quite be said through any other language. It takes thousands of languages to even begin to fathom God's ability to communicate.

God loves and accepts us all, including our languages and cultures. God loves people—and the peoples the Church serves—exactly as they are, too. When we affirm them in their unique languages and cultures, we express the grace and love of God towards them, and we celebrate the craftsmanship of God in his creation.

It is God's desire to open the gates of the kingdom to the peoples of the earth so that they can walk through without having to abandon the unique languages and cultures in which God has placed them.

And so we translate the Scriptures, and we also help stabilize languages that are threatened and cultures that are being eroded. We help people develop their languages so that, in a changing, hostile world, they can continue using their languages to express their unique identity in the face of the onslaught of dominant languages and cultures. We help people understand that their languages are real languages. They can stand as linguistic equals with anyone else on the face of the earth.

God has given us our languages, each one beautiful, full of expressive power and grammatical complexity. When we uncover and display that beauty and complexity through linguistic and cultural study and documentation, we put the workmanship of God on display to a watching world.

People should not be impressed by the skill or scholarship of those working in languages or anthropology. What people learn about the languages and cultures of the world should take their breath away, just as we stand in awe of the wonders and magnitude of the universe when astronomers show us photos of galaxies and nebula millions of light years away. When anyone reads or hears about the peoples and languages of the earth, they should say, "Wow! What special people! What incredible languages!" When Christians learn of the richness of the world's languages and cultures, they should be moved to praise God: "O LORD, marvelous are your works. Your ways are beyond understanding."

As we carry out our work of linguistic and cultural study, Scripture translation, and helping people develop their languages to express their unique identity and meet their particular needs, the world should know that we love God, because we love the peoples he created just as they are. They should be able to see that we are worshiping God with our minds, just as he commanded. It should be obvious that we believe in people, not some sort of spiritual "bottom line" in which progress is measured in verses translated, New Testaments published, and "souls saved". Rather, such activities are means to the end of displaying God's glory in and through the peoples of the earth.

And at the end of the day, the people we work with should know beyond any doubt that we love and value them just as they are, including their unique language and way of life. We want them to know God within their language and culture, not in spite of them. We want to honor them through our research, affirm them through literacy, build them up through training, and love them as God loves them.

Beth

*I have hidden your word in my heart
that I might not sin against you.
(Psalm 119:11)*

2

The Mission of God and the Question of Language

Michael Greed

Layla began to follow Jesus in her late teens. Soon after that she joined the team translating the Scriptures into her mother tongue, Uzbek. She now works as a Bible translation consultant, advising and guiding other translation teams.

In the spring of 2021, Layla visited a translation team in Central Asia. She prayed daily with them in her mother tongue. Although they only recognised a few words, the translation team members were moved by how easily Layla conversed with God. They themselves only ever prayed in the national language because they did not think God would find prayers in their own language acceptable. Layla assured them that God created their language and loves to hear the sound of it—not merely ritual phrases, but heartfelt communication.

This idea astonished the translators! However, the next time the team met with Layla, one of the translators tentatively took the step of praying aloud in his language for the very first time. He discovered he could indeed pray in his own language!

Introduction

In this chapter we will begin by taking a look at the nature of God's mission. We will see that God's mission is to make himself known, known intimately and experientially, and that knowing him leads to flourishing life, which is God's desire for all that he has made. We will then look at language and how it relates firstly to God's endeavours to make himself known and secondly to flourishing life.

It is his desire that every person on earth would know the comfort, joy, and courage of praying to him in their own language, whatever that language might be.

The mission of God is God's self-revelation

"The mission of God is God's self-revelation as the One who loves the world," writes the missiologist David Bosch (1991:10). In a similar manner, the missiologist Christopher Wright writes, "Biblical mission is driven by God's will to be known as God ... The one living God wills to be known throughout his whole creation" (2006:126–127). Both Bosch and Wright present God's mission as one of self-revelation, making himself known. Missiology has often focused in on the practical results of this, the consequences of God making himself known. These include:

- **Restoration:** "The mission of God may be described as God's intention and activity to restore all creation to the purposes for which he created it"—Roger Hahn (2011:40).
- **Reconciliation:** "Mission is first of all the activity of God. The missionary impulse flows from the love of God to reconcile his alienated world. The Father sends the Son to reconcile all things to himself"—Michael Goheen (2014:77).
- **Blessing the nations:** "I believe that the entire canon is about God's mission and it is very clear that God's purpose has always been to reach and to bless all nations"—Antonia Leonora van der Meer (2001:150).
- **Transformation:** "The aim of God's mission is the transformation of life not only of individuals but also of the whole society, even the created order."—Titre Ande (2008:37); "The transformation of all creation into God's home seems to be an appropriate description of the mission of God"—Nelus Niemandt (2020:14).

The theologian Thomas Schirrmacher identifies three steps that God takes to make himself known:

> **Step 1:** God comes close to humanity by speaking their language [and] revealing himself to them, [as recounted in the Old Testament] ...

Step 2: God comes closer to humanity by becoming a human in Christ and by revealing himself directly to humankind ...
Step 3: God comes closer still to humanity by dwelling through his Spirit in all those who believe in Jesus Christ ... (2017:42)

God comes close, closer, and closer still, revealing himself, and making himself known. The central driving force of God's mission is God's desire to make himself known. A statement repeated almost word for word in two Old Testament prophets in quite different contexts illustrates this.

Isaiah is painting a picture of a young branch that will grow from the stump of Jesse, a messianic figure, anointed by the Spirit of God. The result: the wolf will live with the lamb, the lion will eat straw like the ox, and children will play near the cobra's den. All this will happen because

> the earth will be filled with the knowledge of the LORD
> as the waters cover the sea. (Isa 11:9b)

The prophet Habakkuk is wrestling with God. Habakkuk accuses God of being unjust and tells him that he will climb his watchtower and wait there until God gives him an answer. A chapter later Habakkuk is ecstatic at the answer God gives: "Though the fig tree does not bud and there are no grapes on the vines ... yet I will rejoice in the LORD, I will be joyful in God my Savior" (Hab 3:17–18). What is the divine answer that sends the prophet wild with delight? Judgement will come. The phrase "Woe to him who ..." is repeated throughout the chapter, illustrating that evildoers will receive God's judgement. In the midst of it all is the beacon of hope, the knowledge of the glory of the LORD.

> For the earth will be filled with the knowledge of the glory of the LORD
> as the waters cover the sea. (Hab 2:14)

The earth is already full of the glory of the LORD (Isa 6:3). The crucial piece of information in this statement is *knowledge*. The *knowledge* of the LORD (Isaiah), the *knowledge* of the glory of the LORD (Habakkuk)—this will fill the earth.[1]

The missiologist Christopher Wright argues that the mission of God is the overarching theme of the Scriptures and describes it as the Bible's "grand narrative" (2006). The mission of God, he argues, is the framework through which the whole biblical witness is to be understood. Under the title *The God of Mission*, Wright explores how "the living God makes himself

---

[1] While the Hebrew of Isaiah and Habakkuk do not have the same word for "knowledge," they are not different to any significant degree: both are infinitival forms of the same Hebrew root, *yada'* (to know) (Gesenius 1910:69c). They are translated identically in the Septuagint, the Greek translation of the Hebrew Scriptures. McComiskey (2009:869) suggests that Habakkuk is "repeating" the earlier words of Isaiah.

known in Israel", and how "the living God makes himself known in Jesus Christ" (2006, section headings).

> The one living God wills to be known throughout his whole creation. The world must know its Creator. The nations must know their Ruler, Judge and Savior. This is a major subplot of the exodus narrative in the book of Exodus, but later recollections on that great event repeatedly highlight its prime purpose as making a great name for YHWH among the nations. (Wright 2006:127)

Wright then quotes Psalm 22 to demonstrate that the reason the story is to be told from generation to generation is to fill the earth with the knowledge of the LORD.

> All the ends of the earth
>   will remember and turn to the LORD,
> and all the families of the nations
>   will bow down before him …
>
> [because]
>
> future generations will be told about the LORD.
> They will proclaim his righteousness,
>   declaring to a people yet unborn:
>   He has done it! (Ps 22:27, 30–31)

Summarizing, Wright writes of "the driving will of the one true living God to be known throughout his whole creation for who he is, the LORD God, YHWH, the Holy One of Israel, incarnate in Jesus of Nazareth, crucified, risen, ascended and returning" (2006:532).

The mission of the love of God

What is it about the essence or identity of God that gives him this driving will to be known? The answer is: his love. In the words of God to Moses: "The LORD, the LORD, the compassionate and gracious God, slow to anger, abounding in love and faithfulness …" (Exod 34:6b). In the words of John's first epistle: "God is love" (1 John 4:16). In the words of the missiologist How Chuang Chua: "The only motivation for God to create the universe is His gracious love" (2010:5). The Jesuit priest William Barry expands on this.

> As long as we keep in mind that the three Persons are not three beings, we can say that the Trinity is the perfect community where nothing is lacking. These reflections should put an end to the romantic, but ultimately heretical, notion that God created the universe because of his loneliness.

> Precisely because God is the perfect community, God had no need to create anything else. God creates the universe for no other motive than God's gratuitous and unfathomable love. It is as if the three Persons said to one another: "Our life together is so good; why don't we create a universe where we can invite others to share it." (2004:44)

The mission of God, God's reason for creating the universe and being reconciled with it, resides deep in the essence of God's very being, his love.

Writing at about the same time as Chua and Barry, the theologians Henning Wrogemann and Theo Sundermeier come to a very similar conclusion; they put the love of God firmly in the center of the mission of God. "God comes to people as a lover," writes Sundermeier. God is love, and his mission proceeds from his essence, which is love. Over the term *missio Dei*, Wrogemann prefers the term *missio amoris Dei*, the mission of the love of God (Schirrmacher 2017:52–53).

For love to exist, there needs to be a lover and a beloved. God loves us, God loves the whole world that he has created, and everything in it. But God's love did not begin when he created the world. It's the other way around: his creation of the world sprang out of his love. The triune God has existed for all eternity, and love is rooted in God's eternal, essential character: the Father loves and is loved by the Son who loves and is loved by the Spirit who loves and is loved by the Father. Out of that eternally existent love comes the love that God bestows on his created universe.

An invitation to life

The response that the God who wants to be known desires of us is that we get to know him. This brings life. "I have come," says Jesus, "that they may have life, and have it to the full" (John 10:10b). Other translations use the phrase "abundant life" here. This is completely different from what is sometimes called "the good life" where we have all the health and wealth we need (and a little more) to sit back and enjoy ourselves—to eat, drink and be merry (see Luke 12:18–19). The abundant life or flourishing life that Jesus invites us to share in is more like the vision God gave the prophets Micah and Zechariah of sitting with our neighbor under our vine and fig tree, in peace and unafraid (Mic 4:4, Zech 3:10). It is a life lived in shalom and in harmony with God, with neighbors, with society, with the world, with creation, and with ourselves.

The theologian Michael Gorman suggests that the overarching theme of John's Gospel is

> Jesus' singular work of bringing *zoe*, 'life,' which the Gospel also calls 'eternal' life (e.g., 17:2-3) and 'abundant' life (10:10b), or life 'to the full' … Life—participation in the life

of God—[is] the ultimate missional purpose of God and the 'work' of Jesus ... Jesus does not merely *disclose* something, he *delivers* something. That something is life. (2018:44)

Flourishing life is also the picture Paul paints in his epistles. This comes out most clearly in the letter to the Romans where, having said that "just as sin reigned in death, so also grace might reign through righteousness to bring eternal life through Jesus Christ our Lord" (Rom 5:21) and "the wages of sin is death, but the gift of God is eternal life in Christ Jesus our Lord" (Rom 6:23), Paul goes on to describe that life in chapter 8:

> If the Spirit of him who raised Jesus from the dead is living in you, he who raised Christ from the dead will also give life to your mortal bodies because of his Spirit who lives in you. (Rom 8:11)

God's mission is to make himself known. In this, he is motivated by his love. As we respond to God and get to know him, we experience life, flourishing life.

Language

Having introduced the subject of the mission of God, we now turn to language, since the key question this book addresses concerns the relationship between language and the mission of God. If, as we have suggested, the mission of God relates to God making himself known and results in flourishing life, we need to ask: What is the relationship between language and God making himself known? What is the relationship between language and flourishing life?

But first, let's step back and look at language as a phenomenon. What is language? Where does it come from? What is its relationship to culture? We will also take a brief survey of linguistics, the study of language.

What is language?

We speak it. We sign it. We write it. We do so in thousands of different ways. We use words, sentences, and discourse to express it. We use the tongue and the vocal cords, the hands and facial gestures, pen, ink, and computer keyboard to articulate it. Yet, what is *language*?

The Encyclopædia Britannica entry on language is written by the linguists David Crystal and Robert Henry Robins. They define language as "a system of conventional spoken, manual (signed), or written symbols by means of which human beings, as members of a social group and participants in its culture, express themselves. The functions of language include communication, the expression of identity, play, imaginative expression, and emotional release" (2024). While language can be spoken, signed, or written, language itself is higher than the symbols that represent it, for language as a phenomenon is not dependent on the expression of it. Language enables us to make sense of the world.

"We simply don't know how language originated" (Yule 2010:1). George Yule explains, "In most religions, there appears to be a divine source who provides humans with language" (p. 2). We affirm the "divine source" who provides humans with language, and we caught a glimpse of this in chapter 1, a divine source who, as Trinity, had language long before we ever did. However, we do not know the process by which he gave language to humanity.

The anthropologist Matthew Crosland (2022) discusses the relationship between culture and language in Papua New Guinea. He quotes Wenying Jiang, who writes, "Language simultaneously reflects culture and is influenced and shaped by it. In the broadest sense, it is also the symbolic representation of a people, since it comprises their historical and cultural backgrounds, as well as their approach to life and their ways of living and thinking" (2000:328). Crosland also quotes H. D. Brown, who writes, "A language is a part of a culture and a culture is a part of a language; the two are intricately interwoven so that one cannot separate the two without losing the significance of either language or culture" (quoted in Jiang 2000:328). Crosland continues:

> Language is a part of culture and ... the two are connected in such a way that one cannot thrive without the other. In Papua New Guinea I have worked with a number of language communities who have seen the language of wider communication for the area take the place of their local language as the primary language. As the local language begins to lose its place of prominence in the community, so do some cultural values and traditions. Likewise, I have seen communities move away from their cultural distinctives under outside pressure to conform, and the use of their local languages waned as well. (2022:418–419)

Linguistics: The study of language

Linguistics is the study of language, and people have been studying language since antiquity. There is evidence of discussions about language in ancient Mesopotamia, India, and China, and more recently by the Greeks and Romans in classical antiquity. To give a flavor of the different approaches to the study of language, we will briefly survey four that have been prominent in recent years. Before we do so, it is important to note that language is multifaceted, and it is not necessary to select one linguistic theory and disregard the rest. The linguist Mary Pearce comments, "Linguists can be eclectic in their approach. They don't have to choose one and disregard the other approaches. I might get value from a generative approach in phonology, but some other approach in pragmatics of the same language" (Pearce, pers. comm., 2024).

Structuralism

We begin with the linguist and philosopher Ferdinand de Saussure who, during the years 1907–1911, gave a series of lectures in which he demonstrated that language is a logical, structured system of elements that can be analyzed. After his death, Saussure's theories continued to gain traction as others, including the linguist Leonard Bloomfield (1887–1949), continued the research. Bloomfield, whose name is particularly associated with structuralism, "argued that language was a response to external stimuli rather than something innate to the brain" (Noonan 2020:39).

A key feature of structuralism is the contrast between *langue* 'language' and *parole* 'speaking'. *Langue* (French for 'language'), Benjamin Noonan explains, refers to an abstract language system or the common code shared by all speakers of a given language, whereas *parole* (French for 'speaking') refers to the actual use of language by specific individuals. Structuralism argues that it is *langue* (not *parole*) that should be the object of linguistic study.

Generative grammar

The primary proponent of generative grammar is Noam Chomsky (born 1928) who argued that "language stem[s] from some internal, innate ability. Every person possesses a basic linguistic 'competence' in their language without having been taught" (Noonan 2020:41). Thus, there is a "universal grammar" innate to the human brain, and the task of linguistics is to uncover these universal underlying rules. Language, in generative grammar, is part of the mind, not an external system.

Generative grammar contrasts performance and competence, where *competence* refers to a person's innate ability to generate an infinite number of sentences, while *performance* refers to the actual ability of any given individual. It is competence—the idealized, infinite language ability—Chomsky argues, that should be the object of linguistic study.

Functionalism

The focus of functionalism is the role of language in communication. Thus, while structuralism focuses on language as an abstract system, independent from actual use, functionalism focuses on language in real-life contexts, and while generative grammar sees the communication aspects of language as irrelevant for analysis, functionalism puts communication front and center

(Noonan 2020:44). Functionalism sees communication as the primary function of language, and so the meaning conveyed by that communication is central.

Cognitive linguistics

In cognitive linguistics,[2] the grammar and lexicon of language do not simply exist "out there", they are always part of actual language usage, and they have no meaning apart from real usage in the real world. This, therefore, is what linguists should study, not some abstract, idealized system (Noonan 2020:48). *Cognitive* indicates that "language encompasses the way that the brain processes and categorizes our interaction with the world" (p. 47), shaping experience, not just expressing or reflecting it. Thus, language as a phenomenon is deeper than the expression of language.

Summary of linguistic approaches

At the risk of huge simplification, structuralism sees language as a logical, structured system of elements that can be analysed; generative grammar sees language as part of the mind, not an external system; functionalism sees language through the lens of communication; and cognitive linguistics sees language as embedded in a person's overall cognitive capacities.

Deus loquens[3]: The relationship between language and God making himself known

The sociolinguist M. Paul Lewis writes,

> Language is pervasive. While we may declare ourselves, at times, to be speechless, that very claim, whether spoken, written, or thought, proves that we are not ... Speaking (self-revelation) is an essential characteristic of God. In his eternal nature, he is described as "the Word" (John 1:1) and the first of his acts in history that we are made aware of was to speak into being all that exists (Gen 1:3, 6, 9, 14, 20, 24, 26, 28, 29). He contrasts himself with those false and useless gods who do not speak (Hab 2:18–20). He is unknown only because we do not listen or have not heard him (Acts 17:16–34) ... God (*Deus loquens*) has continuously been made known and has communed with humanity in time and space by means of language (Heb 1:1) and continues to speak through creation (Ps 19:1, Rom 1:20) and the Scriptures. (2022:236)

---

[2] See https://www.cognitivelinguistics.org/en/about-cognitive-linguistics
[3] *Deus loquens* is Latin for "the God who speaks".

The first attribute the Bible ascribes to God is speech. God uses declarative speech acts (see chapter 8), to speak creation into existence. Genesis 1:3 records,

> God said, "Let there be light," and there was light.

He could have thought light into existence; he could have reached out and touched the void; he could have stood up and waved a divine staff. But no. God speaks. He uses language, even when the earth is formless and empty. The psalmist celebrates this:

> By the word of the LORD the heavens were made,
>   their starry host by the breath of his mouth. (Ps 33:6)

God's speech acts continue throughout the rest of the chapter, and after each speech act comes the simple "And it was so".

The final speech act is different, and we see a different divine use of language. Genesis 1:26 records,

> Then God said, "Let us make humans in our image." (NRSVUE)

God is using language to discuss within the Trinity his desire to create people in his image. Now, this verse is in the ancient Jewish Scriptures, and the Jewish faith maintains a strict singularity in its monotheism, and so does not see Trinity here. Some Jewish commentators suggest that God is discussing his idea with the angels. Other commentators draw on the "wisdom tradition" and suggest that God was consulting with divine *Sophia*, or Wisdom, as seen, for example, in Proverbs 3:19:

> By wisdom the LORD laid the earth's foundations,
>   by understanding he set the heavens in place.

With reference to Genesis 1, the theologian D. A. Carson writes, "It seems more likely that 'us' and 'our' imply a greater complexity to God's nature as already suggested by the Spirit of God [in Gen 1:2]" (2015).

It is significant for Christian commentators and interpreters researching language that the triune God uses language to discuss amongst themself the creation of those who will bear their image. Language itself is an attribute of the triune God and he shares it with his image-bearers. As the biblical narrative continues, we see how God uses language to make himself known in the developing friendship he has with people.

There is a mystery to language, which we glimpse at the beginning of the story in Genesis. God speaks to create. The members of the Godhead speak amongst themselves, for God is community, God is relationship. Catholic, Orthodox, and Protestant Christians have very different theologies concerning the Trinity, but all are agreed on seeing the Trinity as a community.[4] Language is an innate characteristic of God. This does not

---

[4] See Miroslav Volf (1997), After Our Likeness: The Church as the Image of the Trinity, where Volf discusses the Trinity and the Church as communities.

mean he has vocal cords (for spoken language) or limbs (for sign language). When God "speaks" we do not know what form that speech takes. We may anthropomorphize it into what we know as spoken or signed language, but in the end we do not know what form God's speech took at creation or takes now.

> "For my thoughts are not your thoughts,
>   neither are your ways my ways,"
> declares the LORD.
> "As the heavens are higher than the earth,
>   so are my ways higher than your ways
>   and my thoughts than your thoughts." (Isa 55:8–9)

What we do know is that God shares this characteristic of language with those whom he made in his image. This does not mean that humans have an innate ability to acquire language devoid of any contact with other humans, but it does mean that every child growing up in an environment where language (one or more) is spoken has an innate, untaught ability to acquire that language or those languages in all their nuances and complexities. Deprived of a social environment, a child would not acquire language, for language is innately social, integral to community and relationship, as seen in the Trinity where the members of the Godhead speak amongst themselves.

The first specific task God gives humanity involves the creative use of language: he brings all the wild animals and birds of the sky to Adam for him to name (Gen 2:19), and he respects the names Adam gives them.

Aspects of the relationship between language and God making himself known can be found in part two of this book.

The relationship between language and flourishing life

This is the subject of the next chapter and so we will not expend many words on it here.

What does a vision of a flourishing life look like for speakers of a majority language and speakers of a threatened language, for monolingual people and multilingual people, for those who can enjoy a full education in a language they value and those who struggle in their education because it is in a language that is new to them? Where is the interaction between flourishing and language in the mission of God? What is the role of language in the reconciliation to God of "all things, whether things on earth or things in heaven" (Col 1:20), and thereby enabling them to flourish?

Aspects of the relationship between language and flourishing life can be found in part three of this book.

Conclusion

In this introductory chapter we have seen, firstly, that God's mission is to make himself known. This is the grand narrative of the Scriptures and is summarized in the prophetic statement:

> For the earth will be filled with the knowledge of the glory of the LORD as the waters cover the sea. (Hab 2:14)

In this, God is motivated by his love. "God so loved the world, that he gave his one and only Son ..." (John 3:16a). His mission embraces redemption, reconciliation, renewal, and restoration, and leads to life. "[T]hat whoever believes in him shall not perish but have eternal life" (John 3:16b). This is summarized in Jesus' statement:

> "I have come that they may have life, and have it to the full." (John 10:10b)

Secondly, we have seen that God used language before he gave it as a gift to humankind. The first activity of God recorded in the Scriptures is speaking. "God said, 'Let there be light,' and there was light" (Gen 1:3).

SIL's Vision Statement says that we "long to see people flourishing in community, using the languages they value most" (SIL 2024). This book will identify a variety of ways in which God uses language to make himself known, and a range of aspects of the relationship between language and the flourishing life that God intends for his creation.

This chapter began with the story of Layla praying in her own language, and the impact this had on the translation team. As this book unfolds, we will discover that for people to know God in "the languages they value most"—this is true knowing. Language has a significant place in the mission of God.

References

Barry, William A. 2004. *Spiritual direction and the encounter with God: A theological inquiry.* Revised edition. New York, NY: Paulist Press.

Bosch, David J. 1991. *Transforming mission: Paradigm shifts in theology of mission.* American Society of Missiology Series 16. Maryknoll, NY: Orbis Books.

Carson, D. A., ed. 2015. *The NIV Zondervan study Bible.* Grand Rapids, MI: Zondervan.

Chua, How Chuang. 2010. *Perichoresis* and *missio Dei*: Implications of a trinitarian view of personhood for missionary practice. Unpublished paper presented at OMF Mission Research Consultation 2010. http://www.scribd.com/doc/62278399/A-Trinity-and-Mission-H-C-Chua.

Crosland, Matthew. 2022. Language, culture and the image of God: How God revealed himself to me in Papua New Guinea. In Greed and Kruger, 417–429.

Crystal, David, and Robert Henry Robins. 2024. *Encyclopaedia Britannica, Language.* https://www.britannica.com/topic/language.

Gesenius, Wilhelm. 1910. *Gesenius' Hebrew grammar.* Second English edition. Oxford: Clarendon Press.

Goheen, Michael. 2014. *Introducing Christian mission today: Scripture, history, and issues.* Downers Grove, IL: IVP Academic.

Gorman, Michael J. 2018. *Abide and go: Missional theosis in the Gospel of John.* The Didsbury Lecture Series. Eugene, OR: Cascade Books.

Hahn, Roger L. 2011. The mission of God and a covenant people. In Keith Schwanz and Joseph Coleson (eds.), *Missio Dei: A Wesleyan understanding,* 40–48. Kansas City, MO: Beacon Hill Press of Kansas City.

Jiang, Wenying. 2000. The relationship between culture and language. *ELT Journal* 54(4):328–334. https://doi.org/10.1093/elt/54.4.328.

Lewis, M. Paul. 2022. Language and poverty: Linguistics applied beyond Bible translation. In Greed and Kruger, 233–249.

McComiskey, Thomas E. 2009. *The Minor Prophets: An exegetical and expositional commentary.* Vol. II. Grand Rapids, MI: Baker Academic.

Niemandt, Nelus. 2020. The *missio Dei* as flourishing life. *Ecclesial Futures.* 1(1):11–30. https://www.zora.uzh.ch/id/eprint/204044/1/ZORA204044.pdf.

Noonan, Benjamin J. 2020. *Advances in the study of Biblical Hebrew and Aramaic.* Grand Rapids, MI: Zondervan Academic.

Schirrmacher, Thomas. 2017. *Missio Dei: God's missional nature.* Translated by Richard McClary. The WEA World of Theology Series 10. Bonn, Germany: Verlag für Kultur und Wissenschaft (Culture and Science Publishing). https://worldea.org/resource-pack/.

SIL. 2024. Our vision. Dallas, TX: SIL International. https://www.sil.org/about.

Titre Ande, Georges. 2008. To teach, baptise, and nurture new believers. In Andrew Walls and Cathy Ross (eds.), *Mission in the 21st century,* 37–45. Maryknoll, NY: Orbis Books.

Van der Meer, Antonia Leonora. 2001. The Scriptures, the church, and humanity: Who should do mission and why? In William D. Taylor (ed.), *Global missiology for the 21st century: The Iguassu dialogue,* 149–162. Grand Rapids, MI: Baker Academic.

Volf, Miroslav. 1997. *After our likeness: The Church as the image of the Trinity.* Grand Rapids, MI: Eerdmans.

Wright, Christopher J. H. 2006. *The mission of God: Unlocking the Bible's grand narrative.* Nottingham, UK: IVP Academic.

Yule, George. 2010. *The study of language.* Fourth edition. Cambridge, UK: Cambridge University Press.

Gimel

*Open my eyes that I may see
wonderful things in your law.
(Psalm 119:18)*

3

Flourishing and Language

Michel Kenmogne

Introduction

Building on two vignettes that depict issues and consequences of language use among minority language speaking communities, this chapter briefly examines language as an attribute of God, a distinctive of human beings, and a defining marker of the communities that use it. Moreover, it portrays flourishing as part of God's missional intent for humanity, and indeed, all of creation, as depicted through the grand narrative of the Bible. Therefore, the concept of flourishing is likened to blessing, shalom, and reconciliation. In pursuing these, God centrally uses language, thereby providing a missional basis for engagement with language.

Two stories of the denial of language use

Never again use your mother tongue in the church!

It was barely the first milestone in the Bakoko language development project in Cameroon. After months of working with the speakers of the various dialects of the language, a preliminary alphabet of Bakoko was available for the first time. Several community members gathered to launch and celebrate the creation of their writing system. The advent of this alphabet gave people the hope that they would be able to preserve in writing their ancestral knowledge and wisdom. They would create literature, and increase and own any relevant knowledge that would further their thriving as individuals and community.

When the alphabet was launched and the first demonstration of its use made public, an old man named Dinjeke burst into tears. When asked later why he got so emotional, he told the story of the humiliation that he and his Bakoko people had suffered for decades. While the other two major languages of the region had been written and had the Scriptures translated therein, Bakoko[1] had never received any attention. As a result, outreach work among the Bakoko people was done using the neighboring Bassa language. One day, when he was a young adult, Dinjeke was asked to pray during the church service. Breaking the church tradition, he stood up and prayed in his native Bakoko language. While he was standing and praying, somebody "pulled his cloth downward", i.e., rebuked him from the back, telling him to shut up and sit down. Following that, the church leadership warned him to never again use his mother tongue in the context of worship. Dinjeke was hurt in his innermost being. He lived the ensuing decades with shame, feeling that the Bakoko people were undeserving of the same dignity as other people.

For this reason, the development of a writing system for his language was more than a scientific achievement; it was symbolic affirmation that speakers of this language are not second-class citizens of the world. It also provided the seeds of hope that his people might some day enjoy the same prestige as others, using their God-given language.

A traumatic schooling experience

Eken spoke only his mother tongue until he reached school age. Like all children in the community, he was fluent; he could count and tell the stories

---

[1] In 1989, as a postgraduate student, I was part of a major survey that one of our professors carried out on the Coastal Bantu languages of Cameroon. In the course of this, it occurred to me that Bakoko, with its many dialects, had never been given any attention since the early missionary days. Inquiring about the reason behind the neglect of this language and its speakers, I was told that, in the early days of mission in Cameroon, the Bakoko people strongly opposed the missionaries' efforts to develop their language and introduce Christianity. They claimed that their language would be used to keep their ancestral practices and safeguard their magical rites and witchcraft against any corruption. It was this discovery that led to my decision to study the Bakoko language for my doctoral research, resulting in *The Lexical Phonology of Bakoko* (Kenmogne 2000). Currently, a Bakoko language and Bible translation project is nearing completion, under the auspices of CABTAL.

that he had heard in his family context. As such, he was confident because he had a clear frame of reference in life. Upon entering the classroom, however, Eken, along with all other children in the community, was exposed to a foreign language that he neither spoke nor understood. Worse still, speaking the mother tongue on the school campus was forbidden.

This was a traumatic experience for many children who had to learn both the skill of reading and writing and the language of instruction itself at the same time. To these children, education was not a process of going from what they knew to a gradual discovery of the unknown. Rather, it was a radical and abrupt disruption of their daily reality that made education a painful and sudden adjustment to a foreign and mysterious reality. As such, education violently disconnected the child from his community. He was obliged to forfeit his identity throughout the education process.

It is not surprising that many children were thought by the school staff to be dull, and the majority dropped out of the school system over the years. It remains a miracle that a few in the community did go through such an arduous system and eventually learned to read and write. However, the majority of children whose mother tongue was a language other than the language of instruction missed the possibility to achieve their full potential in life. Such people constitute the critical mass of the population whose job opportunities are significantly limited. Hence, they see themselves as second-class citizens in contrast to the minority of people who were able to make it through the arduous system of education and have their choice of careers.

The stories of the Bakoko alphabet and the traumatic schooling experience point to one basic fact: the language that has framed someone's early encounter with the world needs to be considered in any process that requires the deepest levels of one's personality. The failure to do this results in a profound alteration of the self-image, disrupts the group's sense of community, furthers a discrimination among human beings, and thwarts the ability to have a healthy relationship with God. The result is a deep injustice.

Language and minority language communities

Many controversies surround language and its use. Language diversity (see chapter 9) is often viewed either as a curse or a blessing, as a unifying or dividing factor among communities and nations. Over the past five centuries, the processes of colonization (including the imposition of colonial languages), nationalization (removing choice in favor of enforcing official languages to further national integration), and globalization (fostering the rush towards using languages that offer more socio-political and economic power) have had a remarkable effect on the condition of the world's languages. As people approach language issues from a pragmatic perspective, they tend to pay little attention to its intrinsic nature, its relationship to life, and its centrality in all human undertakings. In hindsight, human beings and the communities they form cannot be dissociated from their languages. Language is so essential to human beings that it would be fitting to refer to people as *linguistic beings* because language uniquely defines and distinguishes them.

Language: An extraordinary endowment

When we use the word *language* in English, we refer to two realities: 1) the faculty that humans have to speak or sign as a means of communicating, and 2) the actual system of sounds and symbols that people use to make meaning and to communicate among themselves. This unique ability to use language is inherent to human beings and has been a matter of wonderment for various observers and thinkers. Much has been written about the theory of language, but in this chapter, I will limit my focus to the following tenets about language:

> **Language is a distinctly human attribute:** While communication systems exist among animals, human language is unique in its complexity and generative capacity. Drawing from the rich creativity that is possible in syntactic structures, Stephen Anderson concludes that "human language makes it possible to express a vast range of notions that have no analogue in animal communication systems" (2004:220). In this, language distinguishes humans among other animal species. Further asserting the human-ness of language, Derek Bickerton writes that "language is what makes us human. Maybe it's the only thing that makes us human" (2009:4).
>
> **Language is essential to human life:** As Robert Longacre (1976) has observed, language enables us to express our emotions and volition, our interactions and observations about the environment in which we live. By it we organize our world temporally (by classifying actions in a successive order), and logically (according to various implicational relationships). In essence, language enables us to understand the world and how we fit in it, thereby giving us a sense of personal and social identity.
>
> **Language is a reflection of God's image in human beings:** Reviewing and dismissing the various speculations about the origin of language, Longacre convincingly argued that "the Judeo-Christian God revealed in the Scriptures ... must be central to a satisfactory worldview" (1983:348) about language. We hold from Scripture that God uses language to communicate within the Trinity (Gen 1:26 and more) and to communicate with humans (Gen 3 and more), to create reality (Gen 1), and to intimately reveal himself (Acts 2). In this regard, language is a bona fide theological category with a deep missional and strategic value. It enables God to reach

out to human beings within their respective and particular cultural contexts in ways that are relevant and appropriate to all.

Language is a social reality: There is no community that is not defined and identified by means of language. The use of a common language or languages provides a shared identity which is the foundation of a community. As a community loses its language[2] and shifts to use another one, it gradually ceases to exist as a distinct social entity. As important as it is to individuals' identity, language is essentially a social construct, a collective possession of all those who use it. Each person carries a bit or piece of the language, and it takes the entire community of speakers to manifest the full expression of the language.

This underscores another aspect of God's image in human beings: they are relational creatures (see chapter 4) who exist and thrive in communities. In this regard, language plays a vital and irreplaceable unifying role beyond its ability to enable a deeper communication and understanding. It represents the collective experience of the community's engagement with reality and conceptualizes its worldview and unique perspectives about life. In this regard, language can be likened to a treasure chest that stores a community's experiences, memories, wisdom, knowledge, and images and thereby expresses their sense of uniqueness in the world.

These key statements about language are essential to understanding the condition of the people who speak the minority languages of the world.

Minority language communities

About 1.8 billion people on the earth speak 92 percent of the world's languages. Most of these languages have a relatively small number of speakers, are often unwritten, and are spoken or signed in communities that lack the institutions and infrastructure to sustain their use. The following general attributes identified by John Watters (2019) characterize minority language communities. They are:

- **Economically**: most often among the poorest.
- **Medically**: most often in the bottom 20 percent of those receiving service.
- **Politically**: most often among the most disenfranchised.
- **Socially**: most often among the least valued.
- **Educationally**: most often among the least educated.
- **Justice-wise**: most often among the least informed of their rights and privileges.
- **Human dignity**: most often the least honored or considered worthy.

---

[2] Or languages. For simplicity, for the purposes of this paragraph the hypothetical language community uses a single language. The concept still applies, with added complexity, to language communities whose linguistic identity involves more than a single language.

As Watters goes on to rightly observe, they live in a context dominated by another language and culture, are in contact with other language communities, and must be multilingual in order to survive. As a result, they have varying needs. Any engagement in meeting those needs should enlist their authentic participation to ensure respect for their dignity and to affirm their sense of worth (see chapter 19).

Javier Pérez de Cuéllar (1996), a previous Director-General of UNESCO, makes a case for investing to preserve or enable the continuing use of minority languages. He argues that

> A people's language is perhaps its most fundamental cultural attribute ... Every single language spoken in the world represents a unique way of viewing human experience and the world itself ... The question of how to accommodate minorities is not of academic interest only but is a central challenge to any human politics ... Indigenous languages continue to be the main medium of expression of aspirations, intimate desires, feelings and local life. They are indeed the living repositories of cultures. (de Cuéllar 1996:59)

Significance of denying someone use of their first language

As language is so inherently connected to life, the denial of people's right to use their languages has important consequences for their identity and carries the potential to seriously affect their ability to flourish. Dinjeke and Eken's traumas affected their self-image, their community wholeness, and ultimately their relationship with God, as seen in the earlier vignettes.

Alteration of self-image

The refusal to allow Dinjeke and Eken to use their native languages in church or school conveys a profound, albeit unstated, message: your language is irrelevant; it doesn't count here. Since their mother tongue is the language that forged and shaped their early encounters with the world, there is a connection between that language and who they think they are and what they think they are worth. As such, the denial of their languages is not just a tactical choice of one language over another; it communicates to Dinjeke and Eken a loud message about their identity and dignity. Put differently, it tells them: just as your language is irrelevant, you also are inferior people.

Over the centuries and all around the world, wherever people's ability to use their languages has been denied or suppressed, the resulting effect has been a deep and disturbing identity issue. Algerian writer Sidahmed Sahla reveals the identity plight of his people when he produces dramas in his native Magribi (Algerian Arabic) language, claiming that it conveys an unequalled level of intimacy, spontaneity, truth, and naturalness (quoted in Skandar 2020:1).

In like manner, the First Nations in North America continue to struggle with their sense of self as a result of the policies that were violently enforced against their languages and cultures in the process of nation-building. Recounting their suffering, Bishop Larry Beardy (native Swampy Cree of Canada) recounts that when "his generation lost their language, they lost their identity and they lost their way. A lot of his brothers are on the streets. They use drugs and alcohol in an attempt to relieve the pain they carry … Their trauma is passed down into the next generation. Indigenous youth today are still struggling with their identity" (quoted in Eyre 2020).

Similar traumatic behaviors were observed among the Breton people of France when they lost their language. When a policy was enforced in the 1970s to reinstate their language, Serota Cote observed that alcoholism and depression subsided as people recovered their lost identity through language revitalization. She went on to write that "every Breton I spoke with who has learned the language as an adult said they feel now that they have been able to close the gap and heal those past wounds of shame. Many described finally discovering their roots by learning the language. One Breton said that the language 'completes the whole' " (quoted in Wallace 2009).

Alteration of the relationship with others

Eken's traumatic schooling experience is that of millions of children around the world. A child's linguistic, cognitive, and academic development happen in parallel. Therefore learning happens best when the language of instruction and the learner's competence in that language coincide.[3]

In southern Cameroon, for example, the imposition of the Bulu language for church and education purposes stirred the revolt of the Ngumba people. Salvador Eyezo'o (2010:102) writes that the Ngumba saw in the introduction of education in a foreign language something tantamount to enslavement. The Ngumba children wasted five to six years learning the foreign language; many dropped out of school and returned to illiteracy. Learning in a foreign language therefore compromised the ability for most of these children to achieve their full potential in life. The people claimed that the adoption of their native Ngumba language would be both efficient and fulfilling for their children's education.

There is more to Eken's trauma than the learning issue. The denial of the use of his native language in the education context subverts and unsettles the perspectives that give the community its sense of uniqueness and allows it to actively contribute to the world's knowledge. More so, it disrupts the education system that Eken was already connected to, with its values and orientations. The denial of the use of the native language disconnects him

---

[3] See Walter (2025) and Thomas and Collier (1997).

from his community values and perspectives and sets him on course to gradually morph into a different system with its own assumptions about life and reality. Cheikh Hamidou Kane writes that "very often, the metamorphosis is not complete; it sets and leaves us in a hybrid situation. Hence, we hide because we are deeply ashamed" (1960:125).

Along the same lines, in his novel, *Mission Terminée*, Mongo Beti (1957:97–98) tells the story of Medza who returns to his village after the successful completion of his high school education only to discover he is completely disconnected, unable to share in his native language about his learnings. He admires and embraces the values and assumptions of his education experience, yet they are incompatible with those that prevail in his own community. The result is cultural alienation and inability to become an active participant and contributor to the well-being of his community. At the Akrofi-Christaller Institute of Theology, Mission and Culture in Ghana, every student presenting a postgraduate degree is required to make a summary of their dissertation in their mother tongue. Through this, the students demonstrate whether or not they truly understand their topic and are able to engage with it in their community context.

In summary, it appears that the denial of the use of the native language in the schooling context is a covert start of an assimilation process that gradually turns the child into a semi-native of the externally imposed language.

Alteration of the relationship with God

Traumatic experiences, such as those of Dinjeke and Eken, also affect people's perception of God. They are creatures of a God who has sovereignly decided to create them within a specific linguistic and cultural setting. The denial of their right to access education or to worship God in their own language is a violent and abusive act that stirs existential questions that linger in their minds. Are we second-class creatures of God? Why has God endowed us with this language if we can't use it even for his worship? Are we God-forsaken? Such existential questions caused the Ghomala' people of Cameroon to refuse to take communion in the church for several years, until the early missionaries approved the adoption of their language for worship.

From what precedes, it appears that the 1.8 billion people (approximately 25 percent of the global population) who speak the lesser-known languages of the world (about 92 percent of the world's languages) have their worldview fractured by the lack of consideration given to their own languages. This has the potential to deeply affect their relationship with self, with others, and with God.

Flourishing as a missional concept

In chapter 2 we examined *flourishing life* as a missional concept and saw that in creating the world God created a relationship and environment for flourishing.

But the interaction recorded between God, Adam, and Eve in Genesis 3:8–13, which follows the rebellion of the humans against God's limitations on their lives, indicates that they wanted to be gods of their own lives rather than submit to God their Creator. As a result, their self-image, their relationships with God and with one another became distorted, causing them to flee from God's presence and become hostile to each other. The originally "good" creation in which they were placed is corrupted, and the cumulative effect of these factors disables their ability to flourish.

Despite human rebellion, God does not give up on his intent to bless people and pursue their flourishing. He calls Abraham out of his nation and promises to bless him and through him to bless all the families or nations of the earth. This promise repeats and summarizes God's missional intent and statement.

Ultimately, the incarnation, life, death, resurrection, and ascension of Jesus Christ achieves and enables the full realization of this blessing. Jesus is our supreme example and model of a flourishing life. People recognized his love for others, including those on the margins, and the ways he demonstrated God's righteousness and justice in caring for the vulnerable. The outpouring of the Holy Spirit at Pentecost inaugurated the church and reaffirmed God's commitment to extend God's blessing and desire for flourishing to all the ethnolinguistic communities of the earth.

Finally, the new creation as pictured in Revelation is a flourishing multicultural and plurilingual community of people who experience the fullness of God's presence. Coupled with this is the absence of any sorrows because "he will wipe away every tear from their eyes, and there will be no more death, or sorrow or crying or pain" (Rev 21:4a, NLT).

In the incarnation, Immanuel, God with us, submitted himself to human institutions and the particularity of culture and language (see chapter 12). He knew what it was to be part of a minority culture, speaking a minority language, being dominated by the trade language (Greek) and oppressed by the colonial power (Rome). In introducing the Kingdom of God that unveils God's blessing to these people in the margins, Jesus chose to speak their ordinary language.

On Pentecost (Acts 2), the Spirit of God made it possible for everyone present to hear the disciples speaking in their own languages. The Spirit respected each person and the language with which they identified. The Spirit spoke directly to each person without an interpreter but directly from the mouths of the disciples. So, Jesus' command to make disciples in every ethnic group converges with the Spirit's respect for language. The result of this command is a gathering of a crowd that nobody could count, of people from every tribe and tongue standing before the Lamb and worshipping God eternally (Rev 7:9). If God's blessing, which results in human flourishing, is so central to what God seeks to achieve within creation, then flourishing becomes a missional concept.

The Bible declares in Matthew that "Jesus traveled through all the towns and villages of that area, teaching in the synagogues and announcing the good news about the kingdom. And he healed every kind of disease and illness. When he saw the crowds, he had compassion on them because they were confused and helpless, like sheep without a shepherd. He said to his disciples, 'The harvest is great, but the workers are few. So pray to the Lord who is in charge of the harvest; ask him to send more workers into his fields'" (9:35–38, NLT).

If Jesus were here today in this twenty-first century, travelling through our towns and villages, he would certainly have compassion on speakers of minority languages who are often "confused and helpless" (Matt 9:36). With the acceleration of globalization, many of them would be found in their homelands where land and nature conservation issues continue to threaten their very existence; others would be migrant workers in diaspora and urban settings; and still others would be refugees in countries or regions of the world where they have to negotiate their integration, often at the expense of their own identities. Unlocking to them what God does to restore his intent for the lives of his creatures represents the best response to their deepest hope and aspirations. The concept of flourishing in its essence captures this intent. In this way, it can be understood through other biblical themes and images such as blessing, shalom, and reconciliation, which I discuss in the following sections.

Flourishing as blessing

In the account of Genesis, God declares all that he created as good. He creates men and women and blesses them to expand humanity, to take care of creation, and rule over it. God's blessing is therefore understood as the pronouncement of a future of goodness and the fulfillment of the person or entity on which the blessing is bestowed. When the blessing is fulfilled in a person, community, or nation, it enables them to flourish, to attain the full realization of what God intended for them. Sarita Gallagher and Stephen Hawthorne (2011:11) depict three broad categories or manifestations of blessing found in the story of Abraham. First, we see blessing as material wealth and fruitfulness (Gen 24:35, 30:27, 30). Second, we see blessing as a favored relationship with God and the experience of his presence (Gen 14:19–20, 21:22, 26:22). And third, we see blessings bringing about a measure of peace amidst families and peoples (Gen 21:22–23, 26:18–29). God called Abraham and his descendants to be the agents of this threefold blessing upon all the peoples.

Ultimately, the incarnation, life, death, and resurrection of Jesus Christ achieves and enables the full realization of this blessing. Jesus declares that his "purpose is to give them a rich and satisfying life" (John 10:10b, NLT). The Church is instituted to participate in this blessing and to enable its experience by all individuals, communities, and nations of the world. The concept of flourishing understood as blessing is therefore a deep expression of the aspiration of the speakers of the minority languages of the earth who long for a right relationship with God and with their fellow human beings so that the cycle of material poverty and political and spiritual alienation that enslaves them can be broken.

Flourishing as shalom

The notion of shalom is a key and prevalent biblical concept. The Hebrew word שָׁלוֹם (*shalom*) can be found 237 times in the Old Testament, while εἰρήνη (*eirēnē*)—the Greek equivalent—can be found ninety-two times in the New. The English rendering of shalom as peace limits the semantic field of the word. The original Hebrew meaning is far richer and conveys the ideas of wholeness, completeness, soundness, well-being, health, prosperity, and salvation. As Paul Hiebert writes, "It is based on three fundamental principles: this world and all in it belongs to God; all humans share equally in God's loving concern; and the reign of God in creation and in human communities leads to peace, justice and truly fulfilled lives" (quoted in Moreau 2000:868). Hiebert's second principle touches on the most fundamental issue of exclusion that mars the condition of the speakers of minority languages as highlighted by Eken and Dinjeke. All human beings are equal in dignity, and God shows no favoritism to any people groups. Therefore, the same good news that invites people into God's kingdom is available to all human beings, irrespective of their languages or their socio-economic or racial status.

In highly individualistic societies, the idea of social well-being tends to be construed as a matter of each individual achieving their full potential. As such, the group thriving is the sum of its individual members thriving. Most often, the speakers of minority languages share different worldviews. The individual's worth does not depend primarily on individual achievement but is a matter of group status or prestige. Therefore, communal harmony takes precedence over individual rights. In fact, the individual's well-being flows out of the person's community's well-being. The worldview orientation of these communities is like that of *Ubuntu*[4] which emphasizes

---

[4] "Ubuntu" is a Nguni Bantu term meaning 'humanity'. It is often translated as 'I am because we are', or 'humanity towards others', or, in Xhosa, *umntu ngumntu ngabantu,* often used in a more philosophical sense to mean "the belief in a universal bond of sharing that connects all humanity." "About the Name." Official Ubuntu Documentation. Canonical. Archived from the original on 23 February 2013. Retrieved 2 February 2017.

interconnectedness. Right behavior is defined by a person's relations with other people or by acts that benefit the entire community. The pursuit of true shalom involves harnessing all initiatives (economic, political, spiritual, cultural, etc.) and using all resources to promote the moral fiber of the community. In this regard, language becomes a critical component of group well-being because it is an intrinsically social issue. As a marker that identifies the group, it becomes essential to the wholeness of the group that speaks it.

Viewed in this way, shalom needs to be construed in its fuller breadth rather than in the reductionist scope of peace. The pursuit of flourishing, understood as shalom, among minority language speaking communities implies engagement in activities that further the presence and reign of God. This includes building a positive context for people to use the languages they value to expand their possibilities through adequate access to and engagement with God's word, education, and integration into the socio-economic life of their nations.

Flourishing as reconciliation

As argued before, minority language speakers like Dinjeke and Eken live with a marred identity. As a result, they don't experience the fullness of life that God intended for them because their relationships with self, with others, and with God have been distorted. The restoration of these relationships back to God's original order is indispensable for them to flourish. Reconciliation is the process through which God works to restore those relationships. In Colossians 1:20, Paul writes that God reconciled "to himself all things, whether things on earth or things in heaven, by making peace through his blood, shed on the cross." The scope of what the cross addresses in order to bring about a full reconciliation with God goes far beyond what we can understand from a human perspective. It is about destroying all that enslaves and separates human beings and creation from the experience of God's intent for them. Looking specifically at the condition of minority language speakers, there is a need to reappraise our understanding of the cross to discern the kinds of missional activities that would bring about effective reconciliation. Language is significant in the definition of people's identity; it plays a key role in their ability to effectively engage with God and with their fellow human beings. Therefore, adequate attention must be given to the role of language in effective reconciliation and in providing the necessary conditions for flourishing.

In summary, we understand the concept of human flourishing to mean the restoration of all that God intended for his creatures. Therefore, human flourishing is central in God's mission. Dinjeke and Eken's stories clearly indicate that language issues have the potential to enable or inhibit people's experience of that fullness of life because "language and human life are ultimately inseparable" (Longacre 1976:319).

Conclusion: Implications for the Church's missional engagement

The process of globalization tends to merge people and nations within a global community that is dominated by a few languages. This fragile community construct has always proven to be problematic. The issue of minority language speakers flourishing is often deeply ingrained in the resulting identity struggles. Undeniably, language is central and essential to this, warranting that we clarify our missional engagement with regard to language.

> **The basis of our engagement:** From what precedes, we understand that language is a unique attribute of God, humans, and communities; it also has an inherent relationship with God's mission. Therefore, issues of language have the potential to deeply affect people and their communities, and thereby compromise their ability to flourish. In consequence, it is important to build our missional engagement on the solid foundation of both the great commission and the great commandment (loving God and loving neighbor). The ethic of love in the great commandment is required to painstakingly engage in the subtle and complex realities of the minority language speaking communities, especially in the twenty-first century.
>
> **Scope of engagement:** If flourishing for minority language communities is indeed about the experience of blessing, reconciliation, and shalom, then it is important to re-envision the full scope of what Jesus' death on the cross is meant to achieve in order to realize God's aims for them. Two extreme views of the gospel continue to create tensions within the worldwide Christian community: a vertical interpretation essentially concerned with God's saving action in the life of individuals, and a horizontal one that is preoccupied with human relationships in the world. As Visser t'Hooft states,
>
>> A Christianity which has lost its vertical dimension has lost its salt and is not only insipid in itself, but useless for the world. But a Christianity which would use the vertical preoccupation as a means to escape from its responsibility for and in the common life of man is a denial of the incarnation of God's love for the world manifested in Christ. (quoted in Padilla 2004:2)
>
> In his own ministry on earth, Jesus models integration between both perspectives by clearly addressing human and physical needs, while undeniably pointing to and converging all his actions to serve the purpose of God's kingdom.

Language and Bible translation: Bible translation has been a driver of the interest in language and its development, especially in the missionary era. As Bible translation becomes more and more of a theological enterprise and an ecclesial activity in the twenty-first century, it is important to reappraise the role of language in Bible translation.

Language beyond Bible translation: The importance of language in God's nature and activity and for the identity of human beings and the communities they constitute warrants a consideration of the value of language beyond Bible translation. The psycho-sociological impact of language and culture loss resulting in ill-behaviors, ethnic strife that endangers peace and democracy in developing nations, and overall justice issues in a fast-globalizing world all point to the relevance of language in the quest to achieve effective flourishing of communities. Such realities provide a wider basis for the interest in language development, language preservation, language promotion, and language use in the various domains of life.

In a fast-globalizing world that tends to merge people into an imagined global space, there is an urgent necessity for a missional engagement with language in order to advocate for the pursuit of God's diverse, plurilingual, and multicultural kingdom as described in Revelation. This missional engagement with language must extend into the academic realm to explore and firm up a theology of language, and to sow and advocate for perspectives that will inform public policies in favor of the flourishing of the speakers of minority languages. In this, we assert that as we engage in God's mission through linguistic initiatives, we are not concerned about language for language's sake, but our concern is for the flourishing of God's people and his plans and purposes in the world.

References

Anderson, Stephen R. 2004. *Doctor Dolittle's delusion: Animals and the uniqueness of human language.* New Haven, CT: Yale University Press.
Beti, Mongo. 1957. *Mission terminée.* Paris: Buchet-Chastel.
Bickerton, Derek. 2009. *Adam's tongue: How humans made language, how language made humans.* New York, NY: Hill and Wang.
De Cuéllar, Javier Pérez. 1996. What benefit for whom? In *Our creative diversity: Report of the World Commission on Culture and Development.* Paris: UNESCO.
Eyezo'o, Salvador. 2010. *L'émergence de l'Église Protestante Africaine (1934–1959) : Enjeux linguistiques, identité kwassio et contextualisation de l'Évangile en situation missionnaire.* Yaoundé, Cameroon: Éditions CLÉ.
Eyre, Roy. 2020. Email message to Wycliffe Canada, 7 August 2020.

Gallagher, Sarita D., and Stephen C. Hawthorne. 2011. Blessing as transformation. *Mission Frontiers* Sept–Oct 2011:11. https://www.missionfrontiers.org/issue/article/blessing-as-transformation.

Kane, Cheikh Hamidou. 1960. *L'Aventure ambiguë*. Paris: Juliard.

Kenmogne, Michel. 2000. The lexical phonology of Bakoko. PhD dissertation. The University of Buea, Cameroon.

Longacre, Robert E. 1976. *An anatomy of speech notions*. PdR Press Publications in Tagmemics 3. Lisse, Netherlands: Peter de Ridder Press.

Longacre, Robert E. 1983. *The grammar of discourse*. New York, NY: Plenum Press.

Moreau, A. Scott, ed. 2000. *Evangelical dictionary of world missions*. Baker Reference Library. Grand Rapids, MI: Baker Books.

Padilla, C. René. 2004. Holistic mission. *Lausanne Occasional Papers* 33:2.

Skandar, Nabila. 2020. Langue et théâtre, une question d'intimité. Viedes libres, 10 August 2020. Accessed 11 September 2020. https://algeriecultures.com/actualite-culturelle/langue-et-theatre-une-question-dintimite/ (site discontinued).

Thomas, Wayne P., and Virginia Collier. 1997. School effectiveness for language minority students. NCBE Resource Collection Series 9. Washington, DC: National Clearinghouse for Bilingual Education (NCBE).

Wallace, Lane. 2009. What's lost when a language dies. *The Atlantic*, 10 November 2009. https://www.theatlantic.com/national/archive/2009/11/whats-lost-when-a-language-dies/29886/.

Walter, Stephen L. 2025. The impact of partial proficiency in the language of instruction on learning outcomes in basic education. In Suwilai Premsrirat and David Hirsh (eds.), *Mother tongue-based multilingual education in the Asia-Pacific region*, 197–221. Bristol, UK: Multilingual Matters.

Watters, John R. 2019. The state of minority languages in the twenty-first century. In Christopher L. Flanders (ed.), *Devoted to Christ: Missiological reflections in honor of Sherwood G. Lingenfelter*, 30–49. Eugene, OR: Pickwick Publications. Original draft of paper 2013.

Daleth

*I run in the path of your commands,
for you have broadened my understanding.
(Psalm 119:32)*

4

Language: The Gift of God's Presence

Dawn Kruger

Introduction

The mission of God radiates from the center of the Trinity (see chapter 2), that place where perfect love and shalom are freely given and received and enjoyed among the three Persons of the Godhead (So 2010:43). From that context and with a desire to share that love and shalom with others, God created people in his image—humans with the capacity to know him and thus to commune with him (Barry 1992:47). One way in which humans reflect the image of God, who is love, is that we, too, are capable of loving. As love is relational, it follows that God is relational. So being created in his image means we are relational beings as well, even as he is.

Thus we can say that we were created for relationship: to enjoy fellowship with God, with others, and even with God's created world, just as God himself does. That capacity for fellowship—particularly with God—is made possible because our relational God, the transcendent Creator, enters into the space of his creation and lives life with his image-bearers. To describe the uniqueness of that relationship, in this chapter I borrow the word *tabernacle*—introduced in the Old Testament (see, for example, Exod 26,

36, and 40) and reiterated throughout the New Testament (e.g., Heb 9:1–11 and Rev 21:3, sometimes translated as "dwell" as in John 1:14)—because, for me, tabernacle conveys a deeper meaning of intimacy and familiarity than other word choices.

Tabernacle expresses well the complex, comprehensive relational initiative of God. In tabernacling with his people, God does more than simply exist in the same place. Rather, God's presence together with his glory fills the space and the surrounding area (see, for example, Exod 16:10 and 19:17–20, Num 9:15–22, 1 Kings 8:10–13), and God himself experiences life in that place in the same way as his image-bearers. Tabernacling speaks to the wonder of God giving himself—his holiness, power, hope, joy, and yes, shalom—and essentially bringing all of his attributes to bear on the experience of his people in the place where he lives with them. Consider these passages from Israel's history:

> Moses and Aaron then went into the tent of meeting. When they came out, they blessed the people; and the glory of the LORD appeared to all the people. Fire came out from the presence of the LORD and consumed the burnt offering and the fat portions on the altar. And when all the people saw it, they shouted for joy and fell facedown. (Lev 9:23–24)

> "For the generations to come this burnt offering is to be made regularly at the entrance to the tent of meeting, before the LORD. There I will meet you and speak to you; there also I will meet with the Israelites, and the place will be consecrated by my glory. ... Then I will dwell among the Israelites and be their God. They will know that I am the LORD their God, who brought them out of Egypt *so that I might dwell among them.* I am the LORD their God." (Exod 29:42–43, 45–46 [emphasis added]).

When the visible manifestation of God's glory, the shekinah[1], filled the tabernacle in Exodus 40:34–38, the people of Israel knew that God himself was in that desert place with them, bringing with his presence an intimate, experiential understanding of them and their situation. Today that same relational God tabernacles with us, his people, and I suggest that he does this through language.

There are many ways and many means by which God is both present amongst and communicates with his people. John 20:22 and other Scriptures tell us that God himself in the person of the Holy Spirit dwells with and in his people (see also Acts 1:5, 1:8, 1 Cor 6:19, Heb 13:5). He also uses a wide variety of ways to communicate (see part two). However, this

---

[1] Literally, "that which dwells," referring to God dwelling with his people; see Exod 25:22.

chapter focuses on God's pursuit of his missional goals to be known and to receive glory by utilizing the missiological strategy of tabernacling with his people in the space and context of language.

Divine missional goal

One goal of God's mission is to display his glory and preserve the reputation of his great name. All that God does, including redemption, is for his glory. Psalm 85:9 says, "Surely his salvation is near those who fear him, *that his glory may dwell in our land*" (emphasis added). Again, in Psalm 79:9, the psalmist cries out, "Help us, God our Savior, for the glory of your name; deliver us and forgive our sins for your name's sake." God receives glory through our salvation.

God receives glory through relationships. The Son glorifies the Father (John 12:28) and conversely, the Father glorifies the Son (John 17:1, 4–5). The book of John tells us that the Spirit also glorifies the Son (John 16:14). Christ in humility obeyed the Father, and the Father in return exalted the Son, giving him "the name that is above every other name … to the glory of God the Father" (Phil 2:9, 11).

If glory is a key element of God's mission, then we need to ask ourselves, "What does the word *glory* mean?" Moran Rosenblit (2022) writes: "In the English translation of Scripture, the Hebrew word 'כָּבוֹד' 'kavod' is translated as 'glory', but in essence there is a much deeper meaning to this word. This word contains the essence of something of value, of great appreciation, wealth, honor and weight." Ursula Niebuhr (1984) describes God's glory as "more than beauty, more than mystery, more than goodness. The Hebrew word KABOD stands for the qualities … of God, and suggests as well as describes his Presence which is too glorious for [people] to behold. [This word] gives us, when we look at the biblical stories, an exact description of God's nature, of his character."

Though the word itself defies a tidy definition, in this chapter, when I speak of God's glory as a missional goal, I am referring to God's desire to be known in the fullness of who he is (his nature and character), which includes his holiness and his tenderness; his majesty and his humility; his power and his grace; his transcendence and his affection. Our relationship with God must be framed within "the knowledge of the glory of the Lord" (Hab 2:14) (see chapter 2).

Divine missional strategy

God's glory is realized as knowledge of him increases. God is constantly revealing his nature and character as he moves toward the day when "the earth will be filled with the knowledge of the glory of the Lord as the waters cover the sea" (Hab 2:14). Revelation of God comes through various means. Scripture speaks of his self-revelation through creation (Ps 19:1–2, Isa 55:12) and his sovereign acts of mercy (1 Sam 12:22, Ps 106:8, Isa 43:25, 48:11). Even his judgment, as described in Ezekiel 36, reveals his holy nature. But two significant ways by which God makes himself known are through his word and through his people (Wright 2006:127).

In Scripture we see God's purposes accomplished through the use of language. The biblical narrative begins with God speaking creation into existence (Gen 1) and, in response, nature proclaims the glory of God (Ps 19:1). On a different level, God uses language to discuss within the context of the Trinity his desire to create people in his own image (Gen 1:26) (see chapter 8 for more on speech acts of God). Isaiah 59:21 tells us how God uses language for his ongoing relationship with his people. "'As for me, this is my covenant with them,' says the LORD. 'My Spirit, who is on you, will not depart from you, and my words that I have put in your mouth will always be on your lips, on the lips of your children and on the lips of their descendants—from this time on and forever,' says the LORD." Language is an attribute of the triune God that he shares with his image-bearers, and, using language, God makes himself known in the developing friendship he has with people (Exod 33:11, Deut 5:24, Isa 41:8–10).

Making himself known

Christopher Wright (2006:95) boldly claims that God's desire to be known is what drives the biblical narrative. God begins by communing with Adam and Eve in the Garden of Eden. This narrative reflects the prototype relationship between the divine and the created. God walked with them and conversed with them in the garden (Gen 3:8ff.). Honoring his image in them, he extended to Adam the privilege of sharing in his creative initiatives by naming the animals. Language was not just a resource to provide noun-names for creatures, nor was it a utilitarian instrument for the transfer of information. Rather God was using language to fellowship with his image-bearers, sharing himself and his activities with them. Eden, then, became the holy place where God was present with his people (Beale and Kim 2014:20). T. C. Moore says, "The garden of Eden is not viewed by the author of Genesis simply as a piece of Mesopotamian farmland, but as an archetypal sanctuary, that is a place where God dwells and where [humanity] worship[s] him" (2015:4).

God's passion to be known and his desire to bless all of creation with his presence are evidenced in his instructions to his image-bearers, when he blesses them and tells them to be fruitful, to multiply, and to fill the earth (Gen 1:28). God's instructions to Adam and Eve and to Noah's family (Gen 9:1), and then, later, his benevolent act of dispersing the people at the Tower of Babel, were intended to fulfill his missional purpose of filling the earth with the knowledge of his glory (see also chapter 10). The call to multiply image-bearers to cover the earth would, according to Beale and Kim, "expand the boundaries of that Garden sanctuary until it [too] filled the whole earth" (2014:34). For with that expansion goes the presence of God himself. "The abundance of life found in the Garden paints a picture of the abundance [of life that can be] found in the tabernacling presence of God" in every place where his image is displayed (2014:20).

Later in Genesis, God chooses Israel to be the nation with whom he would tabernacle—literally, as noted earlier. He displays his loving nature as he gently cares for Israel, carrying them "on eagles' wings" (Exod 19:4) and providing for all their needs (i.e., manna, water, clothing, military success, etc.). To his treasured possession (Exod 19:4–6) God makes promises, using language in its fullness of expression, "I will send you rain in its season, your threshing will continue [from harvest to planting] … I will grant you peace in the land … I will look on you with favor and make you fruitful … and I will keep my covenant with you." Then he says: "I will put my dwelling place among you … I will walk among you and be your God, and you will be my people … I broke the bars of your yoke and enabled you to walk with *heads held high*" (Lev 26:4–13 [emphasis added]). Israel flourished under God's care. As a display people, as Michael Goheen (2011) calls them, Israel was to attract others into a covenant relationship with God, "bringing the knowledge of God to the nations and bringing the nations to the means of atonement with God" (Wright 2006:331). In his covenant relationship with Israel, God was blessing them with the same shalom experienced within the relationship of the Trinity, and missionally revealing himself to the nations (Mangano 2008:74, Köstenberger and O'Brien 2017:34).

Offering his presence

The crowning moment of God's covenant with Israel was sealed on Mount Sinai when God promised his own presence to dwell in their midst. The *shekinah* served as evidence of the presence of God entering the tabernacle; this became the distinguishing feature of that "treasured possession". In Ezekiel 37:27–28 God himself says, "My dwelling place will be with them; I will be their God, and they will be my people. *Then the nations will know* that I the LORD make Israel holy, when my sanctuary is among them forever" (emphasis added). God entering the tabernacle in order to dwell in the midst of his people was for their own flourishing (as he cared for them) and for the good of the nations (as his glory was revealed through them). According to Ida Glaser, the significance of God meeting with Moses on Mount Sinai is "that God is giving Israel his presence; the giving of the law was secondary" (2016:134). Thus it would be safe to say that the presence of God tabernacling with his people is of central importance in the biblical narrative.

Moses understood the weight of this commitment. When Moses spoke with God about entering Canaan, he asked, "What else will distinguish me and your people from all the other people on the face of the earth?" (Exod 33:16b). "Without the presence of the LORD God, Israel would be no different from the rest of the nations. And only by Israel being distinct from the nations was there any purpose in being Israel at all, or any hope for the nations themselves eventually" (Wright 2006:333). God's mission is "a matter of presence—the presence of the people of God in the midst of the nations and the presence of God in the midst of His people" (Martin-Achard 1962:47). As Goheen says, "Israel's identity was wrapped up in one reality: that the Creator and Sovereign LORD stooped down to humanity and dwelt in their midst" (2011:43).

Summation of God's missional intent

As we look at God and his mission as revealed in Scripture, we see that God's desire is to be known among the nations and to receive glory for his name's sake. To that end he gives himself to creation through his promised presence. He began by walking with his image-bearers in the garden sanctuary, then by dwelling in the Holy of Holies in the tabernacle and later in the temple (evidenced by the glowing light of the *shekinah*, visible to all Israelites). Though the glory of God later departed from the temple, God remembered his covenantal promise. In the New Testament, Immanuel appears, and God is once again with his people. When Christ is about to return to the Father, he promises his disciples, "I will ask the Father, and he will give you another advocate, to help you and *be with you forever*" (John 14:16 [emphasis added]). At Pentecost the Spirit of God descends on all God's people and remains with them even as he does with us today. In all this, God continues to move his mission forward toward that day when the holy city, the new Jerusalem, will come down from heaven, shining with the glory of God in all its brilliance, and a loud voice will shout, "Look! God's dwelling place is now among the people, and he will dwell with them. They will be his people, and God himself will be with them and be their God" (Rev 21:3b). "So," Glaser declares, "we could say that the whole Bible is about how God fulfills his desire to live among human beings" (2016:129).

God tabernacling with his people looks backward to his presence in Eden and in Israel and looks forward to his ultimate presence among all nations forever. God tabernacling with his people is at the heart of his mission.

God the Word dwells in language

A passage often quoted by people when referencing God's use of language is the first chapter of the book of John: "In the beginning was the Word" (John 1:1a). Of course, the Word here represents more than a unit of language. It encompasses the full essence of God, an expression of God who existed pre-creation and continues to exist as the Word post-resurrection. This Word is the bridge between divine and mortal, the channel through which we humans are able to commune with a transcendent God, our divine Creator. It is interesting to note that the Word is not a string of words gathered together into many sentences. It is not a complex explanation or a systematic theology. It is simply the Word. God. It is also interesting to note that God projects his identity linguistically through the word *Word*. We, made in his image, also root our identity in language, as a finite reflection of an infinite God. Yet, the Word is not identified as a language, implying that God speaks one particular language and would need to learn other languages in order to communicate with people. Rather, God as the Word represents all that needs to be said and known, anytime, anywhere, in any language. The Word is as transcendent as God himself; it is a language unto itself, knowable in all languages.

"And the Word became flesh and made his dwelling among us. We have seen his glory" (John 1:14a). This verse beautifully connects God the Word with the mission of God as described above. The incarnation of Christ fills the gap between the pre-creation Word that existed as God and the post-incarnation Word that reveals God, establishing continuity between the transcendent expression of God and the physical expression of God normalized through language. The Word entered into the world of words to reveal God's glory. God as the Word tabernacles in language so that we can know him.

From this eternally pre-existent Word, we understand that God has always been a communicating God. God has always been transparent about who he is. A Word eternally spoken, an incomprehensible being ever ready to make himself known. In this Word the fullness of God dwells (Col 1:19), and through this Word God has spoken to us (Heb 1:2). God is and always has been outwardly focused, ready to reveal his nature and his character to any who would listen.

We know that this Word, being God, is omnipresent. This omnipresent expression of God dwells in the midst of all he created. So, in essence, we could say that the earth is and always has been filled with the message of and, thus, the glory of God. However, *knowledge* of that message, *knowledge* of the glory of God, does not yet fill the earth. For that to happen, this Word needs to be proclaimed in the words of all languages. The Word is everywhere present, ready to speak into every language community.

We further learn from the book of John that life resides in the Word (John 1:4). That Word being present in the world of words provides the means by which God offers life to all who believe. Language, then, is one means by which God's abundant life comes to us, for it is available to all who believe in his name, and his name is Word.

John 1:9–12 speaks of the Word coming into the world as "to his own". The Word enters the world of words—of language. We who are uniquely image-bearers of God have now become word-bearers of the Word. The

Word came to his own—to those created in his image. We who are "his own," as word-bearers, often socially organize ourselves and identify ourselves by language. So, we could say that language (as representing people) is his own. The Word coming to language as to his own indicates the missional intent of God to enter into every language, every cultural context, bringing his presence into every community. God is not simply seeking to find practical ways of mechanically spreading the gospel to every language. Rather, he is making himself known through relationship—the Word relating to all words, the Word tabernacling in all languages—not in a linear fashion of text dissemination but in a beautiful, calligraphic relationship unique to each script and sign.

What do we do, then, with John's statement that his own did not receive him (John 1:11)? Sung Chan Kwon (2019:92) speaks of this when he references Jesus' relationship with the first century Jews. He says, "[T]hey [the Jews] are the nation of 'revelation' of God. By being 'with the very words of God', they were expected to recognize the incarnate Word, Jesus." Yet they did not, because they were looking for form (traditions and practices focused on rote action) instead of meaning (the essence of the nature of God himself). The law of God had become a matter of ritual to the Jews; the word of God had lost its meaning for them other than to simply be something they performed. Kwon (see chapter 14) goes on to describe how Jesus' mission was to restore the meaning of God's Word (Immanuel, God with us) as well as the missional identity of God's people.

So, the Word being rejected by his own could be understood as God being rejected by people and nations identified by language because they do not understand the meaning of the Word, that is, they are lacking knowledge of God. The conflict of the Word entering into the world of words is a conflict that happens within the realm of meaning and understanding. But the Word came, and dwelt, and we beheld. In his coming and in his dwelling we experience God's nature; in beholding we see his glory. As a result we grasp afresh the depth of meaning, the magnitude of the Word becoming flesh and dwelling among us (John 1:14). And, like Adam and Eve, we, his word-bearers, have been instructed to spread out and fill the earth with this knowledge of him (Mark 16:15), that this Word may be understood—received by his own—and may thus tabernacle with word-bearers in all languages.

The future Word

God's missional engagement in the world happens in a significant way within the realm of language. In the grand scope of the mission of God, the Word speaks by its very existence of a God who desires relationship, and to that end reveals himself through language.

The story doesn't end there, however. Not only did the Word take on the flesh of language, but "the flesh of language [still] clings to the Word"

(Ambrus 2016:14). Christ before creation was the Word without a physical body. In the advent of his incarnation, that Word was enveloped in flesh and took on language. In his language-flesh Christ lived, died, and was raised back to life. Today he lives eternally as the God-Word embodied in human words. Just as God in Christ came as the eternal Word, so now the human being Jesus has returned to heaven physically, retaining in his human form the capacity—literally—to use language. "What the words of the risen Lord … reveal to us is not only the assumption of Christ's body into heavenly glory, but also the Word's everlasting retention of incarnate language" (Ambrus 2016:14). By remaining now and for eternity both divine Word and incarnate language, Christ forever affirms the treasure of all human languages. Christ taking on the flesh of language both reflects and secures the value that God confers on all languages for all time. God tabernacles in language, and language will forever remain with God.

"So what?"

God tabernacles in language and invites us to meet him there. So now we must ask ourselves: What does that mean to us today?

The presence of God with his people is substantiated through his blessing. Adam and Eve flourished in the garden sanctuary in the presence of God. God's visible presence in the tabernacle (the *shekinah*) was a source of blessing for the nation of Israel. But it was also a means by which surrounding nations would see God's blessing toward his chosen people and thereby be drawn to God himself. Ultimately, Jesus Christ the Word came and, in coming, offered life and meaning to this fractured world.

Yet, do we his people understand the full impact of God's abiding presence with us? We often personalize the gift of God's presence, taking comfort in the gift of the Holy Spirit, quoting such verses as, "I can do all things through Christ who gives me strength" (Phil 4:13), or "My grace is sufficient for you, for my power is made perfect in weakness" (2 Cor 12:9a). We use such verses to pray for help with the difficult burdens we bear personally. But God's missional intention for tabernacling with his people goes beyond simply blessing us with inner strength to endure or overcome personal trials. The goal is that we will experience the fullness of life in Christ, and that the nations will see his character and his nature displayed in how he lives with us and cares for us, *so that* they, too, will be drawn into his presence, into his kingdom. We, like Israel, are to be *so that* people.

That happens individually, yes, but also corporately. As his people, his Church, how do we view our responsibility as God's image-bearers, and—reflecting the character of Christ to the world—as God's word-bearers? The work God's people do is sacred work, for God himself is present in it, whether it be discipleship, caring for the poor and the hurting, offering a cup of cold water in Jesus' name, caring for the planet, and so much more.

Specifically connecting language with the mission of God, then, Scripture translation, education, and language development initiatives (like those described by Kenmogne in chapter 3 and Young in chapter 19) are just some of the many crucial ways in which people working in human and social sciences can promote God's missional activity of making himself known for the glory of his name and for the flourishing of people. As others mention in this book, linguistic hospitality (chapter 21) and linguistic justice (chapter 17), among other attitudes and initiatives, are reasonable expectations of word-bearers, reflecting the character of God in relation to the misunderstood, misrepresented, or marginalized.

Conclusion

So, we have seen that God's mission is to be known and to be in relationship with his image-bearers, which he does by tabernacling with them, for the glory of his name. Language is one means by which he accomplishes this. Because the Word dwells with us, we have the capacity to commune directly with God. We flourish as we fellowship with the transcendent one who stooped down to enter our space. As we view language and its many expressions as the space where God himself meets with his word-bearers, we encourage "his own" to receive him. As the Word finds its home and tabernacles in all languages, the abundance of God's presence enters into all people's stories. And as people enjoy their sacred and bountiful relationship with God through the living Word, God receives glory.

References

Ambrus, Gárbon. 2016. In the beginning was the Word: Theological reflections on language and technical media in the context of the Gospel of John. *AUC Theologica* 6(2):135–151.

Barry, William A. 1992. *Spiritual direction and the encounter with God: A theological inquiry*. Mahwah, NJ: Paulist Press.

Beale, G. K., and Mitchell Kim. 2014. *God dwells among us: Expanding Eden to the ends of the earth*. Downers Grove, IL: IVP.

Glaser, Ida. 2016. *Thinking biblically about Islam: Genesis, transfiguration, transformation*. Carlisle, UK: Langham Global Library.

Goheen, Michael W. 2011. *A light to the nations: The missional church and the biblical story*. Grand Rapids, MI: Baker Academic.

Köstenberger, Andreas J., and Peter T. O'Brien. 2017. *Salvation to the ends of the Earth: A biblical theology of mission*. New Studies in Biblical Theology 11. Downers Grove, IL: InterVarsity Press.

Kwon, Sung Chan. 2019. A missional reading of the Fourth Gospel. PhD dissertation. Oxford Centre for Mission Studies.

Mangano, Mark J. 2008. *The image of God*. Lanham, MD: University Press of America.

Martin-Achard, Robert. 1962. *A light to the nations: A study of the Old Testament conception of Israel's mission to the world*. Edinburgh, UK: Oliver and Boyd Ltd. Digitized 2011.

Moore, T. C. 2015. Toward a temple-city of Shalom: How the Pentateuch anticipates a world indwelled by God. Gordon-Conwell Theological Seminary, Center for Urban Ministerial Education. https://www.academia.edu/12097546/Toward_a_Temple_City_of_Shalom_How_the_Pentateuch_Anticipates_a_World_Indwelled_by_God.

Niebuhr, Ursala M. 1984. Glory. *Biblical Theology Bulletin*. 14(2):49–53. https://journals.sagepub.com/doi/abs/10.1177/014610798401400203.

Rosenblit, Moran. 2022. The weight of his glory. Hope for Israel blog post March 3, 2022. https://hope4israel.org/pequdei-tashpav/.

So, Damon W. K. 2010. *The forgotten Jesus and the Trinity you never knew*. Eugene, OR: Wipf and Stock.

Wright, Christopher J. H. 2006. *The mission of God: Unlocking the Bible's grand narrative*. Nottingham, UK: Inter-Varsity Press.

He

*Teach me, LORD, the way of your decrees,
that I may follow it to the end.
(Psalm 119:33)*

5

Oral Language and the Mission of God

Abou Sama, with Bronwen Cleaver

Introduction

In this chapter we examine oral, that is spoken, language. God's mission is one of self-revelation, to make himself known, and this he does, first and foremost, by means of oral communication. This is seen as he engages with patriarchs and prophets in the Old Testament, and also in the New Testament, where Jesus' teaching was always delivered orally. (The one time when Jesus is said to have written something, in John 8:6–8, we are not told what he wrote.) In the second part of this chapter, we examine the effectiveness of oral communication in God's mission and give some examples of its use. One particular way in which God speaks is through dreams, and two examples are given of lives transformed through God speaking orally in dreams. In the final section, we compare orality and literacy and note some strengths of each.

God's choice to communicate orally

God's spoken word brought the universe into existence. He used the same voice to establish a profound relationship with the patriarchs. To foster a deeper bond with humanity, God communicated his love through his voice, desiring his children to hear him. His voice resonated in both the Old and New Testaments. As David Théry (2022) states, "Indeed, God communicates in numerous ways, but hearing His voice is always extraordinary."

Jesus affirmed, "My sheep *hear my voice*. I know them, and they follow me" (John 10:27, NRSV [emphasis added]). God's communication in the Scriptures took various forms—through angels, visions, dreams, revelations, prophecies, and even, humorously, through a donkey. In all these instances, it is God's voice that is heard. God also enabled humankind to express words and emotions to him orally.

God's oral tradition in the Old Testament

Understanding the relationship between God and humanity in Christianity is rooted in God's communication with humankind, which began with oral exchanges. An essential aspect of this oral tradition can be found primarily in the Old Testament, where various forms of direct communication from God to individuals are experienced along with biblical teachings transmitted through verbal means. These methods reveal crucial elements about divine revelation and human interaction with God since they convey that Scriptures were not transcribed directly but rather were passed down orally for years or centuries before being chronicled into written accounts.

Throughout the Old Testament, God's interactions with humanity have frequently been portrayed as happening through spoken means. The book of Genesis provides one of the earliest instances, when God speaks directly to Adam and Eve in a verbal exchange (Gen 3:8–13). Similarly, an important occurrence of divine oral transmission takes place during Moses' encounter with the burning bush (Exod 3:1–6), where he is called upon by God to lead God's people out of bondage in Egypt. This address from within a fiery manifestation serves not only as proof for divinity but also directs Moses personally toward action. Additionally significant is that this instance marks the initial recorded occasion on which Moses receives direct contact from above by means of the spoken word.

Nonetheless, the majority of people did not hear God's voice directly, and in subsequent Old Testament books, prophets acted as go-betweens connecting God and his people through verbal messages. As an illustration, before communicating divine words to the Israelites, the prophet Isaiah announced, "The LORD has spoken" (Isa 1:2a). This customary process of relaying spoken communication via prophets was consistently employed throughout the Old Testament, which underscored God's preference for speaking directly to his people using messengers of his own choice (Swarr et al. 2017).

The Old Testament's oral lore encompasses more than just messages from God—it includes the dissemination of teachings and stories across generations. This rich tradition is instrumental in safeguarding the Israelites' beliefs and constructing their comprehension of humanity's connection with God. The retelling of fundamental stories, including the creation narrative, the establishment of a covenant with Abraham, and the exodus from Egypt are integral components within the Old Testament's oral tradition. Passed orally through multiple generations, these tales serve as reminders concerning God's faithfulness whilst exemplifying his relationship to his chosen people via a covenant arrangement.

Insight into the significance of oral tradition in Israelite society can be gained from the book of Deuteronomy. In particular, the beginning of a longstanding Jewish prayer centers around the act of hearing—*Shema Yisrael*, meaning "Listen, O Israel!" (Deut 6:4, NLT). The Israelites are commanded to listen and to verbally transmit their cultural faith tradition to the next generation: "When your children ask you in time to come, 'What is the meaning of the decrees and the statutes and the ordinances that the LORD our God has commanded you?' then you shall say to your children ..." (Deut 6:20–21a, NRSV). This emphasis placed on transmitting information orally highlights just how important storytelling and communicating verbally was for molding Israelite identity over time.

The Psalms exhibit the oral traditions of ancient Israel, showcasing many that were constructed as musical or poetic pieces to be recited aloud. These elegant expressions of worship provide a communal means for reflecting on praise, remorse, and gratitude while strengthening the value placed on verbal communication during that era. Furthermore, Proverbs—part of the wisdom literature in this venerable text—holds teachings and adages handed down orally via sages and wise men who have come before us. These sayings offer practical advice for living righteously with integrity and demonstrate how the spoken word plays an integral role within the numerous genres found among the pages of the Bible. This illustrates the complementarity that has existed and continues to exist between written biblical texts and oral tradition. There are many examples of this in the book of Proverbs, as illustrated by the following verse:

> Listen, my son, to your father's instruction
> and do not forsake your mother's teaching. (Prov 1:8)

Several significant implications arise from the prevalence of oral tradition in the Old Testament for understanding divine revelation and human response.

- **First:** Communicating orally emphasizes God's personal and relational interaction with humanity rather than relying on written texts or abstract concepts.
- **Second:** Through spoken words, a direct connection is established between the divine and the individual or community he addresses.
- **Third:** As such, it is also clear that this living word transcends time and culture, which testifies to an active God who communicates personally; he is not silent. Not merely an historical artifact, this living transcendent word continues informing Christian practices today where proclaiming the gospel through speech remains central to faith practice.

God's choice to communicate orally, and the oral tradition in the Old Testament, highlight the dynamic and relational nature of divine revelation.

The continuity of God's oral messages

Divine messages delivered orally by God himself have spanned multiple cultures and generations, forming an enduring legacy that predates the written records of Scriptures. Oral tradition conveys foundational biblical teachings, commandments, and narratives from past eras with remarkable clarity. From patriarchal accounts to Moses' laws and wisdom literature—crucial aspects of faith were carefully passed along in this manner ensuring temporal preservation. Prophets historically conveyed divine communications verbally. Over time the Hebrew Scriptures were written down, and "were viewed as an authoritative collection of writings by about 150 BC at the latest" (Alexander 2015:3).

Jesus continued down this oral route in the New Testament, for, during his earthly ministry, he chose oral communication. He could have opted for other means to interact with his disciples and others, but he favored the exchange of words through human vocal cords[1]. Jesus could have authored great books, novels, or verses to convey his message of salvation. Like his ancestor David, he could have composed psalms for special occasions. However, he chose to deliver his crucial message through spoken words. The oral message of Christ had a significant impact on his audience, eliciting both strong positive and negative reactions. Eliazar Daila Baba (2022) demonstrated that Christ's primary concern when communicating was mutual understanding with his audience.

The early Christians carefully spread information about the life of Jesus Christ through oral means, though within a generation the written Gospels had been created. Yet, though the verbal discourse of God has been

---

[1] Or with gestures and signs, as we see described in chapter 6, exploring Jesus' encounter with the deaf man in Mark 7; the point is that this is person-to-person communication, and by using physical expressions Jesus showed that he "knew the language" of the deaf man.

transcribed into written literature, the obligation to actively internalize and adhere to it is consistently reinforced by numerous scriptural injunctions directing its readership towards committing it to memory, contemplation, and vocalization (e.g., much of Psalm 119).

The power and effectiveness of orality in mission work

The utilization of verbal techniques, specifically storytelling, to spread the teachings of Christ and promote spiritual development among believers is a methodology that has demonstrated exceptional efficacy in societies that primarily rely on spoken language, such as those found in West Africa and elsewhere,[2] where communication is often facilitated through oral traditions like narratives and music.

No doubt, even in the first century, the means of literacy certainly played some part in the spread of the gospel in the early years of the Christian faith. However, as we have seen, the Holy Scriptures bear witness to the fact that our Lord Jesus Christ used oral discourse with his disciples, who effectively conveyed his message. This enabled multitudes of generations to identify with Christ. Most people today still have a predilection for orality as a mode of learning and communication, whether by necessity or choice, and this makes them less receptive to modern Western styles of text-based communication. Bronwen Cleaver, a specialist in orality, sums it up well when she writes,

> Lovejoy (2012) estimates that 5.7 billion people in the world are, in fact, oral preference communicators—over 80 percent of the world population. Sundersingh (2001) notes that there are a growing number of non-literate people, highlighting in particular India and South Asia. He also emphasizes that even among the functionally literate, there has been a reduction in the habit of reading, due to progression in entertainment media. The Lausanne Occasional Paper No. 54 (2004), "Making Disciples of Oral Learners", asserts that approximately two-thirds of the world's population live by orality. Many of these two-thirds are literate but prefer to learn and communicate by oral means. (2022:333)

Cleaver further notes that "Pettitt has labelled our modern era as the 'Gutenberg Parenthesis' (Swarr et al. 2017). This is defined as the textual period between the orality of the past and that of the future, in which technology will allow people to be no longer dependent on print or text" (2022:334).

---

[2] For an excellent article on orality in God's mission that focuses on the people of the Republic of Altai, Siberia, see Bronwen Cleaver's chapter "God as an Oral Communicator—a study of orality, epic tales, and oral performances in Siberia" (in Greed and Kruger 2022).

It is therefore apropos to assert that oral traditions are efficacious not only within historical and biblical contexts but also in contemporary missionary efforts because the majority of the world leans in this direction.

This relative[3] growing preference for orality undergirds what is often termed today as an "orality movement". The focal point of the orality movement is to spread gospel teachings and foster discipleship by implementing oral practices. In so doing, it becomes possible to spread the good news irrespective of literacy rates. Jerry Wiles (2017) suggests that the orality movement aligns with the roots of the early church, emphasizing the timeless effectiveness of oral communication methods in sharing the gospel. Oral approaches possess flexibility that allows them to be integrated into various mission activities; they also prove effective for short-term church-based projects aimed at promoting harmony in businesses with a missional focus while developing leadership capacity amongst communities. These methods are universally applicable, adaptable across diverse cultures, and easy to replicate.

Oral transmission can serve as a powerful tool against deculturalization. Its power in mission work lies in its ability to reach oral cultures, its versatility, its capacity for building relationships, its resilience, and its ability to work hand-in-hand with literature or technological resources. These characteristics make it an effective tool for communicating the gospel and making disciples in diverse contexts.

The impact of orality in proclamation and personal witness

Proclamation and personal witness are experiencing their fastest-ever expansion through orality, changing the face of mission worldwide. This rapid growth is most evident in regions like Africa, where oral cultures thrive, cultures that rely predominantly on storytelling and verbal communication as a way of life. The immense success that personal witness and proclamation have had in these societies attests to how influential they can be amidst such an environment.

The use of storytelling, drama, communal processing, and the asking of questions are powerful tools for communities to use, leading to transformed lives. Adopting these oral-based methods is effective in that it captivates listeners by enlisting tone, inflection, and body language to convey messages with more nuance while spurring greater participation from the listener. This sense of community promotes a shared comprehension experience that cannot be replicated through traditional printed medium alone.

The majority of people groups across the globe that are not engaging with the Scriptures reside in cultures that rely on oral traditions. Nevertheless,

---

[3] While the preference for orality is visible in many ways, it should also be noted that in many parts of the world this trend may be declining or even changing due to the extensive use of the Internet.

many highly educated individuals also prefer learning and communicating through an oral approach. Consequently, methods based on orality prove to be pertinent and efficient for diverse cultural settings. By using these strategies, the gospel can reach a wider audience while remaining culturally appropriate and conscious, thereby enhancing its influence exponentially.

The role of orality in the spread of the Christian faith

The practice of orality has had a profound impact on Christianity's wider adoption over time, as it involves communicating knowledge, culture, and religious principles through spoken rather than written language.

Before the printing press came into existence, hand-copied texts of the Bible were available only to a very few, and remembering and recounting stories was crucial to upholding Christian teachings. The oral tradition effectively assisted in this by employing memory aids and creating a communal atmosphere around storytelling. Through these means, the fundamental tenets of the Christian faith were faithfully transmitted from one generation to another.

In addition, predominant oral traditions highlighted the significance of individual testimony and firsthand observation—essential elements in Christian witness. Conveying one's personal encounter with faith through speech has proven to be a potent means for promoting growth and transformation within a community.

The tradition of oral transmission still persists in contemporary times, impacting the spread of the Christian faith. This is made possible by various media tools such as radio broadcasts, podcasts, and audio Bibles that provide access to Christian teachings for those who cannot read or have no written materials at their disposal. Thus modern technology enables continuity with this age-old practice. In summary, orality is a crucial element in present-day missiology as it presents an efficient means of disseminating the gospel message and nurturing believers, principally in communities that rely on oral communication. This approach coincides with the nature of biblical texts themselves, which were originally oral, alongside Jesus Christ's communication methods during his time on earth. "There is a sense in which God's word and his gospel are to be received through the ear" (Martin 2023).

The message of God in dreams, visions, and revelations

God's oral communication with humanity often takes place in the context of visions, dreams, and revelations. The Bible is replete with examples of this. For example, Job 33:14–18 states that God speaks in various ways, even if people do not always perceive it. He may choose to speak through dreams and visions during a time of deep sleep, providing warnings to deter individuals from wrongdoing and pride and thereby saving them from disastrous consequences. This method of communication is still prevalent in some parts of the world, including Africa and most of the Global South. Many people value these supernatural revelations, often due to their religious traditions.

Stuart Robinson refers to two surveys conducted in Africa and Asia where the objective was to understand why those surveyed chose to follow Jesus. One of the reasons cited was the power of God's word. However, the most common reason was people's encounter with God through dreams and visions. Robinson states, "Dreams and visions have always been two of the media for God's communication with humankind ... [today] they have become a major means used by God for [people] finding their way into his kingdom" (2003:263).

God often chooses to reveal himself through dreams and visions to those who do not yet know him, or to those whom he wishes to guide towards a deeper understanding of him and to strengthen their faith in him. This is evident in Genesis 15:1, where God reveals himself to Abraham, leading him to a profound act of adoration and loyalty.

The following stories highlight how God, even in this present day, often opts to manifest himself through extraordinary signs, wonders, and miracles to those who have pledged their allegiance to other gods. These individuals, without divine intervention, would remain unaware of him or simply possess limited knowledge about him. Furthermore, he unveils himself through dreams and visions to individuals or communities unaccustomed to worshiping him. This revelation serves as a foundation for their future faith.

The case of Salama

Salama was a woman deeply rooted in the faith of her local community. God unveiled himself to her in the following way. The decision of her parents and other paternal family members to follow Jesus profoundly impacted her, leading her to sever ties with these relatives. She confined herself to her immediate family—her husband, children, and in-laws, all of whom followed the dominant religion of the region. However, her Christian family members prayed fervently for her, hoping for divine intervention. One night, she heard a distinct voice in her dream calling her by name. "Salama, follow me, I am Jesus." Realizing the spiritual nature of this visitation, she sought guidance from a local pastor who explained the significance of hearing God's voice in a vision. Encouraged, she chose, without hesitation, to follow Jesus. Today, Salama is a devoted follower of Jesus and her faith is unshakeable due to her divine encounter.

Musa's journey to faith

Musa, a devout believer residing in Sokodé, Togo, was deeply committed to his previous faith and practice. However, he was troubled when his neighbor chose to follow Jesus. Despite his initial reluctance, he agreed to listen to his neighbor's testimony about her transformative experience. The message resonated with him, leading him to seek Jesus himself, but in secret, due to fear of persecution. He chose secluded spots to pray, away from prying eyes. His life took a turn when he had a divine encounter in a vision. Musa recalls, "I saw a bright light at midnight in my room. From this light came a voice: 'Musa, I call you to serve me. Leave everything and come to me.' The voice continued, 'It's me, Jesus, calling you. Why are you hiding? Why won't you openly follow me? Come to me! I am the way, the truth, and the life. No one can see God without passing through me. Choose me. I want you to start worshiping me tomorrow—Sunday—with the brothers and sisters at church. I am the way, the truth, and the life.'" This vision transformed Musa's life completely. The following day, he fearlessly attended church, marking the beginning of his new life as a firm believer in Christ, reaching out to his community.

Today, many individuals are drawn to the Lord, inspired by testimonies of divine oral encounters. It is crucial for the church to document these uplifting stories and disseminate them through various media platforms, enabling hard-to-reach individuals to witness the transformative power of God. God's word has power to transform when it is proclaimed in faith in any given language (Sama 2022).

Complementarity of orality and literacy

Throughout history, the fascinating interplay between orality and literacy in human communication and knowledge transmission has impacted cultures and societies. Orality is characterized by shared stories, traditions, and information through the spoken word that has been a foundation for human interaction since ancient times with its immediate nature being communal as well as inherently pliable to adaptation. Contrarily, writing helps record complex ideas across time while providing precision and permanence unavailable in oral tradition.

The initial spread of Christian teachings heavily relied on orality.

To quote Cleaver once again,

> Rhoads (2012) proposes that biblical authors, like musical composers, did not initially write down their speeches or stories, but composed them orally. These oral compositions were then passed on without the aid of manuscripts, though there were scrolls that did provide a written record of the performance. The performers probably visualized their whole performance, including gestures, movements, and facial expressions, ahead of the actual performance. Music, singing, and chanting were aids to memorization, as were other stylistic features (de Vries 2015).

Steffen (2018) gives many historical examples to show that the use of oral methods, such as storytelling and drama, was common practice from the earliest days of Christianity. He quotes Augustine to show that the catechism of new believers in the early church was done using mostly memorization and oral recitation.

The biblical text contains both oral and literary features. (Cleaver 2022:341)

The disciples deserve credit for meticulously preserving their Master's teachings in written form, following the precedent set by the authors of the Old Testament. This allowed as many people as possible to experience firsthand the truth of Christ's message, the gospel of salvation. Thanks to this written preservation of God's word it is now available, through translation, both written and oral, to different peoples in their own languages.

With the increase of literacy, the Christian tradition found a new avenue for preserving and sharing its teachings through written texts. The teachings of Jesus and the early Christian messages, initially passed down orally, were documented to ensure wider accessibility and consistency in their distribution. Despite this shift, spoken communication remained significant, as written texts were often read aloud to congregations, maintaining an important oral component in Christian practice.

The interdependence of oral and written communication is apparent. Christianity's teachings remain relevant and easy to understand through the continuation of oral traditions, while written works establish a solid groundwork that preserves the message consistently over time. The current digital era adds another layer by combining orality's directness with the extensive dissemination capabilities of the written word, giving further enhancement in modern times. Oral and written forms of communication are not contradictory elements, but rather complementary ones, representing different strengths. The combination of these two modes has created a powerful synergy that has enabled Christianity to prosper along with other forms of knowledge over time. This mutual reliance illuminates how humans communicate and conserve collective wisdom in various ways.

A balance is therefore needed between these two means of sharing the message, as pointed out by Chase Reynolds (2020), who believes that orality and literacy represent points on a communication continuum, and Dick Kroneman (2017), who believes that orality is not only relevant to the unlettered, but also to the learned, since both groups of people depend on oral means of communication. "Literacy and orality serve different needs and purposes in communication, depending on the cultural and situational context, so it is important to keep a balance between the two" (Cleaver 2022:334).

Conclusion

In light of God's mission to make himself known and in light of this probing into the validity and value of orality in a mission context, we must conclude that the use of oral communication is not only beneficial but essential to the ongoing work of God's kingdom. The biblical, historical, and contemporary trends of using orality as a tool for communication and mission enterprise clearly confirm and affirm the significance God himself places on the utilization of orality for the dissemination of his message. From the very first recorded words of God speaking creation into existence, the spoken word has been and continues to be a potent tool for sharing the truth of God and his love for the world expressed in the redeeming work of Christ: the Word made flesh.

References

Alexander, T. D. 2015. Introduction to the Old Testament. In D. A. Carson (gen. ed.), *The NIV Zondervan Study Bible*. Grand Rapids, MI: Zondervan.

Cleaver, Bronwen. 2022. God as an oral communicator: A study of orality, epic tales, and oral Bible performances in Siberia. In Greed and Kruger, 331–347.

Daila Baba, Eliazar. 2022. Jesus' method of communicating the Gospel: Its implications for the missionaries today. *International Journal of Humanities Social Sciences and Education (IJHSSE)* 9(8):129–137. https://www.arcjournals.org/pdfs/ijhsse/v9-i8/13.pdf.

Kroneman, Dick. 2017. Translation, literacy, and orality: Reflections from the domain of Bible translation. *Orality Journal* 6(2):41–60.

Martin, Ryan. 2023. How do we reach oral learners with the gospel? *Center for Great Commission Studies*. Blog post 6 October 2023. https://www.thecgcs.org/resources/post/orality/.

Reynolds, Chase. 2020. Shape of communities along the communication continuum: Considerations for BT and SE strategies. https://map.bloomfire.com/posts/3767692-theshape-of-communities-along-the-communication-continuumconsiderations-for-b.

Robinson, Stuart. 2003. *Mosques and miracles: Revealing Islam and God's grace*. Brisbane, Australia: Cityharvest International.

Sama, Abou. 2022. God, language, and orality in the African context. In Greed and Kruger, 342–356.

Swarr, David, Rick Gidoomal, and Psalm Araujo. 2017. *Master storyteller: God's oral communication in the Bible and Hebrew tradition*. Richmond, VA: Center for Oral Scriptures.

Théry, David. 2022. *21 days of listening to God's voice.* Audio Prayer Guide. https://weare.jesus.net/wp-content/uploads/2022/09/Audio-Prayer-Guide-21-Days-of-Listening-to-Gods-Voice-EXAMPLE.pdf.

Wiles, Jerry. 2017. Orality methods and strategy: A growing movement. Blog post. Missio Nexus, 13 September 2017. https://missionexus.org/orality/.

Waw

*I reach out for your commands, which I love,
that I may meditate on your decrees.
(Psalm 119:48)*

6

Sign Languages in the Mission of God

Stuart Thiessen

Introduction

In my life, I've experienced what it means to be hard of hearing and attempting to fit into a hearing community. And I have experienced what it means to be Deaf and, in my home context of the United States, to become a part of a Deaf community with its rich language and culture. In my work as a translation consultant, I have visited a number of different Deaf communities. Each Deaf community has its challenges that need to be understood in order for us to accomplish God's mission in their context. Because I am more familiar with my own Deaf community, some of my comments may reflect that background. My hope is that in this chapter you will grasp the importance of seeing what God is uniquely doing (and desires to do) in each Deaf community.[1]

---

[1] I appreciate the helpful feedback from my wife Linda, Teri and Rachel Miles, Beth Cook, RuthAnna Spooner, Camille Beckham, Martha Gateley, Janice Silo and others in writing this chapter. In this chapter, I follow a common English convention using deaf/Deaf as a way to distinguish between the physical circumstance (deaf) and a linguistic/cultural identity (Deaf). By contrast, people who hear are generally referred to as hearing people. Use of the first person plural represents what I

A rich understanding of God's mission as it relates to language requires us to consider the breadth of human languages he has given us. Hundreds of sign languages, used by millions of Deaf people worldwide, are part of God's redemptive plan for the peoples of the world. This chapter will lay out who these Deaf communities are, how great thinkers have wrestled with the humanity of Deaf people (and our languages), and what God says about Deaf people. This foundation leads into an exploration of dueling theological truths about Deaf people and offers suggestions for God's people to step forward in God's mission in obedience.

For the uninitiated, what are Deaf communities?

Most people in the world speak languages that use the voice and ear. Yet, for millions of Deaf people, languages using the voice and ear are not the most accessible nor a primary means of communication. The debate has ensued for centuries: are Deaf people a disabled community that needs fixing or are we indeed another group of linguistic and cultural minorities? Certainly, we have ears that do not work to one degree or another. But as Deaf people commonly say, "We can do everything except hear." Our inability to hear (or speak) is not the totality of our identity. Instead, our cultural identity is grounded in our respective sign languages, our shared experiences as Deaf people, and the local Deaf culture in which we live.

While more survey is still needed, we estimate that more than 300 natural sign languages exist worldwide. Most are regional or national sign languages used by specific Deaf communities. Deaf people within these communities develop a distinct cultural identity based on the natural sign language(s) they speak and their shared experiences of what it means to be deaf. Hearing children of Deaf adults (CODAs), sign language interpreters, and other interested professionals or signers are also welcomed into these Deaf communities to varying degrees.

Unlike children in spoken language minorities who receive their language and culture from their parents, most Deaf children will have hearing parents. These hearing parents will likely have little to no experience with the language or culture of the Deaf community in their country. These Deaf children will vary in their cultural proximity to the core Deaf community depending on their identification with that Deaf community's linguistic and cultural values. Factors such as attending a Deaf school, being active in a Deaf association at a local, regional, or national level, or participation in other key Deaf institutions may also play a part in identifying one's proximity to this core. Depending on the advice their parents receive about them and how they and/or their parents respond, these Deaf children may:

---

have seen as a general Deaf perspective. Still, individually, Deaf people (and Deaf communities) have a range of perspectives.

- **Experience Deaf community and sign language access from an early age:** The government, the medical community, and/or the educational community may encourage these hearing parents and their deaf children to learn that community's sign language and become a part of that Deaf community. Deaf children born to Deaf parents who also are a part of that Deaf community will have access to language and community from an early age.
- **Experience a push to become hearing, which often fails to some degree, yet, possibly encountering their Deaf community at some point later in life:** The government, the medical community, and/or the educational community may actively encourage medical solutions intended to "fix" the child's hearing loss[2] and, in effect, link the child's intelligence to their acquisition of speech and lipreading.[3] Though some may "succeed," only a few can use their speech and lipreading skills outside of the highly structured educational context. Children who "fail" are sent to a Deaf school or a special education program, often communicated as a step downward/backward. Interestingly, these Deaf children or teens, even in a context that elevates spoken languages, will often discover and learn their Deaf community's sign language and connect with their Deaf community at some point.
- **Experience "inclusive" education:** Even when no attempt is made to "fix" hearing loss, a deaf child may be pushed into a mainstream classroom setting, attempting to include the child by teaching them alongside hearing children through an interpreter. Except in rare circumstances, the Deaf child often ends up isolated from those same hearing peers, other Deaf children, and from Deaf culture.
- **Experience isolation and language deprivation, becoming limited in their contributions to society:** The government, the medical community, and/or the educational community may not address the needs of Deaf children at all. Parents are left to figure out how to address the needs of their child on their own. In this context, Deaf children may not learn any language until significantly later than hearing children.[4] This phenomenon of language deprivation is unique

---

[2] Hearing aids and cochlear implants are frequently put forward as solutions, but even cochlear implants do not provide "normal hearing", and even when children are implanted early in life, they often lag behind hearing peers or Deaf children with early exposure to sign language in language ability and general cognitive skills (Knoors and Marschark 2020:426–440).

[3] In reality, relatively little speech can be read on the lips, with the majority being entirely guesswork. Context and fluency can often be great allies, but without these, the Deaf person can easily and quickly be lost. Ironically, medical/educational experts will often encourage "baby signs" for hearing infants, but discourage natural sign language for Deaf infants.

[4] Hall et al. (2019:368) estimate that 1 in 1,000 children in developed countries and 6 in 1,000 children in developing countries will have a significant hearing loss

to Deaf people because the limited spoken language input they might visually acquire will be insufficient to learn a spoken language (and later be educated in that spoken language). In order to communicate with those in their immediate circle of relationships, they may develop a basic system of gestures typically known as "home signs" (Woll et al. 2001:9, Torigoe and Takei 2002:282). Yet, without early and regular spoken or signed language input, they often become limited in their ability to express themselves linguistically. Being language-deprived has a significant impact on their cognitive development, their ability to thrive as a person God created and to contribute meaningfully with their community.[5]

A smaller set of sign language communities exist where Deaf people form a noticeable percentage of a community, creating contexts where local sign languages are on equal footing with other local languages.[6] In these shared sign language contexts, Deaf people are less likely to develop a separate cultural identity because their sign language has both hearing and Deaf users and is a significant part of the linguistic milieu of these communities.

What are sign languages?

We have talked about sign languages, but what are they? Contrary to what many hearing people may assume, sign languages are not a manual representation of a spoken language.[7] What hearing people may often see is "code-switching", where Deaf people adopt a form of "contact signing" to bridge the communication barrier. They will borrow lexical items, morphology, and even syntax from a shared spoken or signed language to make communication more efficient. It can be easy to assume that they are using their natural sign language, but in fact it is a mixture of elements from a signed and a spoken language. Deaf people who spend most of their time around those who don't know their sign language well may default to this

---

and, of these, 95 percent will be born in a home where only spoken languages are used. While various situations may allow some children to communicate in a spoken language, a signed language, or both early in life, a significant number of children will not have that opportunity. Regardless of specific cause or degree of impact, language deprivation has a detrimental effect on the lives of Deaf people.

[5] This also has important implications for how the church ministers to them and how language deprivation may impose limits on their ability to actively learn and engage with God's word.

[6] See https://www.ethnologue.com/subgroup/4397/ for some examples of shared sign languages.

[7] While the United States and the UK share the same spoken language, their sign languages are entirely distinct. Educators have developed sign systems to represent spoken languages, but they are not natural sign languages and are not as easily understood.

contact signing simply because it is easier to make themselves understood as a minority in that environment. Contact signing, however, is more like a pidgin; it does not have a fixed form and is not the natural sign language of a deaf community.

Natural sign languages are languages that have a system of phonetics[8] that uses the configurations and movements of the hands, face, and body instead of sounds. Each sign in the language can be phonetically analyzed by identifying the configuration of the hands (including their orientation), movements of the hands, location of the hands with respect to the body, and specific configurations of the face, head, and/or body that happen concurrently. Indeed, some signs in a sign language may in fact not use the hands at all and may simply use some configuration and/or movement of the face, head, and/or body. Sign languages also have rules of phonology, morphology, syntax, and discourse. Their grammar includes special constructions, such as a complex linguistic feature called "classifier constructions", the use of a specific set of handshapes that move in specified ways to allow the signer to represent the size, shape, and/or movements of inanimate or animate objects. A description of a car crash, for instance, will likely include classifiers to depict the event and lexical descriptions to provide more explanation.

How have people thought about deaf people and sign languages?

Historically, hearing people have wrestled with the validity of sign languages.[9] Plato in *Cratylus* (Jowett 2010:422E) quotes Socrates acknowledging sign languages. "Suppose that we had no voice or tongue, and wanted to communicate with one another, should we not, like the deaf and [mute], make signs with the hands and head and the rest of the body?" But within the same discourse, Socrates suggests sign languages are inferior to spoken languages. Aristotle went so far as to say, "It is hearing that contributes most to the growth of intelligence. For rational discourse is a cause of instruction … since it is composed of words, and each word is a thought-symbol. Accordingly, of persons destitute from birth of either sense, the blind are more intelligent than the deaf and [mute]" (1931:437a11–17). This Greek perspective contributed to the idea that acquisition of spoken language is a mark of intelligence.

Neurologist Oliver Sacks (1989:15) noted this idea when he wrote,

---

[8] In the study of spoken languages, phonetics are the sounds that make up words. In sign languages, linguists use this term to describe the smallest components that make up a sign.

[9] Much more could be said in this section to explore both positive and negative aspects of historical and modern views of Deaf people. See Further Reading at the end of chapter 6.

But what was all-important and had been a source of fundamental confusion since Aristotle's pronouncements on the matter was the enduring misconception that symbols [of communication] had to be speech. Perhaps indeed this passionate misperception, or prejudice, went back to biblical days: the subhuman status of mutes was part of the Mosaic code, and it was reinforced by the biblical exaltation of the voice and ear as the one and true way in which man and God could speak ("In the beginning was the Word").

I will soon discuss what the biblical text actually says about Deaf people, but I raise this quote to point out a common assumption that even the religious sphere elevates spoken language. While "the subhuman status of mutes" can nowhere be found in the Mosaic code (i.e., the Torah), Jewish tradition recorded in the Babylonian Talmud does contain discussions among the rabbis suggesting that if a person lacked both speech and hearing, he or she was also lacking in intelligence, competency, or a certain legal standing.[10] A person with speech or with hearing had a better standing than one who lacked both. In the rabbis' discussion, they wrestle with whether competence requires the ability to make and understand intelligible sounds.

"In the beginning was the Word" from the Gospel of John, though, is an entirely separate topic from the Mosaic code. Sacks conflates the two, supposing that the term *Word* here represents an auditory word and reinforces this spoken language bias. However, looking more closely, the semantic range of *word* here (Greek λόγος *logos*) encompasses the idea of an account, a message, or a statement. In Greek philosophy, λόγος represented rationality or the unifying principle of the universe. In ancient Jewish thought, we see the personification of Wisdom and the creative act of God using his word. John appeals to both perspectives and announces that this λόγος who has existed since the beginning has now come as a flesh-and-blood human to bring God's message to people. So rather than exalting the voice-ear as the one way to God, "the Word" reflects God's desire to meet us relationally as people (see chapter 4).

Some people have used Paul's words in Romans 10:17 (NKJV)—"So then faith comes by hearing, and hearing by the word of God"—to support an argument that Deaf people, not having physical hearing, are thus excluded from faith in God. While this seems an obvious exegetical and hermeneutical fallacy, there are church leaders who have believed this. But when we read this verse again in context, *hearing* is clearly focusing on someone receiving the message of the gospel in a language they understand regardless of how the message is transmitted.

---

[10] Examples include b.R.H.29a; b.Hag.2a, 2b, 3a; b.Hull.2a, 2b; b.Arak.2a, 5b, 17b, 18a. That said, one statement in b.Git.71a does imply that a "deaf-mute" could be married using "gesture".

While some segments of the church have matured in their responses to Deaf people, an undercurrent of the medical model of deafness where Deaf people are considered to be damaged and primarily in need of having their hearing restored can still be found (however subtly) in the modern church. Examples include:

- One interpreter trainer mentioned a conversation where a "religious hearing person" said, "I can't wait until you get to heaven and you will be able to hear and talk!" and the Deaf person responded, "How do you know that there won't be sign language in heaven?"
- Sometimes family or friends of Deaf people will bring them to a healing service only to have the healing "fail" and the Deaf person is blamed for a lack of faith or apparent sinfulness.
- Sometimes Deaf people (and sign language interpreters) are relegated to the back of the sanctuary or the far side of the church, far from the action out of fear that sign language interpreters will distract from the service.
- Sometimes well-meaning church people may come up and say, "Oh, I'm so sorry that you cannot hear!" or "I'm sorry that you cannot sing (or cannot worship)!"
- Sometimes Deaf people can be made to feel they are too expensive to be included in the life of the church.

Responses such as these reflect a focus on the hearing loss, but completely overlook God's perspective of Deaf people.

So, what does the Bible really say about deaf people?

Leaving aside the metaphorical uses of deafness, let me briefly walk through the passages in the Bible that can give insight into God's view of Deaf people and address some controversial passages.

Exodus 4:11

The first mention of "deaf" in the Bible occurs in the exchange between God and Moses when Moses offers the excuse that he has a speech impediment (or he is too rusty in his Egyptian). God's response in Exodus 4:11 reads: "The LORD said to him, 'Who gave human beings their mouths? Who makes them deaf or mute? Who gives them sight or makes them blind? Is it not I, the LORD?'" I and others talk about this passage as the "creation story of the Deaf". We are not accidents of biology or the victims of disease or people who missed the "normal" boat. God says, "I have a purpose for you, Moses. You are not a mistake." At the same time, he lets us know, "I have created deaf people (and blind people, mute people, lame people, etc.) just as they are and they are not mistakes either." So rather than calling Deaf people subhuman or mistakes, God in fact singles them out as his creations.

Leviticus 19:14

God instructs Moses, "Do not curse the deaf or put a stumbling block in front of the blind, but fear your God. I am the LORD." This instruction out of the blue is quite interesting. The semantic range of the verb translated "curse" here (קלל *qll*) includes lightly esteeming someone, speaking disparagingly about someone, uttering violent reproaches on someone, or imprecating evil towards someone. I admit that I often wonder how much is said against us or about us in frustration that we do not hear. Note the contrast "do not curse the deaf ... but fear your God". *Fear* here has more to do with a healthy awe or respect of God that recognizes our appropriate place in relation to him as our Creator. To speak or act in a demeaning way toward a deaf or blind person is not showing this awe or respect of God. Or, to state it positively, a healthy awe or respect of God expects that we respond to people he has created in ways that honor him as their Creator.

Isaiah 29:18

Isaiah writes, "In that day the deaf will hear the words of the scroll, and out of gloom and darkness the eyes of the blind will see." Taken in context, Isaiah 29:18 is frequently seen as a metaphorical reference to deafness to point out Israel's seeming inability to understand God's truth. Other commentators allow for a reference to physical deafness but consider a metaphorical reference as more likely. However one takes this passage, the focus of the passage is not so much about regaining physical hearing or sight but gaining meaningful access to God's words.

Admittedly, it can feel uncomfortable to see blindness and deafness used as metaphors for being spiritually unable to perceive truth from God. Metaphors like these can sometimes be misconstrued as being true of those of us who are physically deaf and/or blind. However, the point of metaphors is to create vivid imagery by emphasizing a specific point of comparison. I would be hard pressed to think of more vivid imagery to depict Israel's apparent inability to receive God's words. It truly seemed as though they were unable to see or hear his message. I can think of somewhat comparable visual metaphors used in American Sign Language to represent how information may be "received" but not understood.

Isaiah 35:5

This passage from Isaiah may be a clearer reference to physical deafness. He writes, "Then will the eyes of the blind be opened and the ears of the deaf unstopped." In the context of this verse, the lame leap and the mute shouts and water gushes forth in the desert. This passage is the depiction of a reversal of all that sin has damaged. There is a theme in Scripture that God will restore his creation back to his original design where sin does not win. Suffice it to say that Scripture maintains this tension where "disabled" people are both people who experience a consequence of that first sin *and* people who are a creation of God, precious in his sight. I will discuss this more in the next section.

Matthew 11:2–6, Luke 7:18–23

Here, Matthew and Luke record Jesus' report to John the Baptist when John asks, "Are you the One or should we look for another?" Both Gospels summarize Jesus' ministry as "The blind receive sight, the lame walk, those who have leprosy are cleansed, the deaf hear, the dead are raised, and the good news is proclaimed to the poor" (Matt 11:5, Luke 7:22b). It is one thing for Jesus to proclaim that he has been sent to restore people and creation from the consequences of that first sin. It is quite another to take action to restore what sin had destroyed. As Jesus preached the good news of the Kingdom of God, these miracles and healings were the testimonies that Jesus is the one that God had promised to send.

Mark 7:31–37

The only account we have of Jesus ministering specifically to a Deaf person is here in Mark. Some people jump to where he heals the Deaf man, but we should first examine how Jesus responds to the Deaf man. Step for a moment into the shoes of this deaf man. Whatever he may have been doing that day, this group ("some people") likely pulled him away and escorted him to Jesus. Did they explain to him in his language, or did they enunciate very carefully in hopes he would understand, or did they just pull him along with no explanation? What did he understand? Once they arrived, they took it upon themselves to ask Jesus *for* him. In addition, there was already a large crowd around Jesus with a lot of people talking and gesturing and pointing. In a word, visual chaos! But notice what Jesus did.

First, Jesus took him aside, away from the crowd, reducing the visual distractions so that the two of them could truly communicate. Next, Jesus visually communicated what he would do. We don't know if these were part of a sign language or home signs that this Deaf man knew or if Jesus simply used familiar hearing gestures. He touched the man's ears and his tongue, indicating he planned to provide hearing and speech. He looked up to heaven, a non-manual gesture that indicated the source of this healing would be God. With that look into heaven, he sighed deeply. The Greek verb here for a deep sigh (στενάζω *stenazō*) suggests a sigh that was easily visible. Sometimes I wonder if Jesus sighed about what this man had experienced all his life as a Deaf man in a hearing world. After all that manual and non-manual communication, Jesus only speaks one word: "*Ephphatha!* (Be opened!)"[11] Interestingly enough, this Aramaic word has mouth movements that are very visual so if this Deaf man had any knowledge of Aramaic, that word was likely easily understood.

---

[11] As a humorous side note, I am forever thankful that Jesus' first words were not, "Can you read my lips?" That question is among the most predictable first questions people ask us. See chapter 8 for more about this Aramaic word.

Now, on to the healing itself. While giving him hearing is certainly a miracle, the more remarkable miracle is that he had instantaneous language fluency. Note what Mark writes: "… his ears were opened, his tongue was loosened, and he began to speak *plainly*" (emphasis added). In the blink of an eye, this man went from someone who likely had little or no knowledge of Aramaic to being a fluent speaker (and hearer) of Aramaic. *Nobody* learns a language that quickly! Jesus understood that to address the consequences of sin in this instance required not just the provision of physical hearing but also the provision of full communication. You can see the astonishment of the people. They realized Jesus provided much more than mere hearing. Lest you look at this and think that this is an example of exalting the voice and ear, I think the clear actions of Jesus before the healing and the significance of how he healed the man shows that he was focused on what we always want: full communication.[12]

Mark 9:14–29

In this passage, there is a boy who is mute because of a demon that possessed him. Jesus calls this spirit a "deaf and mute" spirit. Once this "deaf and mute" spirit departs, the boy's muteness also disappears. Some people take the interpretation that John Van Cleve and Barry Crouch (1989:3) attribute to Mark and Luke:

> The Old Testament book of Exodus had reminded the people of Israel that deaf people were part of the Lord's creation and therefore deserving of respect, but both Mark and Luke took an opposite approach. They portray deafness as an indication that an individual has been possessed by a demonic, evil being. … [T]he boy apparently was cured, but deaf people now could be viewed as persons somehow inhabited by an evil presence. This is a remarkable turnabout from the Old Testament view that certain people were deaf because God made them that way.

They presume the New Testament takes a negative view of Deaf people. Given Jesus' commitment to the Law (Matt 5:17), that seems rather unlikely. Jesus' demeanor is clearly compassionate toward the boy. His consternation is reserved for the disciples and the religious leaders whose faith was insufficient to meet the boy's need. He only gently rebuked the father for his doubt ("… if you can …"). A more likely interpretation is that this particular demon may have caused muteness (among other things).[13] Also, verses 28–29 could imply that the phrase "deaf and mute" reflects the stubbornness and intransigence of that particular spirit. After all, Jesus

---

[12] I know this healing is somewhat of a sensitive topic for some Deaf people. For whatever reason, Jesus decided that this was the best outcome for this Deaf person. We simply do not have enough context to understand why.

[13] Note that the text does not indicate if the boy was deaf or not.

explained to his perplexed disciples that this kind of demon requires prayer to cast out. In any case, neither Jesus nor the gospel writers teach here or elsewhere that deafness is generally caused by demons or that Deaf people have lost that status God first accorded them in Exodus.

How do we reconcile the ideas of consequence of sin versus creation of God?

How do we reconcile the tension of disabilities as one consequence of that first sin with a high view of Deaf people as creations of God who have been given a precious gift of sign language and Deaf culture? Hearing people generally want to fix Deaf people to become like themselves, but is that how God views Deaf people?

Table 6.1 demonstrates several common theological statements drawn from Scripture. As those with disabilities come to know very early on, the "Consequence of Sin" statements must be held in tension with the "Creation of God" statements.

Table 6.1. Consequence versus Creation

Consequence of Sin	Creation of God
Imperfection, thus disabilities did not occur until after sin entered the world (Gen 1:31, 2:17, 3:16–19)	Even after the fall, we are products of his creation (Ps 139)
God is not responsible, nor can we blame him for sin or its results (Gen 3:12, Rom 5:12–19, 9:15–23)	Scripture does teach that God is involved somehow in disabilities (Exod 4:11)
Usually, the cause of disabilities is original sin rather than personal sin (John 9:1–3)	God uses our disabilities to show his glory and grace (John 9:1–3, 2 Cor 12:7–10)

In Genesis, when our first parents disobeyed God by eating the fruit he commanded them not to eat, their action had significant negative consequences for them, for their descendants, and for the earth they were given responsibility to steward. Not everyone experiences the consequences of that first sin in the exact same way. Among the consequences of that first sin are the various ways in which our bodies do not function as God originally designed them to function. Some people blame God, but, clearly, that first sin was the choice of our first parents. And offering them that choice was necessary because God had no interest in making us automatons. He wanted an authentic relationship with us. Genesis 4 through the end of Revelation is about God acting to restore our relationship with him and offer us (and his creation) a way to finally be free from sin and its effects.

The beauty of the biblical narrative is that God did not abandon humanity when we turned away from him. Psalm 139 describes God's creative attention to the very details of our bodies, using words like *created*, *knit*, *made*, and *woven together*. Exodus 4 describes God as the Creator even of those with disabilities. Every baby receives the attention of the Master Designer. All their days are written in his book and are precious to him. He is the expert at taking those whom sin wishes to destroy and intervening to transform them into beautiful creations. As George W. Veditz (1934), a past president of the U.S. National Association of the Deaf, reminds us in his famously preserved speech, "As long as we have deaf people on earth, we will have signs. ... It is my hope that we all will love and guard our beautiful sign language as the noblest gift God has given to deaf people".[14] And being dependent on God can mean more effectiveness in God's kingdom than being independent (2 Cor 12:9).

How should all this background impact the Church's work among sign language communities?

"The only thing we cannot do is hear." The real barrier for Deaf people is not actually a lack of hearing itself, but a lack of access to relevant information and communication we need for life. The most important thing hearing people can do is adjust their thinking about deaf people. Deaf people are not helpless objects of ministry who need to be fixed in the image of hearing people. Rather, we are people created in the image of God to whom God has given a solution that does not depend on our ears.

With this background I have shared, allow me to propose some suggestions that can lead to more effective work among deaf communities:

- Hearing people need to welcome the necessity that living in community with Deaf people means that they should learn at least one sign language well to communicate effectively. Expand your view of language from merely auditory to encompassing the visual. After all, "We cannot learn to hear, but you can learn to sign." We are very thankful for the work of sign language interpreters who help bridge the gap between hearing people and Deaf people and their work remains vital, but it is always refreshing to be able to communicate directly. Generally, sign languages are much faster to acquire than spoken languages, and the value to the community is significant.
- Recognize that some solutions to needs within specific Deaf communities may be larger than any one organization or any particular network of organizations. A broader coalition may be essential. In fact, we will need to build relationships with the broader community in that country. Many of the unique challenges that Deaf communities face have one

---

[14] This quotation on video is available at www.youtube.com/shorts/4t8VUm1RnIY.

or more of the properties of so-called "wicked problems"[15]. Among these properties, a lasting solution to "wicked problems" requires seemingly simultaneous intervention on many levels (e.g., family, education, government, community, church) and each of these actors will themselves have their own perspective of what a lasting solution might look like. Also, there is rarely a simple, easy solution that is free of potential drawbacks. C. West Churchman (1967:B142) discusses the challenges of attempting to resolve only part of a "wicked problem," to find that the solutions have "not tamed the whole problem, just the growl; the beast is still as wicked as ever."

- Keep in mind that hearing ministry strategies and programs may not always work exactly the same for the Deaf context. To be sure, we need to explore what can be learned from hearing ministry strategies and programs. Yet, in the Deaf context, we have unique challenges related to how language is passed down (including the phenomenon of language deprivation), how education is provided to Deaf children, how education is provided to Deaf leaders, how well Deaf people can access hearing networks for funding and collaboration, etc. This is where it is vital that Deaf people take the leadership in exploring best options for initiatives that seek to serve Deaf people ("nothing about us without us" is a common encouragement).
- It may seem "faster" to train and send hearing people to work with bibleless Deaf communities because of the ready availability of tools in spoken/written languages, but there are two main issues with this. First, equipping Deaf believers is more in rhythm with God's method of reaching the world. God does not intend for his mission to be administered only by the most powerful language communities—instead, he calls all believers to the redemptive work he is doing. Second, Deaf believers are strategically positioned to engage bibleless Deaf communities. Because of the cultural and linguistic similarities between Deaf communities globally, the most local expression of the church to an unreached Deaf people group—the one that would have the lowest barriers to effective engagement—is very often another Deaf people group (even if that Deaf group is in another country). For these reasons, it is far more strategic for all of us to invest in Deaf people to do this work. This may mean rethinking compensation, training, and content resources to make all three more feasible for Deaf people to engage in this work.

    Compensation: Often, compensation depends on the ministry person's home church community, but that presumes that the home church community is ready and able to provide those funds. Unfortunately,

---

[15] "Wicked problems" is a way to describe problems that seem more complex than we realize. It was first noted by Horst W.J. Rittel in 1973.

even in the United States, Deaf churches often can barely support their own pastor, let alone contribute significant funding to send other Deaf people for ministry work. This means the Deaf person who wishes to be involved in other ministry work must build partnerships with hearing churches. This raises questions such as:

- Who pays for the interpreters when they speak at hearing churches? If the Deaf person pays, then it makes it that much slower to build that financial partnership.
- Often, hearing churches or church networks only fund people who belong to their churches or church networks. If none of them provide direct ministry to Deaf people, how can Deaf people belong to these church networks to earn the opportunity to request their funding?

Training: Traditionally, training has required formal education which, in turn, has required fluency in English or some other language of wider communication. Depending on a Deaf person's education and language background, this may or may not present a challenge. Fortunately, competency-based evaluation which allows for both formal and informal educational approaches has become more prominent. We need to continue to explore training that is provided directly in a sign language by Deaf people or hearing people who are fluent in a sign language.

Content Resources: Traditionally, content resources are provided first (and more abundantly) in English as the global business language with other languages like French, Spanish, or Indonesian, serving a similar role in their contexts. But without fluency in one of these key languages, access to resources becomes more limited. In the Deaf context, merely translating the spoken language content is insufficient because Deaf people need resources that frame the information in ways in which Deaf people think. Ideally, we should invest in the development of sign language resources that are designed by Deaf people for Deaf people. While there are legitimate funding and logistical questions about how to make that possible, a solution is essential.

There are significant challenges that face sign language communities and Scripture work in sign languages specifically. It can feel overwhelming if our focus is solely on the problems. As the story of the twelve spies in Numbers 13–14 reminds us, nothing is impossible for God when he calls us to a task. God has given us the beautiful gift of sign languages. He has given us qualified and capable Deaf people who are eager to serve him and use the gifts his Spirit has given to them. How can we make the most of this opportunity to come alongside our Deaf brothers and sisters to serve Deaf communities worldwide?

References

Aristotle. 1931. *Parva naturalia*. Translated by William David Ross. Oxford: Clarendon Press.

Churchman, C. West. 1967. Free for all. *Management Science* 14(4):B-141–B-146.

Hall, Matthew L., Wyatte C. Hall, and Naomi K. Caselli. 2019. Deaf children need language, not (just) speech. *First Language* 39(4):367–395. https://doi.org/10.1177/0142723719834102.

Jowett, Benjamin. 2010. Cratylus. In *Dialogues of Plato: Translated into English, with analyses and introduction*, 617–715. Cambridge: Cambridge University Press.

Knoors, Harry, and Marc Marschark. 2020. Accommodating deaf and hard-of-hearing children with cognitive deficits. In Mark Marschark and Harry Knoors (eds.), *The Oxford handbook of deaf studies in learning and cognition*, 426–440. Oxford: Oxford University Press.

Rittel, Horst W. J., and Melvin M. Webber. 1973. Dilemmas in a general theory of planning, *Policy Sciences* 4(2):155-169.

Sacks, Oliver. 1989. *Seeing voices: A journey into the world of the deaf*. Berkeley: University of California Press.

Torigoe, Takashi, and Wataru Takei. 2002. A descriptive analysis of pointing and oral movements in a home sign system. *Sign Language Studies* 2(3):281–295.

Van Cleve, John Vickrey, and Barry A. Crouch. 1989. *A place of their own: Creating the Deaf community in America*. Washington, DC: Gallaudet University Press.

Veditz, George. 1934. Preservation of the sign language. Original version 1913. National Association of the Deaf. https://youtu.be/XITbj3NTLUQ?feature=shared. For a captioned version, see https://youtu.be/F7BLC0uu_zU?feature=shared.

Woll, Bencie, Rachel Sutton-Spence, and Frances Elton. 2001. Multilingualism: The global approach to sign languages. In *The sociolinguistics of sign languages*, 8–32. Cambridge: Cambridge University Press.

Further Reading

Ayres, Bob, and Rick McClain. 2019. *DEAFCHURCH21: Vision for a new generation*. Louisville, KY: Ayres & McClain Publishing.

Ladd, Paddy. 2003. *Understanding Deaf culture: In search of Deafhood*. Bristol, UK: Multilingual Matters Ltd. https://www.multilingual-matters.com/page/detail/Understanding-Deaf-Culture/?k=9781853595455.

Oates, Rosamund. 2021. Speaking in hands: Early modern preaching and signed languages for the deaf. *Past & Present* 256(1):49–85. https://doi.org/10.1093/pastj/gtab019.

Zayin

*I remember, LORD, your ancient laws,
and I find comfort in them.
(Psalm 119:52)*

7

Language and the Wider Mission Movement

Michael Greed and Evan Falk

Introduction

The previous chapters have explored the topics of mission and language largely from the perspective of a mission practitioner in the field of language. Stepping back, this chapter locates that conversation within the broader modern mission movement, both historically and conceptually. How have we found ourselves where we are, and where do we go from here?

The mission of God in church history

Christendom

To look forward, the study of mission must also look backward and face a mixed history. As of the seventh century, the concept of "Christendom" took hold. Christendom countries (mostly located in Europe) sought "the establishment of a unitary Christian society". With the notable exception of

Jews, everyone in the society was Christian, with baptism required by law (Kreider and Kreider 2011:38).

Where did mission fit into this world? With faith and citizenship thus melded together, expansion of Christendom was essentially political, not theological, and was therefore a matter for the state (Bosch 1991:251). The legacy of this uneasy, and unnatural, relationship between evangelism and expansionism has plagued the mission movement, and is still being reckoned with today, for example in South Africa, where apartheid was long supported by colonial theology (Mukuka 2012:116), or in Canada where Indigenous children were taken from their homes and placed in religious residential schools (Truth and Reconciliation Commission 2015:25).

This is not to say that mission activity was unquestioningly loyal to the colonial agenda—there are significant examples where mission practitioners thwarted the colonial powers by humanizing Indigenous populations (Tizon 2018:42–44). Even then, though, as Indigenous American theologian George Tinker observes, while mission workers "surely did not intend any harm to Indian people, yet their blindness to their own inculturation of European values and social structures meant that complicity was unavoidable" (Tinker 1993:15). As church and state slowly began to decouple in late Christendom, and the Protestant mission movement took form, this inculturation would not so easily be jettisoned.

The modern mission movement

In this newly blossoming Protestant mission movement, William Carey (1761–1834) stands out as something of a giant. In 1792 he published a short book, *An Enquiry into the Obligations of Christians, to Use Means for the Conversion of the Heathens* [sic]. It was a call to action, and the keyword in the title was "means". No one in the church doubted that the "heathen" needed to be converted. The issue was whether God was in need of human participation—that is, *means*. Basing his argument on Matthew 28:18–20, Carey argued that "Go!" means "Go!" Stirred by Carey and others, the Protestant Church got involved in mission. Numerous missionary societies were formed, and countless missionaries were sent to foreign lands, many to perish there.

The twentieth century saw a series of significant mission gatherings, the first one being the World Missionary Conference in Edinburgh in 1910. This was a multi-denominational (though largely Western and Protestant) meeting, and could be described as "the climax of the missionary zeal that had marked the nineteenth century" (Gnanakan 1993:15). Held in the closing years of colonialism's heydey, Edinburgh 1910, while inspirational, could also be said to be in many ways symptomatic of the unhealthy relationship between Christendom and following Christ, ending with John Mott's closing address proclaiming that the "end of the conference is the beginning of the conquest" (quoted in Gnanakan 1993:15). Edinburgh spawned a "continuation committee" that continued to organize large missionary gatherings, but subsequent conferences struggled with denominational disagreements and the seismic shifts in society that defined the first half of the twentieth century.

Willingen 1952 and the emergence of missio Dei

One of the gatherings that followed on from Edinburgh was held in Willingen, Germany, in 1952. By this time, following two world wars, the first stirrings of the Cold War, and increasing restrictions on missionary activity, the conference was faced with rethinking the model of mission that had seemed so exciting forty-two years earlier. Further, at Willingen, delegates were not bound by the same prohibition on discussions of doctrine or theology that had kept Edinburgh delegates' differences in check and kept the conversation to commitment and strategy (Guder 2003:39–40). The Willingen conference was marred by disagreements, with delegates eventually rejecting the drafted final statement. The respected missiologist Lesslie Newbigin was recruited to rework the statement, and is said to have retreated into a room on his own and spent the night feverishly attempting to find common ground (Flett 2010:154). Newbigin's revised report was accepted, and formed the foundation of the concept of mission that later came to be referred to as *missio Dei*.

The ambiguity of Newbigin's revised statement was part of what allowed the statement to be embraced in the face of such disagreement, and even today this ambiguity continues to be reflected in the many different interpretations of *missio Dei* that have arisen (Stroope 2017:17–18). Still, there are several key innovations that mark *missio Dei* as a significant paradigm shift in modern mission.

- Mission is seen "primarily as flowing from the missionary heart of God", rather than "as the 'obligation' of the church" (Bosch, quoted in Laing 2012:78). Thus, "It is not the church that has a mission of salvation to fulfil in the world; it is the mission of the Son and the Spirit through the Father that includes the church" (Moltmann 1977, quoted in Bosch 1991:390).
- Following from this, mission is understood as "an attribute of God", not "an activity of the church" (Bosch 1991:390). In a post-Christendom[1] world, this was a significant reversal, as here neither the state nor the church could lay claim to authority over mission; mission belonged to God alone. "In this view the mission is the greater reality, the Church the lesser" (Newbigin 1977:261). The Church does not set the terms

---

[1] Not to be confused with "post-Christian", post-Christendom marks the end of the intertwined social, political, and religious realities that defined the "Christendom" states from the seventh century until the early twentieth century.

for its engagement with the mission of God. "There is church because there is mission, not vice versa" (Aagard, quoted in Bosch 1991:390).
- All this is built on the foundation of a trinitarian grounding for mission. While the trinitarian theology of Willingen 1952 is often criticized for its weakness and ambiguity (Laing 2012:79–80), it anchored mission within inter-trinitarian sending: the Father sends the Son, the Father and Son send the Spirit, and the Son sends the Church (Schirrmacher 2017:33). It is this anchoring that took mission out of the hands of a faltering Christendom and restored it to God alone.

With mission belonging to God, not to the Church, as Karl Harteinstein explained in his summary of the Willingen proceedings, "[Mission] is participation in the sending of the Son" (quoted in Schirrmacher 2017:11). The Church is invited to participate in the mission of God. This mission is much bigger than the Church; it is of the essence of God. All of this flows from Newbigin's appeal for the missional church "to bind to itself afresh the strong Name of the Trinity" (1963:31).

Within all this grand talk of the Trinity and the attributes of God, practical questions persist: which activities fall into the category of "mission", and which do not? *Missio Dei* has redefined significant paradigms of *why* and *how*, but we are still left with the challenge of describing *what* we are now to do. This dilemma has frequently been described in the words of Bishop Stephen Neill's famous lament that "if everything is mission, nothing is mission" (Neill 1959:81–82). Christopher Wright responds that it would be more biblical to say that "if everything is mission" then "everything is mission". Thus, "everything a Christian and a Christian church is, says and does should be missional in its conscious participation in the mission of God in God's world" (Wright 2010:26).

This exchange (albeit across the span of more than half a century) is perhaps one of the best illustrations of the sea change of *missio Dei* thinking: we can no longer define mission by activity, but by character. Mission is part of who God *is*, not merely something God *does*. Similarly, we are to *be missional*, not to *do mission*. "Mission ... unlocks the whole grand narrative of the canon of Scripture", says Wright (2006:17). It is not so much that there is a "biblical basis of mission", Wright continues, but that there is a "missional basis of the Bible"—that the Bible is itself a product of God's mission (2006:22).

The working out of this new paradigm is particularly evident in mediating the age-old tension between evangelism and social action, which has continued to challenge the mission movement. This conversation has been one of the most prominent features of the Lausanne conferences which were to follow.

Lausanne, Bible translation, and Vision 2025

The first Lausanne International Congress on World Evangelization took place in Lausanne, Switzerland, in 1974. The resulting "Lausanne Covenant", which is still used widely by mission organizations, was notable for its commitment to balancing evangelism and social concerns. In many ways echoing the *missio Dei* paradigm, the Covenant identifies these concerns in light of who God is, and thus declares that the Church should share God's "concern for justice and reconciliation throughout human society and for the liberation of men and women from every kind of oppression". Evangelism and social action are both "necessary expressions of our doctrines of God and Man, our love for our neighbour and our obedience to Jesus Christ" (Stott 2009: section 5; see also Lausanne Movement 1974). This was a significant development, particularly in evangelical circles.

With "Let the earth hear his voice" as its theme, God's communication was central to the congress, but any question of the languages with which the earth was to hear that voice was notably absent from the Covenant. The "authority and power of the Bible" warranted its own section, but the accessibility of those Scriptures in languages people would understand was not mentioned. That had to wait until Lausanne II.

Lausanne II was held in Manila in 1989. The question of Scripture translation was nearly left out of the conversation once again (Kyoungah White 2020). Fergus MacDonald, then General Secretary of the United Bible Societies (UBS), questioned its absence. As a result, he and John Bendor-Samuel (then Executive Vice President of SIL) were invited to organise and lead the track.

> Despite the small numbers, the history of rivalry [among Bible agencies], and the fact that the track had been thrown in at the last minute, something beautiful happened. "There was a sense of the Lord's presence each day of the track which reinforced the belief that we all belonged together," says MacDonald. "At our last workshop, the Bible agency people said, 'This has been great. We must do it again.'"
> (Kyoungah White 2020)

Out of this, the Forum of Bible Agencies International (FOBAI) was born. Further, UBS and SIL realized they needed to take action to promote the importance of the languages of the heart, Scripture translation, and dedicated engagement with the Scriptures; that is, they recognised that the mission of God could not be meaningfully engaged without Scriptures in the language of the heart.

In 1999 SIL International and Wycliffe Bible Translators International (now Wycliffe Global Alliance) embraced *Vision 2025*. The Vision states:

> Motivated by the pressing need for all peoples to have access to the Word of God in a language that speaks to their hearts, and reaffirming our historic values and our trust in God to accomplish the impossible,

> We embrace the vision that by the year 2025 a Bible translation project will be in progress for every people group that needs it. (Wycliffe Global Alliance 1999)

Embracing this vision transformed the Bible translation movement in the twenty-first century, bringing the urgency of the task into focus. It was not a matter of "doing the best we can", but of making significant changes in attitudes and ways of working. Vision 2025 is not phrased in terms of missiology. The mission of God is not mentioned in the document, but it is not far below the surface. The preamble recognizes that God is our adequacy, our confidence, our safety, and our satisfaction (Watters 1999:4). It asks what results God might desire of us in the twenty-first century (p. 6) and seeks alignment with what God is doing (p. 12). "The intent is to focus on the living reality of God in our world and his call on our lives" (p. 13).

As SIL and Wycliffe embraced this vision and began to look at how it could be put into practice, a need for missiological reflection was identified, beginning with reflection on the mission of God. Wycliffe produced a range of missional papers rooting Scripture translation in the mission of God,[2] while SIL created missiological reflection materials on, amongst other topics, the mission of God and the role of language in the mission of God.

Consideration of language and the mission of God begin to meet

Missiology in the twenty-first century is polycentric: mission is from everyone to everywhere. Large mission gatherings continue, but they are spread around the world, and the makeup of the delegates is very different than it was in the early twentieth century. In 2010 several significant mission conferences were held to commemorate the centenary of the 1910 Edinburgh World Missionary Conference. One of these was once again held in Edinburgh.

> The spirit of the conference was largely gracious, and the major consensus lay in the universal agreement about the *missio Dei* (the mission of God—that all mission must start from the Trinity and not from humans), as well as the emphases on social justice, prayer and creation care. There was no need to convince people of the validity of these issues.
>
> The idea behind the *missio Dei* is that it is God, and not us, who is the initiator of mission. (Yeh 2016:111)

At least among theologians and practitioners attending this meeting, *missio Dei* and its trinitarian roots appear to have become *de rigueur*. So, too, was the need to reflect *all* of God's missional character and concern towards

---

[2] See https://www.wycliffe.net/what-we-do/philosophy-and-principle-papers/

his creation. Similarly at Lausanne III held in Cape Town that same year, *missio Dei* was a given, and mission was viewed holistically.

> Though the Bible studies each morning were focused on the book of Ephesians, the theme of the conference came from 2 Corinthians 5:19, "God in Christ, reconciling the world to himself." This is perhaps the best definition of mission in the Bible, with the acknowledgment of the *missio Dei* (God as prime mover) and taking the broken and restoring it to wholeness, whether that be the physical body or the spirit or institutional structures or relationships. (Yeh 2016:114)

Following its formation after Lausanne II in Manila, FOBAI, now under the leadership of John Watters of SIL, developed the theme "Eradicating Bible Poverty" for Lausanne III in Cape Town (Watters 2010). While language issues may not yet feature prominently at these gatherings, they do, at least, feature.

As this volume was nearing publication, the 4th Lausanne Congress convened in Seoul under the theme, "Let the Church declare and display Christ together." Hong-Tae Jang, one of those representing SIL Global at the Congress, writes, "Expectations were high that the congress would continue recent efforts to elevate the role of minority languages—not merely as obstacles to mission work but as essential components of cultural identity and unique gifts from God. Nevertheless, preliminary versions of the Seoul Statement suggest a potential retreat from the precedent set by previous Lausanne gatherings in prophetically addressing linguistic challenges integral to fulfilling the Great Commission and proposing viable solutions."

Globalization, virtual communication platforms, and advances in language technology driven by Large Language Models (LLMs, often referred to as "AI"), which became widely referenced and assumed as normative, seem to have fostered the impression that they could bridge the gap for minority language communities. As a result, linguistic issues received less focus relative to other pressing topics. Yet, Jang argues, "it would be premature to conclude that [they] have significantly reduced the number of unreached people groups in linguistic terms. On the contrary, polarization appears to be worsening, primarily because these communities often lack the economic resources and infrastructure to leverage such technologies. Furthermore, many of their languages remain largely undocumented, limiting the capacity of technological solutions to effectively engage with their unique linguistic structures."

As God expresses his loving, relational nature, and outpours his trinitarian self into the world, he uses language, and that is where the present book is contributing to the wider conversation. In this book we are intentionally introducing the concept of language, as we believe that it has not received the prominence in missional thinking that it warrants, given its centrality in our day-to-day lives.

Conclusion

In this chapter we have given a high-level overview of the development of modern missional thinking, and noted points where language and the contemporary Bible translation movement intersect with it. One such key point was the formation of the Forum of Bible Agencies International in 1989, a result of the intentional collaborative engagement of the heads of the two largest Scripture translation agencies, Fergus MacDonald and John Bendor-Samuel. This was followed by Vision 2025 which SIL and Wycliffe embraced in 1999. These milestones were key to the Bible translation movement becoming more fully rooted in the mission of God.

However, as the missiologist Chip Sanders (2022:105) has surveyed the mission literature, looking for references to language in what scholars and practitioners have written about the mission of God, he has found very little. Sanders wonders whether we view language instrumentally, and have therefore simply taken it for granted. However, that leaves us with the weighty question of how language fits into the mission of God. Looking to the literature, to the mission gatherings, and to the missiologists who have paved the road for us, we find this question barely addressed, let alone answered. As mission practitioners, called and equipped to serve the language communities of the world, SIL has something critical to add to this conversation. This book aims to contribute towards a greater understanding of language and the mission of God, both in theory and in practice.

References

Bosch, David J. 1991. *Transforming mission: Paradigm shifts in theology of mission.* American Society of Missiology Series 16. Maryknoll, NY: Orbis Books.

Carey, William. 1792. *An enquiry into the obligations of Christians, to use means for the conversion of the heathens.* Leicester, GB: Ann Ireland, et al.

Flett, John G. 2010. *The witness of God: The Trinity, missio Dei, Karl Barth, and the nature of Christian community.* Grand Rapids, MI: Eerdmans.

Fung, Patrick. 2024. *Let the Church declare and display Christ together.* Lausanne Movement. https://lausanne.org/about/blog/let-the-church-declare-and-display-christ-together.

Gnanakan, Ken. 1993. *Kingdom concerns: A biblical theology of mission today.* Leicester, UK: Inter-Varsity.

Guder, Darrell L. 2003. From mission and theology to missional theology. *Princeton Seminary Bulletin* 24(1):36–54.

Kreider, Alan, and Eleanor Kreider. 2011. *Worship and mission after Christendom.* Harrisonburg, VA: Herald Press.

Kyoungah White, Sara. 2020. *The friendship that changed the world of Bible distribution and translation.* Lausanne Movement. https://lausanne.org/about/blog/friendship-changed-world-bible-distribution-translation.

Laing, Mark T. B. 2012. *From crisis to creation: Lesslie Newbigin and the reinvention of Christian mission.* Eugene, OR: Pickwick Publications.

Lausanne Movement. 1974. *The Lausanne covenant.* https://lausanne.org/statement/lausanne-covenant#cov.

Mukuka, Tarcisius. 2012. Reading/hearing Romans 13:1–7 under an African tree: Towards a lectio postcolonica contexta Africana. *Neotestamentica* 46(1):105–138.

Neill, Stephen. 1959. *Creative tension.* London, UK: Edinburgh House Press.

Newbigin, Lesslie. 1963. *The relevance of trinitarian doctrine for today's mission.* London, UK: Edinburgh House Press.

Newbigin, Lesslie. 1977. Recent thinking on Christian beliefs: VIII. Mission and Missions. *The Expository Times*, 88(9):260–264. https://doi.org/10.1177/001452467708800902.

Sanders, Chip. 2022. Judgment, language and the mission of God. In Greed and Kruger, 152–165.

Schirrmacher, Thomas. 2017. *Missio Dei: God's missional nature.* Translated by Richard McClary. The WEA World of Theology Series 10. Bonn, Germany: Verlag für Kultur und Wissenschaft (Culture and Science Publishing). https://worldea.org/resource-pack/.

Stott, John. 2009. The Lausanne covenant: Complete text with study guide. Published online. Boston, MA: The Lausanne Movement. https://lausanne.org/wp-content/uploads/2021/10/Lausanne-Covenant---Pages.pdf.

Stroope, Michael W. 2017. *Transcending mission: The eclipse of a modern tradition.* Downers Grove, IL: IVP Academic.

Tinker, George E. 1993. *Missionary conquest: The gospel and Native American cultural genocide.* Minneapolis, MN: Fortress Press.

Tizon, Al. 2018. *Whole and reconciled: Gospel, church, and mission in a fractured world.* Grand Rapids, MI: Baker Academic.

Truth and Reconciliation Commission of Canada. 2015. Canada's residential schools: The history, Part 1 Origins to 1939. *The Final Report of the Truth and Reconciliation Commission of Canada* Vol. 1. Montreal: McGill-Queen's University Press. https://archives.nctr.ca/NCTR-EDU-003-001-016.

Watters, John. 1999. Vision 2025 resolution. (Restricted access) https://gateway.sil.org/x/PIABCQ.

Watters, John. 2010. *Scripture in mission: Three major priorities in eradicating Bible poverty.* Lausanne Movement. https://lausanne.org/content/scripture-in-mission-three-major-priorities-in-eradicating-bible-poverty.

Wright, Christopher J. H. 2006. *The mission of God: Unlocking the Bible's grand narrative.* Downers Grove, IL: IVP Academic.

Wright, Christopher J. H. 2010. *The mission of God's people: A biblical theology of the Church's mission.* Grand Rapids, MI: Zondervan.

Wycliffe Global Alliance. 1999. Vision 2025. https://www.wycliffe.net/what-we-do/philosophy-and-principle-papers/vision-2025/.

Yeh, Allen. 2016. *Polycentric missiology: 21st-century mission from everyone to everywhere.* Kindle edition. Downers Grove, IL: InterVarsity Press.

Part Two

The Bible

In chapter 16, at the end of this part of the book, the question is posed, "What is the Bible? Is it God's direct revelation or is it a witness of God's revelation, in a more indirect sense?" However we choose to answer that question, the role of the Bible is crucial in God's revelation of himself. It bears witness to Jesus and to God's communications with humanity, and, as Paul writes to Timothy, "All Scripture is God-breathed" (1 Tim 3:16). Olivia Razafinjatoniary (2022:73–75) introduces some of the ways God speaks in the Bible:

> We have many instances when God speaks to people directly. These are his one-way styles where he does not give room for his audience to speak back to him. It does not mean that he wanted to dictate something, but, rather, he wanted people to understand that what he was communicating is not debatable. We see this during the baptism of Jesus in Matthew 3:17, where "a voice from heaven said, 'This is my Son, whom I love; with him I am well pleased.'"
>
> In Genesis 3, we not only see that God was *talking to* Adam and Eve but he was *interacting with* them as well. His style of communication with them was like the relationship of a father to his children, a father who does not delight in what is not good but remains a loving father, nonetheless.
>
> Many times, God talks to people in a conversational style where he listens and answers questions. He also asks questions, warns, rebukes, and encourages. This is the style that he uses most often in

the Bible, though not always in direct communication, but rather through an intermediary.

One intermediary that God uses is his angels. In Genesis 18, for instance, God used his angels in the form of three men to tell Abraham that his wife Sarah would give birth to a son. Further, in the Gospels he used his angel to tell Joseph in a dream not to be afraid to take Mary as his wife (Matt 1:18–25), and to tell Mary that she would conceive and give birth to the Son of the Most High (Luke 1:26–38). (See chapter 5 to read more about how God speaks through dreams.)

God also uses the prophets to communicate with his people. In many parts of the Bible, no matter what message God wanted to send his people, he used the prophets to pass on his message.

Another means that God uses to communicate with people is nature. For example, in Jonah we see that God expressed through the great wind that he was not pleased with Jonah running away from him. He showed Jonah how merciful he is by allowing the big fish to swallow him yet keep him alive in its stomach for three days.

In one instance when Saul and his troops were fighting against the Philistines, God remained silent and did not answer them (1 Sam 14:37). That was a loud silence because Saul knew right away that something was wrong. Yes, God also uses silence to communicate.

The examples mentioned above are all from the Bible. God can still communicate in these kinds of ways in our daily lives today, but he also chooses to use his word to communicate what he has in his heart for us. For every question we may have in our life, the Bible has guidance for us. At the same time, we are free to talk to God in many ways: through prayers, songs, reading, writing, and even silence. He says in Jeremiah 33:3: "Call to me and I will answer you and tell you great and unsearchable things you do not know."

Yet, above all these different communication styles that God has used, the ultimate and best way he has chosen to communicate with us is when he became a human being like us. He identified himself with human beings in order to reach their communities and cultures. He lived among people and spoke and used their languages.

This part explores language in relation to Scripture: the languages of the Bible, how language is used in the Bible, the level of importance the Bible gives to language, and translation of the Bible. It examines key biblical texts related to language, including the story of the Tower of Babel.

Part Two: The Bible

This part consists of the following:

Speech acts in the Bible (**chapter 8**), the story of the Tower of Babel (**chapter 9**), language diversity (**chapter 10**), language use in the Bible (**chapter 11**), the languages of Jesus (**chapter 12**), and Koine Greek (**chapter 13**). There are then three chapters particularly addressing the question of the translation of the Scriptures: the role of language and translation in advancing God's mission (**chapter 14**), the continuum between language and the mission of God (**chapter 15**), and a case study in contextualization in translation (**chapter 16**).

Reference

Razafinjatoniary, Olivia. 2022. God's inclusive mission through languages. In Greed and Kruger, 71–80.

Heth

I have sought your face with all my heart;
be gracious to me according to your promise.
(Psalm 119:58)

8

Speech Acts in the Bible

Michael Greed

Introduction

In this chapter we will begin with a brief definition and description of the linguistic concept of speech act theory. Then we will look at three groups of speech acts in the Bible: firstly creation, secondly from the lips of Jesus, and finally in the writings of the Apostle Paul.

Speech act theory

Speech act theory was introduced by the Oxford philosopher John Austin (1911–1960) and developed by the Berkeley philosopher John Searle (born 1932). It is used to study how words are used not simply to present information but to perform actions. An act of speaking may include several levels. Austin (1962:99–106) defines the following:

- **Locutionary act:** the *act* of speaking itself, of making a meaningful utterance.
- **Illocutionary act:** an act performed by the speaker by virtue of having been spoken. In focus is the ***force*** of the utterance.
- **Perlocutionary act:** the consequence of the speaker's speaking. In focus is the ***effect*** of the utterance.

The latter two are of interest to us here. There is no agreed taxonomy amongst linguistic philosophers of the different types of illocutionary speech acts. They include *commissive*, where the speaker commits to doing something; *directive*, where the speaker tries to get their hearers to do something; and *declaratory*, where the speaker does "things in the world at the moment of the utterance solely by virtue of saying that they do" (Vanderkeven and Kubo 2002, quoted in Nordquist 2024).

Examples of declaratory speech acts include:

- We, the jury, find the defendant to be 'not guilty'.
- I now pronounce you man and wife.

Taking the second example, the illocutionary force of the utterance is to make the man and woman a married couple. The perlocutionary effect of the utterance is that they are now married "to love and to cherish, till death us do part". A speech act with illocutionary force and perlocutionary effect changes present or future reality.

Creation: "And God said"

There are many speech acts in the Scriptures where present or future reality is changed as a result of the force and effect of what is said. In this study we will focus on just three: first, the speech acts God used when creating the world; second, the speech acts Jesus used in his ministry which impacted Mark the Evangelist so deeply that he retained Jesus' original Aramaic; and third, the speech act described by the Apostle Paul that takes place within our hearts.

The Bible begins with a series of speech acts.

> In the beginning God created the heavens and the earth. Now the earth was formless and empty, darkness was over the surface of the deep, and the Spirit of God was hovering over the waters.
>
> And God said, "Let there be light," and there was light. God saw that the light was good, and he separated the light from the darkness. God called the light "day," and the darkness he called "night." And there was evening, and there was morning—the first day. (Gen 1:1–5)

"Let there be light" and God's successive creation utterances in Genesis 1 are speech acts with illocutionary force and perlocutionary effect. The illocutionary force of "Let there be light" is that light is created. The perlocutionary effect is that light exists. The divine speech acts continue.

> And God said, "Let there be a vault between the waters to separate water from water." (v. 6)
>
> And God said, "Let the water under the sky be gathered to one place, and let dry ground appear." (v. 9)
>
> Then God said, "Let the land produce vegetation: seed-bearing plants and trees on the land that bear fruit with seed in it, according to their various kinds." (v. 11)
>
> And God said, "Let there be lights in the vault of the sky to separate the day from the night, and let them serve as signs to mark sacred times, and days and years, and let them be lights in the vault of the sky to give light on the earth." (v. 14–15)
>
> And God said, "Let the water teem with living creatures, and let birds fly above the earth across the vault of the sky." (v. 20)
>
> And God said, "Let the land produce living creatures according to their kinds: the livestock, the creatures that move along the ground, and the wild animals, each according to its kind." (v. 24)

When God creates humankind, he does not use the third person imperative form ("Let the water teem …", "Let the land produce …"). Rather, he uses the first person imperative. "Let us …" Strictly speaking, this is not a speech act but a statement of intentionality, as God is addressing himself.

> Then God said, "Let us make humans in our image, according to our likeness, and let them have dominion over the fish of the sea and over the birds of the air and over the cattle and over all the wild animals of the earth and over every creeping thing that creeps upon the earth." (v. 26, NRSVUE)

After the seven speech acts there is a simple "And it was so."[1] When God creates humankind there is a fuller statement, indicating its significance.

---

[1] According to the traditional Hebrew Masoretic text, the words "And it was so" do not follow the divine utterance in verse 20. But they do appear in the Septuagint (the Greek translation of the Hebrew Scriptures).

> So God created humans in his image,
>> in the image of God he created them;
>> male and female he created them. (v. 27, NRSVUE)

God creates the universe in seven speech acts and a statement of intentionality.

Divine speech acts continue throughout the Old Testament. An area for further study is how the prophetic oracle and its introductory phrases "This is what the Sovereign LORD says" (e.g., Isa 7:7: "Thus saith the LORD God" in the KJV) and "… declares the LORD" (e.g., Jer 1:8) can be understood through the frame of speech acts.

The Gospels: *"Talitha koum!"*

In the Gospels, Jesus performs declarative speech acts throughout his ministry. Limiting our search to the opening chapters of Mark, Jesus is performing speech acts with illocutionary force and perlocutionary effect when he says to a demon, "Be quiet! Come out of him!" (Mark 1:25); to a man with leprosy, "Be clean!" (Mark 1:41); to a paralyzed man, "Son, your sins are forgiven," and "I tell you, get up, take your mat and go home" (Mark 2:5, 11); to a man with a shriveled hand, "Stretch out your hand" (Mark 3:5); to the waves, "Quiet! Be still!" (Mark 4:39); to a dead girl—but that is something special and we will consider it in some detail in this section.

Mark wrote his Gospel in Greek, even though Jesus' primary language was Aramaic (see chapter 12). However, there are four occasions where Mark, in the midst of his Greek-language narrative, uses Aramaic as the verbatim words of Jesus, which he then translates into Greek.[2]

> He took her by the hand and said to her, *"Talitha koum!"* (which means "Little girl, I say to you, get up!"). (Mark 5:41)

> He looked up to heaven and with a deep sigh said to him, *"Ephphatha!"* (which means "Be opened!"). (Mark 7:34)

> *"Abba*, Father," he said, "everything is possible for you. Take this cup from me. Yet not what I will, but what you will." (Mark 14:36)

> And at three in the afternoon Jesus cried out in a loud voice, *"Eloi, Eloi, lema sabachthani*?" (which means "My God, my God, why have you forsaken me?"). (Mark 15:34)

---

[2] The form "koum" (κούμ, a transliteration of the Aramaic קוּם) occurs in some early manuscripts, but it is grammatically incorrect since it is the masculine form. Other early manuscripts read "koumi" (κουμι, a transliteration of the Aramaic קוּמִי), which is the feminine form.

Amongst the four Gospels, the inclusion of Aramaic is unique to Mark. Jesus' words *Talitha koum* occur in the story of Jesus raising Jairus' twelve-year-old daughter to life. While both Matthew and Luke tell this story, they do not include any Aramaic. In Luke's Gospel (7:14) Jesus raises a widow's son in Nain with the words, "Young man, I say to you, get up!" But no Aramaic is recorded. In John's Gospel (11:43) Jesus raises Lazarus with the words, "Lazarus, come out!" But we are not given Jesus' original Aramaic words. We note, too, that the raising of this twelve-year-old girl is the only account in Mark's Gospel of Jesus raising someone from the dead.

Jesus' word *Ephphatha* is found in the story of the healing of a man who was deaf and mute in Mark 7, which is exclusive to Mark.

Matthew and Luke both record Jesus' prayer in Gethsemane but do not include the Aramaic word *Abba*.

Matthew, like Mark, records Jesus' cry of dereliction from the cross and then translates it into Greek. However, in Matthew's Gospel, Jesus cries out in Hebrew (Buth 2014).

The insertion of key phrases in Aramaic is unique to Mark. It is not our intent here to discuss why Matthew, Luke, and John did *not* include Aramaic phrases. Perhaps Mark was particularly linguistically astute. Limiting our study to Mark, though, it is important to ask, Why these phrases and no others? Why "*Talitha koum!*" in Aramaic, while "Be clean!" (Mark 1:41) is recorded in Greek?

Delgado Gómez gives a number of general functions for the use of these Aramaic phrases including placing the author "in the superior position of being a translator, interpreter and guarantor of the tradition that goes back to Jesus" (2020:404–405). By this means, both Jesus and Mark are characterized as native Aramaic speakers, thereby providing reliability and historicity to the narrative.

The question still stands: Why these particular phrases and not others? We will consider *Abba* and *Eloi, Eloi, lema sabachthani* in chapter 12. Our present interest is with *Talitha koum!* and *Ephphatha!*

Talitha koum! Ephphatha!

The question we are examining here is why Mark retains the Aramaic in the two phrases *Talitha koum!* and *Ephphatha!* He does not do so when telling of how Jesus healed a paralyzed man in 2:11, where the healing command is the same as that used in raising the girl, "Get up!", or in 1:41 where he cures a man with leprosy with the words, "I am willing. Be clean!" What is so special about the phrases *Talitha koum!* and *Ephphatha!*?

Commenting on the raising of the dead girl, Tom Wright suggests that "the crucial words made such a deep impression on Peter and the others that whenever they told the story afterwards, even to non-Jewish audiences, they kept the crucial words as they were" (2001:63). I hold Wright in the greatest respect, but I dare to suggest that he might have probed a little more deeply here, in line with his own statement summarising this section of Mark's Gospel where he writes of "the life-giving power of God ... breaking into, and working through, the ordinary details of life" (2001:63–64).

Another suggestion comes from the Norwegian scholar Harris Birkeland. Birkeland (1954, quoted in Barr 1970) argues that Jesus taught in Hebrew. One of his key arguments is the existence of these four Aramaic phrases: that is, Mark recorded them because they were not in the language Jesus normally used. Birkeland is right in seeing that the reason Mark preserved Jesus' Aramaic words on these four occasions was because they were exceptional. However, most scholars agree that Aramaic was Jesus' mother tongue, and he used it for most of his ministry. The exceptionality of these words lies not in their language but in their (illocutionary) force and (perlocutionary) effect.

Some commentators (summarised in Buth, 2014:409–410) write of "local color", others of a "sense of mystery". Randall Buth himself suggests, "Mark wants the readers to know the plain, ordinary meaning of the words and Mark wants to produce a literary effect" (p. 410). That is to say, these words are not magic incantations in a cultic language but down-to-earth words in the home language of those to whom they are addressed. While in agreement with Buth, I believe Mark is doing something more profound, more earth-shattering here, and that is where speech act theory and the philosophers John Austin and John Searle are relevant.

Speech acts

I propose that *Talitha koum!* and *Ephphatha!* are best understood as speech acts with illocutionary force and perlocutionary effect. More than that, they are speech acts of such exceptional power that they stand in a league of their own. In her unpublished 2008 essay, Teija Greed emphasizes the role of the hearer as well as the speaker in the context of a speech act, using the Finnish term *dialoginen*, which translated means "having the nature of a dialogue". In order to demonstrate the superlative nature of these speech acts preserved in Jesus' original Aramaic, let us view them as the instigators of interactional dialogues. We will do this by looking at the following question:

> Did the girl to whom Jesus said *Talitha koum!* and the man to whom Jesus said *Ephphatha!* hear these commands of Jesus?
>
> The answer is *No*. They were dead and deaf respectively.
>
> The answer is a resounding *Yes*. They obeyed him.

The illocutionary force of Jesus' speech act brings forth a dialogue as the dead girl and the deaf man hear the words of Jesus and respond. Jesus' words have penetrated the impenetrable, cut through the liminal space between the living and the dead, between those able to hear and those unable to hear; the words *Talitha koum!* have smashed through the gates of Sheol where the dead girl was residing; his utterance *Ephphatha!* has burst with a shout of triumph into the linguistic isolation imposed by the hearing people amongst whom the deaf man lived. The effect of Jesus' words is so palpable and profound that Mark records them in the language Jesus used.

Mark tells us that the girl got up immediately; that the man's ears were opened, his tongue loosened, and that he began to speak plainly (see also chapter 6). Such was the perlocutionary impact of the words of Jesus!

There is the echo of a parallel here with the very first speech act, when God spoke into the darkness, "'Let there be light,' and there was light" (Gen 1:3). The illocutionary force of Jesus' speech act to the dead girl is visible as it penetrates beyond the world of flesh and blood, invoking the power of God, the progenitor of all speech acts. Its perlocutionary effect is seen in the fact that she got up, alive, a speech act as effective as God's creational speech acts in Genesis 1.

Paul: "Let light shine out of darkness"

In 2 Corinthians 4:6, Paul writes, "For God, who said, 'Let light shine out of darkness,' made his light shine in our hearts to give us the light of the knowledge of God's glory displayed in the face of Christ." He is quoting Genesis 1:3, "Let light shine out of darkness." This phraseology is Paul's own paraphrase because neither the Hebrew nor the Septuagint (the Greek translation of the Hebrew Scriptures) include "out of darkness". Both have simply, "Let there be light." The darkness comes from the context in Genesis: "darkness was over the surface of the deep" (v. 2). However, Paul was not simply misremembering his Scriptures. He has good reason for including the phrase "out of darkness".

By bringing the darkness from the context into the quote, Paul is creating a parallel design, a comparison between "Let light shine out of darkness" and "made his light shine in our hearts". The source of the light on both occasions is God. The darkness into which God spoke the creative word in Genesis 1 is set alongside the darkness of our hearts into which he makes his light shine. Genesis 1:2 reads, "Now the earth was formless and empty, darkness was over the surface of the deep, and the Spirit of God was hovering over the waters." By inserting "out of darkness" into his Genesis quote, Paul is equating the description of the dark and formless earth in Genesis 1:2 with our hearts: formless, empty, dark; and yet the Spirit of God is at work.

The result of the light shining in Genesis is, "and there was light. God saw that the light was good, and he separated the light from the darkness. God called the light 'day,' and the darkness he called 'night.' And there was evening, and there was morning—the first day" (Gen 1:3–5).

The result of the light shining in 2 Corinthians is described in this way: "[God] made his light shine in our hearts to give us the light of the knowledge of God's glory displayed in the face of Christ" (v. 6). This light, too, is good, and whether or not actual words were used when God caused it to shine, it shines with (illocutionary) force and (perlocutionary) effect. God's locutionary act is found in the words, "made his light shine in our hearts". God is the agent, the source and initiator of the light that shines in our hearts.

No speech is explicit in the phrase "made his light shine in our hearts," so we need to pause and ask whether it is possible to have a locutionary act without speech. Language is deeper and more profound than the spoken word. Language may be spoken, signed, or written, but as was argued in chapter 2, it is not dependent on any of these manifestations for its existence. So whether God spoke, signed, or wrote anything when he shone his light into our hearts is not the point. God has transformed us in the same way as he transformed the void on that first day of creation.

Separating light from light

We have already observed the parallel between the light shining in the darkness of the void in Genesis and the light shining into the darkness of our hearts in Corinthians. There is also a development in this parallel. When Paul is quoting Genesis, the word for "light" is φῶς (*phós*)[3]—the normal Greek word for light, which is also found in the Septuagint translation of Genesis 1:3. The second occurrence of the word "light" in the NIV cannot be found in the Greek, which simply has ἔλαμψεν (*elampsen*, shone), the "light" being assumed by the verb. Compare the NRSVUE, "For it is the God who said, 'Let light shine out of darkness', who has shone in our hearts to give the light of the knowledge of the glory of God in the face of Christ." When we come to the "light" in the phrase "to give us the light of the knowledge of God's glory displayed in the face of Christ" we find a different word in the Greek: φωτισμὸν (*phótismon*).

From the noun φῶς (*phós*, light) is derived the verb φωτίζω (*phótizó*), which is what light does, and so it is most often translated as "to shine" or "to give light". Derived from the verb φωτίζω (*phótizó*) is another noun, φωτισμός (*phótismos*), of which φωτισμὸν (*phótismon*, the word found in

---

[3] The Greek of this verse reads: ὅτι ὁ θεὸς ὁ εἰπών Ἐκ σκότους φῶς λάμψει, ὃς ἔλαμψεν ἐν ταῖς καρδίαις ἡμῶν πρὸς φωτισμὸν τῆς γνώσεως τῆς δόξης τοῦ θεοῦ ἐν προσώπῳ ['Ιησοῦ] Χριστοῦ. Literal translation:

"For the God the having-said Out-of darkness light shall-shine who shone in the hearts of-us for-the-purpose-of illumination of-the knowledge of-the-glory of God in face of-Jesus of-Christ."

2 Cor 4:6) is the accusative. And so, derived from the verb "to shine" or "to give light", the noun φωτισμός (*phótismos*) conveys the meaning of illumination, enlightenment, or radiance. It is light on the move, light being shone.

The light that God gives us in the face of Christ is derived from the Genesis light, but is more than that. It is light on the move. In chapter 2 we saw how intra-trinitarian sending is of the essence of God. The Father sends the Son, the Father and Son send the Spirit. In this complex of sending, God sends forth his light, and he does so in the face of Jesus Christ.

The Greek word φωτισμός (phótismos) occurs only twice in the New Testament.[4] The other occurrence is two verses earlier in 2 Corinthians 4 where the NIV translates it as "light": "The god of this age has blinded the minds of unbelievers, so that they cannot see the light of the gospel that displays the glory of Christ, who is the image of God" (v. 4).

The gospel is light on the move, light that has been sent.

The content of the light or radiance in 2 Corinthians 4 that is transmitted to us in the face of Christ is "the knowledge of God's glory". Habakkuk 2:14 states: "For the earth will be filled with the knowledge of the glory of the LORD as the waters cover the sea." God's mission is to fill the earth with the knowledge of his glory—or the knowledge of himself (cf. Isa 11:9), which is more or less the same thing (see chapter 2). Our verse in 2 Corinthians tells us that God is bringing his mission to fulfilment in the face of Jesus. Jesus is the means by which God accomplishes his mission. It is his mission that everyone get to know him, in all his glory. We see God and his glory displayed in the face of Jesus Christ.

Jesus, the Word of God, is God's speech act. In him are illocutionary force (there is power in the name of Jesus) and perlocutionary effect (through him, with sins forgiven, we draw near to God).

"We do not lose heart"

This light-drenched picture that Paul paints may seem to be at odds with reality, for he continues:

> But we have this treasure in jars of clay to show that this all-surpassing power is from God and not from us. We are hard pressed on every side, but not crushed; perplexed, but not in despair; persecuted, but not abandoned; struck down, but not destroyed. We always carry around in our body the death of Jesus. (2 Cor. 4: 7–10)

---

[4] It is also used six times in the Septuagint. Twice it describes light on the move: Job 3:9 ("May its morning stars become dark; may it wait for daylight in vain and not see the first rays of dawn") and Psalm 78:14 ("He guided them with the cloud by day and with light from the fire all night."). Twice φωτισμός is coupled with πρόσωπον (face) (Ps 44:3 and 90:8). The other two occurrences are Psalm 27:1 and Psalm 139:11.

The end of the story, though, is resurrection:

> We know that the one who raised the Lord Jesus from the dead will also raise us with Jesus and present us with you to himself. (v. 14)

Paul's application of the truth of God's light shining in our hearts comes at the beginning and end of the chapter. Verse 1: "Therefore, since through God's mercy we have this ministry, we do not lose heart." Verse 16: "Therefore we do not lose heart. Though outwardly we are wasting away, yet inwardly we are being renewed day by day." Understanding the force and effect of divine speech acts is not a linguistic or theological curiosity. It is what keeps us going.

Jesus' speech act in Mark 5, *Talitha koum*, was a precursor of our resurrection. Thus, the three speech acts of Genesis 1, Mark 5, and 2 Corinthians 4 form an interconnecting triangle, each pointing to the other and all ultimately pointing to resurrection, the illocutionary force and perlocutionary effect of God's word.

Conclusion

Speech acts have a pivotal role in God's mission as he engages with his creation. God brought the universe into being with a series of speech acts. While Jesus performed many speech acts, *Talitha koum!* and *Ephphatha!* are in a league of their own, and by retaining the original linguistic form, Mark draws the attention of his reader to them. The dead and the deaf—those who would normally be unable to hear him—hear and obey. In recording the Aramaic, Mark is highlighting the power of the words of Jesus, words which, as Paul reminds us, are equally powerful today. The (illocutionary) force and (perlocutionary) effect of the speech acts of God give us the assurance of resurrection (2 Cor 4). Paul's application of God's speech acts comes at both the beginning and the end of 2 Corinthians 4: "We do not lose heart" (v. 1 and 16). This is one of the many perlocutionary consequences of God sending forth his word.

> "Send forth your word, Lord, and let there be light!" (Graham Kendrick 1987)

References

Austin, John. 1962. *How to do things with words.* Oxford: Oxford University Press.

Barr, James. 1970. *Which language did Jesus speak? Some remarks of a semitist*. Bulletin of the John Rylands Library 51(1):929. https://www.manchesterhive.com/view/journals/bjrl/53/1/article-p9.xml.
Birkeland, Harris. 1954. The language of Jesus. Oslo: Dybwad. Quoted in Barr 1970.
Buth, Randall. 2014. The riddle of Jesus' cry from the cross: The meaning of ηλι ηλι λαμα σαβαχθανι (Matthew 27:46) and the literary function of ελωι ελωι λειμα σαβαχθανι (Mark 15:34). In Randall Buth and R. Steven Notley (eds.), *The language environment of First Century Judaea*, 395–421. Leiden, Netherlands: Brill.
Delgado Gómez, Alfredo. 2020. Get up! Be opened!: Code-switching and loanwords in the Gospel of Mark. *Journal for the Study of the New Testament* 42(3):390–427.
Greed, Teija. 2008. Sosiaalinen instituutio á la Searle [Social institution à la Searle]. Ms.
Kendrick, Graham. 1987. *Shine Jesus shine* (song). Make Way Music.
Nordquist, Richard. 2024. *What is the speech act theory: Definition and examples*. ThoughtCo. https://www.thoughtco.com/speech-act-theory-1691986.
Wright, N. T. 2001. *Mark for everyone*. London: SPCK.

Teth

*The law from your mouth is more precious to me
than thousands of pieces of silver and gold.
(Psalm 119:72)*

9

Language Diversity: Curse or Blessing? The Story of the Tower of Babel

Gary Simons

The most iconic story of language in the Bible

When contemplating the topic of language in the Bible, the account of the Tower of Babel in Genesis 11:1–9 is probably the first thing that comes to mind for most people. There we read about a project that attempted to build a city with a tower that would reach to the heavens, but it ended in disaster when the LORD intervened to "confuse" the language of the people, with the result that they scattered over all the earth. In the Western world, the Tower of Babel has emerged from the pages of Scripture to become a cultural icon that represents the multiplicity and diversity of languages across the globe. Witness, for instance, its appearance in the titles of books like the following, which have nothing to do with the Bible.

> *The Ascent of Babel: An Exploration of Language, Mind, and Understanding* (Altmann 1998)
>
> *The Power of Babel: A Natural History of Language* (McWhorter 2003)
>
> *Babel: Around the World in Twenty Languages* (Dorren 2018)

Similarly, the "curse of Babel" has emerged as a term in public discourse. It is much more than a phrase uttered from the pulpit when the Tower of Babel story is featured in a sermon. It has become an idiom in the English language for referring to the challenges of global language diversity, casting these challenges in a negative light. Searching on Google for "curse of Babel" and related phrases yields hundreds of thousands of results. For instance, these are examples of representative titles in the media.

> *Esperanto: Undoing the Curse of Babel* (Halpern and Schor 2016)
>
> *Overcoming the Ancient Curse of Babel with English* (WSJ 2015)
>
> *Technology to Reverse 'Curse of Babel?'* (Arutz Sheva 2011)

However, the notion that the multiplicity of languages is a curse does not actually appear within the biblical text. Where did that idea come from? The next section explores that question.

The most popular reading of the Babel story: Pride and punishment

The idea that the multiplicity of languages on earth is a curse on humanity stems from what commonly has been the most popular way of understanding the Tower of Babel story over the centuries, namely, that the diversification of languages was a divine judgement for the hubris of the tower builders. Any regular churchgoer is likely to have heard a sermon about how the over-reaching pride of the people who attempted to build "a tower that reaches to the heavens" (Gen 11:4) was punished by confusing the language of the people so that they could no longer communicate with each other and were forced to stop the project.

Theodore Hiebert (2007a) traces the history of this pride-and-punishment reading of the Babel story, beginning with the pseudepigraphical *Book of Jubilees* (ca. 200 BC) which provides the first extant interpretation of Genesis 11:1–9. This ancient retelling adds a detail not found in the biblical text, namely, that the intent of the tower builders was to "ascend thereby into heaven" (Jubilees 10:19). Early rabbinic interpreters identified Nimrod, the empire builder in Genesis 10:8–11, as the leader of this arrogant assault on heaven. For the early interpreters, "the diversity at the end of the story—the division of languages and scattering of peoples—can only be understood as a divine punishment for human wickedness" (Hiebert 2007a:127). Hiebert goes on to quote from the writings of Augustine, Luther, and Calvin to show that this interpretation was carried forward by these luminaries from Christian history.

Language diversity as a divine punishment against humanity continues to this day as a common framework for the exegesis of Genesis 11:1–9. The following are some exemplary quotations:

> The multitude of nations indicates not only the manifold quality of God's creative power but also a judgment, for the disorder in the international world, which our narrative regards as the sad conclusion, was not willed by God but is punishment for the sinful rebellion against God. (Von Rad 1973:152)

> Genesis is affirming that the diversity of languages represents a divine judgment on mankind ... Genesis holds that the confusion of languages is a divine antidote to human arrogance. (Wenham 1987:237)

> Linguistic and cultural diversity is presented in Scripture as a whole, and in Genesis especially, as a result of the fall, an act of judgment on humanity. As judgment, it is the deprivation of original harmony and understanding. (Hill 1996:15–16)

But the biblical text does not explicitly identify God's intervention of "confusing the language" as a punishment, nor does the text contain the word "curse". Why, then, has it been so readily interpreted in this way? The Genesis account begins with three classic tales of sin and punishment—the garden of Eden, Cain and Abel, and the great flood—and the word "curse" does occur with reference to punishment in each of these stories (Gen 3:14 and 17, 4:11, 8:21). Hiebert (2007b:47) suggests that interpreters have been inclined to extend the same pattern to the Babel story, even though the language of curse is missing.

While the diversity-as-curse interpretation may resonate with people who see the multiplicity of languages and cultures as a problem, it does not make sense in light of the overall sweep of the biblical narrative from creation to new creation. The tree of life introduced at the beginning of the story (Gen 2:9) ends up being for "the healing of the nations" in its climax (Rev 22:2). In the new city, there will no longer be any curse (Rev 22:3), but there will be diversity as the glory and honor of the nations are brought into it (Rev 21:26). As theologian Christopher Wright observes, "God's mission is what fills the gap between the scattering of the nations in Genesis 11 and the healing of the nations in Revelation 22. It is God's mission in relation to the nations, arguably more than any other single theme, that provides the key that unlocks the biblical grand narrative" (Wright 2013:455)—a narrative "which glories in diversity and celebrates multiple human cultures" (Wright 2013:47). The idea that the diversity of languages and cultures we see in the world today is the result of a punishment inflicted upon humanity is incompatible with the narrative as a whole. We need look no further than the creation story itself for the explanation of linguistic and cultural diversity.

Diversity as the blueprint for creation

The very blueprint of creation is a blueprint for diversity. In the opening chapter of the Bible, we read that God created the great diversity of plant and animal life. We see in the world around us a degree of diversity that can readily be characterized as exuberant (Greeley 1976:152). The blueprint for this diversity is expressed in what Francis Collins (2006) has called "the language of God", namely, DNA. Through the mechanisms of genetic recombination and mutation, the language of DNA is the engine behind ongoing diversification in nature as it spawns new variations in succeeding generations.

In the opening chapter of the Bible, we also read that God created humankind in his own image (Gen 1:26–27). That image includes the capacity of language and rational thought and the creativity that would be needed to fulfill what has come to be known as the cultural mandate, "Be fruitful and increase in number; fill the earth and subdue it" (Gen 1:28a). In the second chapter, we read of the first task explicitly assigned under this cultural mandate, namely, to give names to all the animals (Gen 2:19). As Andy Crouch describes it:

> God [is] making room for his image-bearers to begin to grow into the vast cosmic purpose that was disclosed in Genesis 1. God is perfectly capable of naming every animal and giving Adam a dictionary—but he does not. He makes room for Adam's creativity ... allowing Adam to be the one who speaks something out of nothing, a name where there had been none, and allowing that name to have its own being ... The Creator graciously steps back just enough to allow humankind to begin to discover what it means to be a creator. (2013:109–110)

The creativity inherent in the language capacity is the engine that lies behind language diversification. As Adam began to name the animals, the language began to change. Thus language change was not introduced in Genesis 11 as part of a curse, it was introduced in Genesis 2 as an essential component of what it means to be created in the image of God. And as humankind moved out in different directions from the original garden to begin filling the earth, language would need to keep changing in different ways in different places because there would be new things in every place that would need to be named—not just things in the natural world, but also the new cultural artifacts that people were creating.

Humans are not just language users; they are more fundamentally language makers (Harris 1980:i). As a social practice that is handed down from one generation to the next, a language is constantly changing as each new generation makes the language its own. Throughout history, when peoples who do not share a language have come into extended contact, they have solved the communication problem by making a rudimentary language called a *pidgin* (McWhorter 2003:132–137). Then, when that language is learned by children as their native language, they make it into a full-blown language through a process called *creolization* (McWhorter 2003:212–214, 137ff.). The need to make a language also occurs when Deaf children are born into a community that does not have a sign language (see chapter 7). In *Talking Hands*, Margalit Fox (2007) tells the fascinating story of a remote Bedouin community in Israel making a full-fledged language within just a few generations.

Humans were created to be language makers, and language diversification is what naturally happens when a community of language makers splits into separate communities that live in different places and are no longer in contact with each other. This is exactly the picture that is painted in the "Table of Nations" of Genesis 10 which describes the dispersal of the descendants of the three sons of Noah following the great flood; it describes the diversification of peoples into their own territories, "each with its own language" (Gen 10:5, see also Gen 10:20 and 10:31).

When the Apostle Paul was invited by the philosophers in Athens to address them at the Areopagus, he framed the diversification of the nations as an act of creation. He had observed an altar with the inscription "To an unknown god" and used that as a jumping-off point to introduce the scholars of Athens to the God of the Jews. He began by describing the unknown god's acts of creation as a means of establishing that god's credentials. First, he is "the God who made the world and everything in it" (Acts 17:24a); and then, "From one ancestor he made all peoples to inhabit the whole earth" (Acts 17:26a, NRSVUE). The text of Genesis itself offers some evidence that the diversification of the nations was an action on par with the creation of the first humans. These two acts happen to be the only occurrences within the text of the primeval history in Genesis 1–11 of the first person plural cohortative as spoken by God (Strong 2008:628), "Let us make humans in our image" (Gen 1:26a, NRSVUE) and "Come, let us go down and confuse their language" (Gen 11:7a).

Given the grand narrative of the Bible as God's mission to bless the nations, and given that diversity is in the very blueprint of creation, the conclusion commonly drawn from Genesis 11:1–9, that language diversity is a punishment for human pride, does not make sense. Is there a way of interpreting the story of Babel that is more faithful to the grand narrative from creation to new creation? The next section suggests that there is.

Another reading of the Babel story: Rebellion and restoration

Another way of reading Genesis 11:1–9 begins with the story of creation. As already noted, the account of the sixth day reports that God blessed the humans he had created, saying, "Be fruitful and multiply and fill the earth and subdue it" (Gen 1:28a, ESV). Following the great flood, this same blessing is repeated three times in the text, once over the animals (Gen 8:17) and twice over Noah and his family (Gen 9:1, 7).

After recounting in Genesis 10 how the descendants of Noah did begin to disperse over the earth, the story hits a bump in chapter 11 when the people who have settled on the plain of Shinar decide to halt the process. They propose an alternative plan: "Come, let us build ourselves a city ... so that we may make a name for ourselves; otherwise we will be scattered over the face of the whole earth" (Gen 11:4). This line of action is in direct rebellion against the mandate to fill the earth. The divine response of "confusing their language" solves that problem. Unable to communicate, the people stop building the city and resume the divine plan of filling the earth. The conclusion of the story twice states that they were scattered over the whole earth (Gen 11:8, 9) thus emphasizing that the restoration of the original blessing is what the story is really about.

"Confusing the language" is certainly a divine intervention, but how can language diversity be seen as a divine punishment against humanity when that diversity was in the blueprint from the beginning? Rather, fast-tracking diversification at Babel is more like a stratagem for restoring the original creation blessing. It is reminiscent of the story in which God sent hornets[1] to help clear the land of the Canaanites ahead of the advancing Israelites (Exod 23:28). The stratagem is summarized in a pair of lines from the *Hornet Song*: "He did not compel them to go against their will, He just made them willing to go" (Ingersoll 1954).

Understanding the Babel story as narrating a rebellion against God's original mandate to fill the earth and the restoration of the creation blessing has a long history. In the first century, Flavius Josephus in his *Antiquities of the Jews* (Whiston 1737) framed the story of Babel in terms of this disobedience. He wrote:

> God also commanded them to send colonies abroad, for the thorough peopling of the earth ... But they were so ill instructed, that they did not obey God. For which reason they fell into calamities, and ... God admonished them again to send out colonies. But they ... did not obey him. (*Antiquities* 1.4.1, in Whiston 1737)

Josephus then gives an account of how a tyrannical leader "excited" them to this disobedience and persuaded them to build a tower, but the project came to an abrupt end

---

[1] This obscure Hebrew word can also be translated "panic", "terror", or "discouragement".

> when God saw that they acted so madly ... [he] caused a tumult among them, by producing in them diverse languages; and causing, that through the multitude of those languages, they should not be able to understand one another. (*Antiquities* 1.4.3)

> After this they were dispersed abroad, on account of their languages, and went out by colonies everywhere. And each colony took possession of that land ... unto which God led them. (*Antiquities* 1.5.1)

This way of understanding the text continued in Jewish commentaries of the Middle Ages. For instance, the tenth century rabbi Saadia Gaon taught that "their sin was wanting to stay in one area and not filling the earth as God commanded, which led him to disperse them" (Ron 2014:116).

A number of modern commentaries echo the conclusion that the primary sin in the Babel story was not an arrogant pride, but the deliberate choice to cease the process of filling the earth.

> The sin of the generation ... consisted of resistance to the divine will that the children of men be dispersed over the whole world. (Sarna 1966:72)

> The sin of the generation of Babel consisted of their refusal to "fill the earth". (Plaut 1981:83)

> The basic human failure in this text is not easy to discern, but it seems focused in the motivation, "otherwise we shall be scattered abroad upon the face of the whole earth". (Fretheim 2005:89)

Gunther Plaut goes on to observe that God's action in confusing the language "was not so much a punishment as a carrying out of His plan" (1981:83). A growing chorus of modern scholars has similarly concluded that the scattering at Babel is better understood as a resumption of the creation mandate than as a divine punishment.[2] In the words of one contemporary scholar:

> God's multiplication of languages in this narrative is not a curse, but God's solution to human intransigence, and the catalyst for doing what God had instructed Noah and his sons to do from the beginning, as they first descended from the ark. (Coleson 2012:295)

Many of the recent interpreters also see the dispersal from Babel as an act of deliverance for peoples who were being oppressed under imperial domination. This is the topic of the next section.

---

[2] Anderson 1978, Smith 1996, Kass 2003:232, Hiebert 2007b, Green 2008:211, etc.

Yet another reading: Domination and deliverance

The retelling of Genesis 11:1–9 by Josephus adds a main character to the story.

> Now it was Nimrod who excited them to such an affront and contempt of God ... He also gradually changed the government into tyranny; seeing no other way of turning men from the fear of God, but to bring them into a constant dependence on his own power. (*Antiquities* 1.4.2, in Whiston 1737)

Nimrod is a character introduced in the preceding chapter of the biblical text (Gen 10:8–12). There he is identified as the builder of an empire that began with Babel and extended to other cities in Shinar and Assyria. Influential Christian thinkers like Augustine, Luther, and Calvin continued to name him as the tyrant who instigated the building of the tower (Hiebert 2007a:131, 132, 135).

The Babelite declaration of "Come, let us make bricks" may sound to a modern reader like the beginnings of a benign communal building project. However, it must have had a very different ring to the original readers of the Torah who would have been attuned to the intertextual connections between Genesis 11 and Exodus 1 (Smith 1996, Smith and Carvill 2000:215–216, Sherman 2013:58–60). In addition to the prominence of bricks in both stories (Gen 11:3, Exod 1:14), the "Come, let us ..." formula that is used in the Hebrew text to announce the plan of the tower builders (Gen 11:3, 4) is also used by Pharaoh (Exod 1:10) to announce his solution to the problem of the growing Hebrew population. The Babel narrative has echoes of the tyranny that prevented the ancestors of the Jews from returning to their homeland by enslaving them in Egypt to make bricks for building cities that brought renown to Pharaoh.

The popular understanding of the Babel story takes the opening sentence as a declaration of the original state of humankind—"The whole world had one language and a common speech" (Gen 11:1). This poses a problem for the chronology of the text, since the incident that follows is understood to be the logical precursor to the diversification of languages that is already described in the Table of Nations in Genesis 10. That chapter lists the descendants of the three sons of Noah and states for each line of descent that the various clans had their own languages (Gen 10:5, 20, 31, also see chapter 9).

A more literal translation of the first two nouns in the opening sentence would be, "The whole land had one lip". There is a line of scholarship that interprets this as putting forth an introductory problem statement, rather than as describing the primeval state. In this reading, the first sentence sets the stage for the story by summarizing the problem that God's action seeks to remedy, namely, that a state of linguistic hegemony had arisen throughout an entire land.

The word that is most commonly translated as "earth" or "world" in the opening sentence is the Hebrew word *eretz*. While this term may be used to mean the entire world, it has multiple senses. Across the whole text of the Hebrew Bible, it is more commonly used in reference to a territory or region or country. The word in verse 1 is, in fact, the same word that occurs in verse 2 in the phrase "land of Shinar". Thus the land referred to in the first sentence can be readily interpreted as the same land that is specifically named in the second sentence (De Witt 1979:17, Gousmett 2018:36).

The word that is most commonly translated as "language" in the opening sentence is the Hebrew word *saphah*. The primary meaning of this word is "lip" as a body part. In other occurrences where *saphah* is translated as "language" or "speech", it refers to the content of what is said, rather than to the language as a system (Gousmett 2018:42–43). The usual Hebrew word for a language is *lashon* "tongue" and that is the term used in Genesis 10 in naming the descendants of Noah by their "clans and languages". The seeming discrepancy between chapters 10 and 11 can be solved if the "one lip" is taken to be a lingua franca that makes it possible for people of different "tongues" to communicate (Hamilton 1990:350, Marlowe 2011:30). As explained by Cyrus Gordon, a major proponent of this interpretation, "the meaning is that while the component ethnic elements of the International Order had their speech for family and ethnic communication, there was an international lingua franca that made communication possible so that great projects like the Tower of Babel could be constructed" (Gordon 1988:295).

Christoph Uehlinger's (1990) monograph on the exegesis of Genesis 11:1–9, *World Empire and "One Speech"*, establishes the context for such an interpretation by investigating the rhetoric of empire in the written records of ancient Mesopotamia. He finds that three of the motifs found in the Babel story—one speech, city building, and making a name for oneself—are also recurring themes in the ideology of Mesopotamian kingship. He finds that the "one speech" motif is "a metaphor for the subjugation and assimilation of conquered peoples" (Smith 1996). For instance, he discovered an epithet for the Assyrian king Ashurbanipal which named him as "he who made the totality of all people use one speech" (Uehlinger 1990:464).

Against this backdrop, we can identify a third major way of reading the Babel story—as a tale of domination and deliverance. In this reading, the sin that needed to be addressed was the act of dominating diverse peoples through imperial power that sought to stop their scattering and to rule them through a common language. "Confusing the language" was thus a divine intervention that was effective in eliminating the power of empire afforded by imposing "one speech". The subjugated peoples were thereby delivered from domination and were free to scatter once again as they resumed the original trajectory of diversification that was implicit in the creation blessing to fill the world. Many modern scholars have embraced the interpretation that Babel is a story of the oppression of dominated peoples[3] including those from the global South where the domination of local peoples by imperial powers from the global North characterizes their recent history.[4]

We have reviewed three ways of reading the text—as a story of pride and punishment, of rebellion and restoration, or of domination and deliverance. Do these readings need to be mutually exclusive? It might seem so, since the traditional pride-and-punishment interpretation portrays the diversification of languages as a "curse" and something negative, while the other two interpretations portray it as something positive. This discrepancy stems from interpreting the punishment in the pride-and-punishment reading as a judgement against all of humanity. But who was guilty of prideful sin against God? Was it all of the people, or was it imperial rulers who decided on the project and compelled the rest to carry it out? If we adopt the latter view, then all three ways of reading the story can be true at once. There is an element of pride and punishment in the story, but "confusing the language" is a means of punishment only for the rulers since it takes away their hold on power. For the people at large, it is a means of restoring them to the trajectory of the original creation mandate and of delivering them from the domination of an oppressive empire.

Language diversity as blessing

We conclude, therefore, that the multiplicity of languages on earth is not the result of a divine "curse" imposed on all of humanity. Belief in the "curse of Babel" rests on the assumption that language diversity was not God's original intent, but this does not make sense in light of the grand narrative of the Bible. That narrative begins with a mandate to fill the earth (Gen 1:28) and to be creatively changing the language in the process (Gen 2:19) and ends with the vision of an ultimate future including every language (Rev 7:9) and a city filled with the glory of all the nations (Rev 21:26).

As one seminal study of the Babel story has concluded, "God's will for his creation is diversity rather than homogeneity. Ethnic pluralism is to be welcomed as a divine blessing" (Anderson 1978:75). Just as we can find joy in the exuberant variety of the non-human creation (Greeley 1976), we can also take delight in the rich variety of human languages and cultures. But more than being just a source of pleasure, they are a basis for knowledge and personal identity and building relationships. Language diversity is a blessing for the individual, in that knowing multiple languages provides many benefits for one's personal and professional life over knowing just one (Haugen 1987, Leveen 2021).

---

[3] For example: Klingler 2004; Green 2008:209–211; Marlowe 2011; Kim 2013:108–109.
[4] For example: Croatto 1998; Miguez-Bonino 1999; Andiñach 2016.

Diversity is also a blessing for society, in that every language and culture embodies a different way of knowing and understanding the world around us. This diversity of views is an essential resource in the ages-long quest for goodness, truth, and beauty. One commenter explains the desirability of the outcome of Babel in this way: "Awareness of the multiplicity of human ways is also the necessary precondition for the active search for the better or best way" (Kass 2003:238). A political scientist observes that participatory democracy needs the perspective of every language group within a society "to build more beautiful, enriching, and transformative ways of living together" (Schmidt 2014:405).

Finally, diversity is a blessing for the church. A statement by the Lausanne Movement (1997) declares "that no culture can see its own blind spots and that every culture has something to offer to all other cultures". It further describes "diversity as God´s gift to the church and the means by which the true fullness of his good news and the reality of his kingdom may be discerned". Larry Hayashi (2017:71ff.) gives examples of how translating Scripture into a language for the first time reveals fresh insights about the meaning of the text. In chapter 10 of this volume, Watters and Watters expand on this idea, proposing that only through the multiple vantage points afforded by the "harvest of Babel" can the Church come to a full understanding of God and his ways.

If there is a "curse of Babel," it is not the multiplicity of languages. It is that peoples who have risen to power have persisted to this day in using their "one speech" as a tool of assimilation and domination. Ironically, the "curse of Babel" meme that has arisen in the culture of the West serves to perpetuate this real curse as it perpetuates the claim that language diversity is not what God originally intended but is the unfortunate consequence of human sin. To the contrary, the Bible's grand narrative embraces diversity from beginning to end. The Babel story fits into that narrative by restoring the creation blessing of diversity filling the earth as the divine response to a human attempt to dominate others by imposing one language.

References

Altmann, Gerry T. M. 1998. *The ascent of Babel: An exploration of language, mind, and understanding.* Oxford: Oxford University Press.

Anderson, Bernhard W. 1978. Unity and diversity in God's creation: A study of the Babel story. *Currents in Theology and Mission* 5(2):69–81.

Andiñach, Pablo R. 2016. Denouncing imperialism: An Argentine rereading of the Tower of Babel (Gen 11:1–9). In Susanne Scholz and Pablo R. Andiñach (eds.), La Violencia *and the Hebrew Bible: The politics and histories of biblical hermeneutics on the American continent*, 105–119. Semeia Studies 82. Atlanta: SBL Press.

Arutz Sheva. 2011. Technology to reverse "Curse of Babel?" *Israel National News*. 4 December 2011. http://www.israelnationalnews.com/News/News.aspx/150386.

Coleson, Joseph. 2012. *Genesis 1–11: A Bible commentary in the Wesleyan tradition*. Kansas City, MO: Beacon Hill Press.

Collins, Francis S. 2006. *The language of God: A scientist presents evidence for belief*. New York, NY: Free Press.

Croatto, J. Severino. 1998. A reading of the story of the Tower of Babel from the perspective of non-identity. In Fernando F Segovia and Mary Ann Tolbert (eds.), *Teaching the Bible: The discourses and politics of biblical pedagogy*, 203–223. Maryknoll, NY: Orbis Books.

Crouch, Andy. 2013. *Culture making: Recovering our creative calling*. Downers Grove, IL: InterVarsity Press.

De Witt, Dale S. 1979. The historical background of Genesis 11:1–9: Babel or Ur? *Journal of the Evangelical Theological Society* 22(1):15–26.

Dorren, Gaston. 2018. *Babel: Around the world in twenty languages*. Illustrated edition. New York, NY: Atlantic Monthly Press.

Fox, Margalit. 2007. *Talking hands: What sign language reveals about the mind*. New York, NY: Simon & Schuster.

Fretheim, Terence E. 2005. *God and world in the Old Testament: A relational theology of creation*. Nashville, TN: Abingdon Press.

Gordon, Cyrus H. 1988. Ebla as background for the Old Testament. *In* J. A. Emerton (ed.), *Congress volume: Jerusalem* 1986, 293–297. Vetus Testamenttum, Supplements 40. Leiden, Netherlands: Brill.

Gousmett, Chris. 2018. The confusion of language in the interpretation of Genesis 11. *The Evangelical Quarterly* 89(1):34–50.

Greeley, Andrew M. 1976. A theology of pluralism. In Andrew M. Greeley, *The communal Catholic: A personal manifesto*, 151–162. New York, NY: Seabury Press.

Green, Joel B. 2008. 'In our own language:' Pentecost, Babel, and the shaping of Christian community in Acts 2:1–13. In J. Ross Wagner, C. Kavin Rowe, and A. Katherine Grieb (eds.), *The Word leaps the gap: Essays on Scripture and theology in honor of Richard B. Hays*, 198–213. Grand Rapids, MI: Eerdmans.

Halpern, Gilad, and Esther Schor. 2016. Esperanto: Undoing the curse of Babel. Podcast. *Tel Aviv Review*, 28 November 2016. https://tlv1.fm/the-tel-aviv-review/2016/11/28/esperanto-undoing-the-curse-of-babel/.

Hamilton, Victor P. 1990. The book of Genesis: Chapters 1–17. *The New International Commentary on the Old Testament*. Grand Rapids, MI: Eerdmans.

Harris, Roy. 1980. *The language-makers*. Ithaca, NY: Cornell University Press.

Haugen, Einar. 1987. *Blessings of Babel: Bilingualism and language planning: Problems and pleasures*. Contributions to the Sociology of Language 46. Berlin: Mouton de Gruyter.

Hayashi, Larry S. 2017. The blessing of Babel: A theology of languages. CanIL Electronic Working Papers 3:64–76. https://www.canil.ca/wordpress/student-services/academic-resources/electronic-working-papers/.

Hiebert, Theodore. 2007a. Babel: Babble or blueprint? Calvin, cultural diversity, and the interpretation of Genesis 11:1–9. In Wallace M. Alston and Michael Welker (eds.), *Reformed theology: Identity and ecumenicity II, Biblical interpretation in the Reformed tradition*, 127–145. Grand Rapids, MI: Eerdmans.

Hiebert, Theodore. 2007b. The tower of Babel and the origin of the world's cultures. *Journal of Biblical Literature* 126(1):29–58.

Hill, Philip D. 1996. Comment on language in God's economy: A Welsh and international perspective. *Themelios: An International Journal for Pastors and Students of Theological and Religious Studies* 21(3):15–16.

Ingersoll, Clayton (performer). 1954. Hornet song. Ozark Folksong Collection. University of Arkansas Libraries, Fayetteville. https://digitalcollections.uark.edu/digital/collection/OzarkFolkSong/id/2960.

Jubilees. n.d. Book of Jubilees. In R. H. Charles (ed.), The Apocrypha and Pseudepigrapha of the Old Testament. Oxford: Clarendon Press, 1913. Scanned and edited by Joshua Williams. http://www.pseudepigrapha.com/jubilees/10.htm.

Kass, Leon R. 2003. *The beginning of wisdom: Reading Genesis*. New York, NY: Free Press.

Kim, Daewoong. 2013. Biblical interpretation in the Book of Daniel: Literary allusions in Daniel to Genesis and Ezekiel. PhD dissertation. Rice University, Houston, TX. https://repository.rice.edu/server/api/core/bitstreams/8627c3a2-4817-4de3-99a0-05d477d0b234/content.

Klingler, Al. 2004. Tower of Babel. *Denison Journal of Religion* 4:34–44.

Lausanne Movement. 1997. Gospel contextualisation revisited: Haslev 1997 Consultation statement. Lausanne Movement. https://www.lausanne.org/content/gospel-contextualisation-revisited.

Leveen, Steve. 2021. *America's bilingual century: How Americans are giving the gift of bilingualism to themselves, their loved ones, and their country*. Delray Beach, FL: America the Bilingual Press.

Marlowe, W. Creighton. 2011. The sin of Shinar (Genesis 11:4). *European Journal of Theology* 20(1):29–39.

McWhorter, John. 2003. *The power of Babel: A natural history of language*. New York, NY: Harper Perennial.

Miguez-Bonino, Jose. 1999. Genesis 11:1–9: A Latin American perspective. In Priscilla Pope-Levison and John R. Levison (eds.), *Return to Babel: Global perspectives on the Bible*, 13–16. Louisville, KY: Westminster John Knox Press.

Plaut, W. Gunther. 1981. *The Torah : A modern commentary*. Fourth edition. New York, NY: Union of American Hebrew Congregations.

Ron, Zvi. 2014. The book of Jubilees and the Midrash: Part 3: The Tower of Babel. *Jewish Bible Quarterly* 42(3):165–168.

Sarna, Nahum M. 1966. *Understanding Genesis: The world of the Bible in the light of history.* New York, NY: Shocken Books.

Schmidt, Ronald. 2014. Democratic theory and the challenge of linguistic diversity. *Language Policy* 13(4):395–411.

Sherman, Phillip Michael. 2013. *Babel's tower translated: Genesis 11 and Ancient Jewish interpretation.* Biblical Interpretation 117. Leiden, Netherlands: Brill.

Smith, David I. 1996. What hope after Babel? Diversity and community in Gen 11:1–9, Exod 1:1–14, Zeph 3:1–13 and Acts 2:1–13. *Horizons in Biblical Theology* 18(1):169–191.

Smith, David I., and Barbara Carvill. 2000. *The gift of the stranger: Faith, hospitality, and foreign language learning.* Grand Rapids, MI: Eerdmans.

Strong, John T. 2008. Shattering the image of God: A response to Theodore Hiebert's interpretation of the story of the Tower of Babel. *Journal of Biblical Literature* 127(4):625–634.

Uehlinger, Christoph. 1990. *Weltreich und "eine Rede": Eine neue Deutung der sogenannten Turmbauerzahlung* (Gen. 11,1–9). Orbis Biblicus et Orientalis 101. Freiburg, Schweiz: Universitätsverlag.

Von Rad, Gerhard. 1973. *Genesis: A commentary.* Revised edition. Philadelphia: Westminster Press.

Wenham, Gordon John. 1987. Genesis 1–15. Vol. 1. *Word Biblical Commentary.* Waco, TX: Word Books.

Whiston, William, trans. 1737. *The works of Flavius Josephus.* http://penelope.uchicago.edu/josephus/index.html.

Wright, Christopher J. H. 2013. *The mission of God: Unlocking the Bible's grand narrative.* Kindle edition. Downers Grove, IL: InterVarsity Press.

WSJ. 2015. Overcoming the ancient curse of Babel with English. *Wall Street Journal: Opinion.* 9 January 2015. https://www.wsj.com/articles/overcoming-the-ancient-curse-of-babel-with-english-letters-to-the-editor-1420840424.

Yodh

*May those who fear you rejoice when they see me,
for I have put my hope in your word.
(Psalm 119:74)*

10

Language Diversity: A Greater Glory

Based on a paper by Stephen Watters and Zachary Watters

Introduction

The previous chapter argued that diversity is the blueprint of creation, demonstrating that "language change was not introduced in Genesis 11 as part of a curse, it was introduced in Genesis 2 as an essential component of what it means to be created in the image of God".

Like the other aspects of diversity shown in Genesis 1, language diversity is part of the warp and woof—the essential foundation or base—of creation.

Genesis 10, sometimes known as the Table of Nations, lists the descendants of Noah. It begins by stating:

> This is the account of Shem, Ham and Japheth, Noah's sons, who themselves had sons after the flood. (v. 1)

Japheth's descendants are then listed, with the concluding summary:

> From these the maritime peoples spread out into their territories by their clans within their nations, each with its own language. (v. 5)

Next, the sons of Ham, with the concluding statement:

> These are the sons of Ham by their clans and languages, in their territories and nations. (v. 20)

Then the sons of Shem, concluding:

> These are the sons of Shem by their clans and languages, in their territories and nations. (v. 31)

While recognising that clans, languages, territories, and nations are a means of cataloguing the human race, it is evident that language diversity was *already a feature pre-Babel*, alongside geographical, familial, and ethnic diversity.

The following chapter traces the use of language through the Old and New Testaments. For our present purposes, in our examination of language diversity we will examine the legacy and challenge of Pentecost, that is, Christianity's penchant for translation.

The legacy and challenge of Pentecost

Pentecost set in motion one of the unique characteristics of Christianity as a world religion, and this is its penchant for translation (Sanneh 2009, Cowan 1979, Beckner 2015). The Hebrew and Aramaic spoken by Jesus were translated into Greek; Greek was translated into a host of contemporary languages of that time: Syriac, Arabic, Coptic, and Latin. Latin was translated into the Romance and Germanic languages, as well as Polish; Greek into the Slavic languages, and so on (Jeffrey 2011, Gerner 2018). But this is not true for the other religions of the world. When the Qur'an is translated into other languages it loses its religious authority; Muslims throughout the world must learn classical Arabic if they are to read the authentic Qur'an. In Buddhism and Hinduism, the efficacy of certain sayings is as much in the sound as it is in the meaning. To alter the original language and pronunciation in which a saying is uttered is to take away its power. For Christians, however, the Bible is seen as the word of God, whether it is in Spanish, Korean, Mandarin (Cowan 1979), or the languages spoken by remote ethnicities such as the Magar Kham (see below). What is important to the Christian is the meaning of Scripture and its translatability, not the form (Sanneh 2009). This, in part, accounts for the amazing fact that, whereas there is only one sacred text for the Muslim or the Buddhist, portions of the Bible have been translated into over 3,600 languages of the world (Wycliffe Global Alliance 2023), and, in each language it is given the authority of the Bible.

Even so, the legacy given to us in the birth of the Church at Pentecost is often misunderstood, and the diversity of languages is seen as an impediment to the global mission of the church. While one might expect the average Christian to understand linguistic diversity as an inconvenient barrier, the Bible translation movement itself struggles with the legacy of Pentecost. One of its principal difficulties is with the sheer number of languages spoken in the world today. However, perhaps the daunting number of languages without Scripture is not a problem to be overcome, but is part of the beauty of God's design.

Another of the difficulties presented by language diversity has to do with the incompatible nature of any two languages. Linguistic relativity asserts that no one language is the same as another, and that although the terms of two languages appear to be similar, they in fact describe somewhat different conceptual models of the term.[1] Bible translators, however, seek to preserve the meaning of the original text and attempt to transmit full equivalence of meaning from one language to another. The first task of translation is to understand the original intent of the author with a focus on historical and literal accuracy. The second task is to translate into the receptor language no more or less than what the source communicates, insofar as this is possible. In reality, translation is seldom so straightforward.

There are different ways of viewing the translation process. In the "conduit metaphor", Michael Reddy (1979) depicts a view of language wherein meaning equivalence is fully possible. Meaning is packaged into words, sent down a conduit, unwrapped, and extracted intact at the other end. Meaning is distinct from the package in which it comes. This understanding of communication has influenced much Bible translation practice.[2]

As has been noted by numerous writings on translation theory and practice, the conduit metaphor is not consistent with our current models of language, nor with our understanding of what happens in communication or translation. Meaning cannot be so readily separated from form (Givón 1995) or the cultural context into which it is placed. Reddy (1979) then proposes another model which he calls "The Toolmaker's paradigm" as one that gives a more accurate analogy of what happens in communication. In this model, the speaker has to modify what they say, depending on the context, while the listener will interpret what they hear according to their context. Reddy's observations were remarkably perceptive, given the subsequent development of communication theory. These theories of language and communication cast doubt on the possibility of full meaning-based equivalence, let alone word-based equivalence.

It is not our intention here to argue for one model of communication over another or to review how Bible translation practice overcomes the problems of linguistic and cultural incompatibility, but to simply arrive at a common starting point. Bible translation practice, in spite of taking great care to remain faithful to

---

[1] See Levinson 2003, Slobin 1987, and Pinker 1994 for varying views on linguistic relativity.

[2] The theories and practices of translation that are based on the Conduit Metaphor are referred to as the Code Model. See Kerr 2011 as an illustration of how Nida's 1964 dynamic equivalence model is described as such.

the original documents, is necessarily varied across time and space. It has varied through history because of changing beliefs about what constitutes translation and how equivalent meaning can be achieved. It has varied in geography by the specifics of linguistic and cultural distance between source and target language (McElhanon 2007, Pym 2014). If the original meanings of Scripture end up being changed because of linguistic incompatibility, even if only by nuance and force of assertion, can Bible translators say that they are being faithful to the word? Is this not a fault—an unfortunate state of affairs brought on as a consequence of our fallen state, and (forgetting the diversity of languages in Genesis 10) God's "curse" on us after the Tower of Babel (see chapter 9)? Would it not work better if we all spoke the same language?

Created diversity

The differences between languages and their cultural context on the one hand, and the resultant differences between the translations into those languages on the other, present a challenge to the Church. The major schismatic split between the Western and Eastern churches in 1054, for example, can arguably be demonstrated, in part, to have come from controversies over difficulties in translating from Greek to Latin (McGrath 2013). But what about in our day, where there are noticeable differences between translations in the major languages, and what of the more salient differences found in the non-dominant languages that may not have the philosophical categories of the major world religions? Once we get past the pleasantries of how good it is to have linguistic diversity and grapple with the realities of distinct conceptual worlds made evident in linguistic categories, can we say that linguistic diversity is a blessing? Is the universal truth of Christianity not changed as it is adapted to specific linguistic and cultural worlds? The answers to all of these questions are beyond the scope of this short chapter, but we believe that the recognition of God's intentional creation of diversity provides helpful insights by which to investigate these questions and to understand the place of language diversity in the mission of God. We suggest that although language diversity may thwart perfect communication among the human race, it brings about an even greater good.

Linguistic differences create real barriers to communication. These are felt in the mission of the Church, and nowhere more acutely than in the Bible translation task. On the other hand, as the linguistic nations of the world express the truths of the gospel and give worship to God in their own languages, we see the value of God's generous gift of language diversity playing out before us. God is choosing to redeem us through the expression of the incarnation in the thousands of (incompatible) linguistic worlds scattered across the globe. We need only imagine a monolingual and monocultural world to understand how the multilingual expression of God's revelation of himself brings about a greater good.

Canonical exegesis: A help to translators

In addition to the difficulties that come with language diversity, the Bible translation task must also contend with the widely held belief that there is one, and only one, authorial intent in the Scripture text, and it alone is to be translated. Here, too, Reddy's conduit metaphor influences the traditional approach to interpreting the text. The metaphor would have us focus on translating the text's singular facts, packaged neatly into discrete word units, often without recognition of its "polyvalent" nature. By polyvalent, we simply mean that the text can be read with multiple understandings; for example, figurative meanings may often overlay the literal factual meaning of a text.

In a polyvalent approach, the divine meaning of the text can never be fully restricted by the human text, and must be greater than the historical intention of the author. This means that coming to a good understanding of the text cannot be achieved solely through an objective, scientific study of the author's intentions. It follows, therefore, that inspiration cannot be limited to the author of a text, but must also be found in the reading and reception of the text. Canonical exegesis helps us understand why a book or portion of a book became part of the canon of Scripture, and helps us interpret it in the light of that. As the Church wrestles with the biblical text today, we are dependent on the inspiration of the Holy Spirit to guide our interpretation (Boersma 2017).

The result of this is that our understanding of the text is limited to our ability to receive it. Different linguistic groups can receive the text and understand its meaning differently because their culture and ways of thinking are different from our own. This means that our understandings are *incomplete* without theirs, as theirs are without those of the rest of the Church.

This polyvalent, canonical approach is a help to us in our quest to understand God's purposes with the multiplicity of languages. We suggest that it opens up the possibility of being less slavish to the original texts, at least less slavish than the proponents of literal translations that package and unpackage meaning as in the conduit metaphor. It gives freedom to use the natural categories of the language to make the incarnation translatable into the new linguistic and cultural context. Here, too, we see God's redemption at work, allowing the incarnation to be translated once again with meanings and nuances that are invariably somewhat different from when they came 2,000 or more years ago in Aramaic, Hebrew, and Greek, but which, as then, are now also buttressed by the Spirit's inspiration of the reading and reception of the text in its new context.

Animal categories in Magar Kham

We illustrate what we believe to be an acceptable instance of using natural linguistic categories in service of translatability into the new context. The passage in question is Romans 1:23, which has been translated into English as: "and exchanged the glory of the immortal God for images made to look like a mortal human being and birds and animals and reptiles," and we look at the translation of this passage into Magar Kham, a Tibeto-Burman language spoken in central-western Nepal by about 70,000 people.

The English "birds and animals and reptiles" follows the Greek πετεινόν (*peteinon*) bird, τετράπουν (*tetrapoun*) four-footed animal, and ἑρπετόν (*erpeton*) creeping things, reptiles. The translation of these three categories seems straightforward enough. However, as we have argued from the beginning of this chapter, every language represents, in some sense, a different window on the world, a different "conceptual universe," to borrow George Steiner's (1992) phrase.

In our rationalistic Western world, we categorize the animal kingdom according to the morphological characteristics of anatomy, giving us categories such as mammals, birds, reptiles, insects, and so on. In Magar Kham, animals are classified according to their relationship to people, and not according to their anatomy. In the Magar Kham classification, mammals and birds can be lumped together, as in "leopard-eagles," "deer-birds," "bird-rats," and "bug-worms" (see table 10.1). These are superordinate categories that give classification to a group of animals: *la:* is a leopard, and *ga:* is an eagle, and the combination refers to animals that prey, like leopards and eagles prey on other animals. Similarly, *sya:* is a deer and *ba:* is a bird, and as a superordinate category refers to game animals, or animals which are preyed on, and so on and so forth.

Table 10.1. Animal classification in Magar Kham (D. Watters 2002)

Kham	Literal translation	English category
la: ga:	leopard-eagles	predators
sya: ba:	deer-birds	game animals
baza biza	bird-rats	critters
kahza baza	puppy-chickens	pets
rwihza wanza	bug-worms	repugnant creepy crawlies
kanga moN	crow-vultures	scavengers, carrion-eaters

While Magar Kham has the category of bird of Romans 1:23, it does not have the category of four-footed animal, or reptile. It would have been possible to translate "four-footed animal" in Kham with a descriptive phrase, but such a translation draws attention to the fact that these are animals that have four feet, in contrast to animals with two feet. Translated this way, it would sound as though it is acceptable to worship two-footed animals, just not four-footed ones. Such a translation would be literally correct, but would fall short of Paul's point, which seems to be arguing for the ludicrousness of worshiping an idol in exchange for the glory of God.

The translators of Magar Kham, then, took liberty with the categories of animals in this passage, translating it in the following way.

(1) bənəi   [zəgəi magəiw]   udʒiuni   liʒyaw   khərkə   zə
    very-much [glory majesty] his-life having-one whenever FOC

    makhemʒaw   isware   opolə   dzɦan   [dzai dzantu]
    not-coming-to-an-end God-of   his-place-in even-more   [animal beast]

    [baza biza] [rwihza wanza] mirae   angya
    [bird rat]   [bug worm]   people-of   images

    Dzaida   norae   yasewa   doʒyara
    Making   those-of   their-service   they-do

"Furthermore, in place of God, (glorious and majestic), full of life, and never-ending, they make images of **[animal-beasts]**, **[bird-rats]**, **[bug-worms]**, and a human being, and worship them instead."

The translators played on two lists of supergenerics in this verse to emphasize the foolishness of idolatry. Supergeneric adjectives associated with God are glorious and majestic, full of life, and never-ending. Supergenerics associated with idols are animal-beasts, bird-rats, and bug-worms (see table 10.1). The Magar Kham translation captures the sense, or polyvalent nature of the passage, even as it sidesteps the literal accuracy of Greek animal categories. Although not accurate in a historical sense, the translation uses categories natural to the language to point to spiritual realities, namely the worship of the one true God over and above idolatry.

We suggest that the animal categories in Magar Kham as employed in the New Testament translation are an example of the God-given benefits of language diversity. Although the Magar Kham categories are incompatible with the Greek categories, and although the translation is historically inaccurate, the Kham categories capture the central component of the polyvalent meaning referred to in the text. The result is a richer revelation inasmuch as the Magar Kham categories bring a unique focus to the worship of the immortal God for this culture.

The diversity of conceptual universes given to us through the world's languages, such as the Magar Kham animal categories, function in a similar way to the myth of which C. S. Lewis speaks: they are unfocused gleams of divine truth at first (Lewis 1972:139), but find fulfillment as they find expression in Christ (Watters et al. 2011). These incompatible linguistic worlds then expand and add nuance to the original deposit of revelation found in the Greek.

Further directions

We have given one short example of the way in which language diversity helps us interpret and understand how the natural categories of language used in Bible translation give a unique focus to biblical truths. In fact, the story of the translation of the Bible illustrates this repeatedly for every language. The incarnation comes over and over again, each time graciously accepting the (imperfect) hospitality of its linguistic and cultural hosts.

We recognize that not all linguistic categories are usable in the translation of the Bible, that not every translation is of equal quality, and that some translations may go too far in appropriating the natural categories of the language for the biblical message. Nevertheless, we believe it is worthwhile to study the range of words and grammars used for equivalent concepts found in the worldwide translation effort. We refer to this as the "harvest of Babel", wherein language diversity is studied for how it is employed to convey the concepts of the Bible. Such a study will demonstrate some of the treasures of the mission of God as they are being used to redeem every nation, tongue, and tribe.

We concur with Lamin Sanneh that the translation of the gospel into the mother tongue brings about a fresh theological discourse because of its employment of categories of African life and belief (Sanneh 2009), and, by extension, those of the other peoples of the world. We agree also with many aspects of mother tongue theologies which suggest that local language communities be encouraged to pursue the development of theology using the linguistic categories of their mother tongues (Bediako 2001, Ahaligah 2020). Where there are errors and undue emphasis in one particular direction, reference to the original languages and the Church universal will serve as a self-corrective, as has been the case repeatedly for the English-speaking church (Jeffrey 2003).

Conclusion

There is no doubt that language diversity results in barriers, breakdowns, and inaccuracies in communication. And yet, the thousands of conceptual worlds found in each language represent a potential that is far greater than if the world were monolingual and monocultural.

One potential is that, as the Bible is translated into each language, the deposit of revelation is newly unpacked and expounded, giving nuance to the understanding of the Church universal that was not there before. The conceptual categories of a single language give a partial revelation of the incarnation, but collectively the representation of the incarnation in every language builds a conceptual universe that far more adequately expresses its glory (see chapter 1).

It is tempting to see the daunting number of languages without Scripture as a problem to be overcome, but this misses the beauty of God's design for language and cultural diversity. As the Scriptures are translated into an increasing number of the languages of the world, each language increases the collective beauty and glory in the kaleidoscope of language diversity. Imagine how beautiful it will be when all 7,000+ languages each tell God's story, not in uniformity, but in harmony.

References

Ahaligah, Kwame Aidan. 2020. Mother-tongue theology: Akan Christian Christological re-interpretations. *Pentecostalism, Charismaticism and Neo-Prophetic Movements Journal* 1:10–18.

Beckner, W. Benjamin. 2015. Eugène Casalis and the French mission to Basutoland (1833–1856): A case study of Lamin Sanneh's mission-by-translation paradigm in nineteenth-century southern Africa. *Missiology: An International Review* 43(1):73–86.

Bediako, Kwame. 2001. *The role and significance of the translation of the Bible*. Paper presented at the Wycliffe Bible Translators International Africa Area Forum, Limuru, Kenya, 16-18 May 2001. https://www.wycliffe.net/what-we-do/articles-for-further-reflection/the-role-and-significance-of-the-translation-of-the-bible/.

Boersma, Hans. 2017. *Scripture as real presence: Sacramental exegesis in the early church*. Grand Rapids, MI: Baker Academic.

Cowan, George M. 1979. *The Word that kindles*. Chappaqua, New York, NY: Christian Herald Books.

Gerner, Matthias. 2018. Why worldwide Bible translation grows exponentially. *Journal of Religious History*, 42(2):145–180.

Givón, Talmy. 1995. *Functionalism and grammar*. Amsterdam: John Benjamins.

Jeffrey, David L. 2003. *Houses of the interpreter: Reading Scripture, reading culture*. Waco, TX: Baylor University Press.

Jeffrey, David L. 2011. *Pentecost, the great commission, and Bible translation*. Ms.

Kerr, Glen J. 2011. Dynamic equivalence and its daughters: Placing Bible translation theories in their historical context. *Journal of Translation* 7:1–19.

Levinson, Stephen C. 2003. Language and mind: Let's get the issues straight! In Dedre Gentner and Susan Goldin-Meadow (eds.), *Language in mind*, 25–46. Cambridge, MA: MIT

Lewis, C. S. 1972. *Miracles*. New York, NY: Macmillian.

McElhanon, Kenneth A. 2007. Cognitive linguistics, biblical truth and ethical conduct. *Journal of Interdisciplinary Studies* 19(1/2):119–138.

McGrath, Alister E. 2013. *Christian history: An introduction.* West Sussex, UK: Wiley-Blackwell.

Nida, Eugene A. 1964. *Toward a science of translating.* Leiden, Netherlands: Brill.

Pinker, Steven. 1994. *The language instinct: How the mind creates language.* London: The Penguin Press.

Pym, Anthony. 2014. *Exploring translation theories.* New York, NY: Routledge.

Reddy, Michael J. 1979. The conduit metaphor: A case of frame conflict in our language about language. In Andrew Ortony (ed.), *Metaphor and thought,* 284–324. Cambridge: Cambridge University Press.

Sanneh, Lamin. 2009. *Translating the message: The missionary impact on culture.* Revised and expanded edition. MaryKnoll, NY: Orbis Books.

Slobin, Dan I. 1987. Thinking for speaking. Proceedings of the Thirteenth Annual Meeting of the Berkeley Linguistics Society 13:435–445.

Steiner, George. 1992. *After Babel: Aspects of language and translation.* Second edition. Oxford: Oxford University Press.

Watters, David E. 2002. *A grammar of Kham.* Cambridge: Cambridge University Press.

Watters, David E., Steve Watters, and Daniel Watters. 2011. *At the foot of the snows: A journey of faith and words among the Kham-speaking people of Nepal.* Seattle, WA: Engage Faith Press.

Watters, Zachary J., and Stephen Watters. 2022. Language diversity: A "happy fault" for the church. In Greed and Kruger, 364–379. Wycliffe Global Alliance. 2023. *2023 Global Scripture Access.* https://www.wycliffe.net/resources/statistics/.

Kaph

*In your unfailing love preserve my life,
that I may obey the statutes of your mouth.
(Psalm 119:88)*

11

Language Use in the Bible

Michael Greed, with Paul Frank and Mamy Raharimanantsoa

Introduction

This chapter explores how language and languages are used in the Bible, the shift in language over time, and the implications of multilingualism. After a brief overview of the languages of the Old Testament it moves on to specific instances of language use and change. It then considers the New Testament in a similar manner. The chapter concludes that, based on language use in the Bible, within the mission of God no single language is central or more special than other languages, and there is a clear preference for language that communicates clearly and meaningfully.

This chapter is based on articles written by the linguist Paul Frank and the theologian Mamy Raharimanantsoa for SIL International's God and Language Forum (2020) and the subsequent book, *God and Language: Exploring the Role of Language in the Mission of God* (2022), both of which are quoted and referenced extensively in the course of the next few pages.

The Old Testament

Multilingualism and monolingualism

Most of the Old Testament is written in Biblical Hebrew, a Semitic language related to the ancient Ugaritic, Phoenician, and Moabite languages. It consists of twenty-two consonants, with vowel signs later added above, below, and within the consonants to aid pronunciation. Early Hebrew was written in what is known as the paleo-Hebrew script. During the exile, the "square" Aramaic script was adopted; this is the script we are familiar with in our Hebrew Old Testament today (Benner 1999).

Some sections of the books of Ezra and Daniel are written in Aramaic (see below). Aramaic, also a Semitic language, co-existed with Hebrew throughout Old Testament times—see, for example, Genesis 31:47 where Laban gave a heap of stones an Aramaic name while Jacob gave the same stones a Hebrew name (see below). During the exile there was a shift from Hebrew to Aramaic such that, by New Testament times, Aramaic was the language spoken by the majority, particularly in Galilee. Hebrew was the language of scholarship, liturgy, and worship, and was possibly the dominant language in Judean villages (Fernandez 1999:2–4, see also chs. 12, 13, and 20).

At the beginning of chapter 10, we looked at the Table of Nations in Genesis 10 where it is recorded that the descendants of Shem, Ham, and Japheth—the sons of Noah—spread out into the world according to their clans and languages, territories and nations. This is the first reference to language—or rather, languages—in the Bible. In the first nine chapters of the Bible, individuals and communities speak with one another and with God, but the language or languages they use is not in focus.

In the story of the Tower of Babel in Genesis 11, God "confused the language" of humanity (Gen 11:9) (see chapter 9). From then on language is seldom the focus of the narrative, and the writers of the Hebrew Scriptures rarely comment on what language is used in communication.

From Genesis to Kings

Paul Frank writes that Genesis records "Abraham talking to Pharaoh (Gen 12), Melchizedek and the King of Sodom (Gen 14), Abimelech, King of Gerar (Gen 20), and the Hittites (Gen 23). Who was speaking what language? We don't know" (2022:84). Frank continues,

> Genesis provides many instances in which people from different ethnicities (and, presumably, different languages) interacted. There is Lot in Sodom (Gen 13–20), Hagar the Egyptian in Abraham's household (Gen 16), Abraham negotiating with the Hittites for a piece of land (Gen 23), and Abraham sending his servant to find for Isaac a wife from among his own

relatives rather than a wife from the Canaanites amongst whom he was living (Gen 24). Later, Isaac and Rebekah are with Abimelech, a Philistine king (Gen 26), Jacob and his family are interacting with the Hivites (Gen 34), and Judah marries the daughter of a Canaanite man (Gen 38). (2022:84)

Bilingualism on the part of some is assumed, but this is never the focus of the story. In the story of Jacob and Laban, Genesis 31 recounts how they gathered a heap of stones to serve as a witness to the agreement they made with one another. Verse 47 tells us, "Laban called it Jegar Sahadutha, and Jacob called it Galeed." Jacob gave it a Hebrew name, while Laban, who lived in Aram, gave it an Aramaic name (see chapter 20). Both mean "witness heap" (Carson 2015).

Paul Frank continues his survey of multilingualism in the Old Testament:

> When Joseph was sold as a slave and ended up in Egypt, he learned Egyptian. The story of Joseph interacting with his brothers in Egypt demonstrates that he was bilingual in Egyptian and Hebrew, as was his interpreter (see especially Gen 42:23).
>
> Moses, having grown up as an Egyptian in Pharaoh's court, was presumably bilingual, but there is no indication of what language was used when he and Aaron spoke to Pharaoh.
>
> As the people of Israel entered the promised land, there are many instances that must have involved two or more languages. An early example is the two Jewish spies and Rahab talking to one another in Jericho (Josh 2).
>
> The building of Solomon's temple involved Jewish craftsmen, workers from Lebanon, and workers from Babylon (1 Kings 5:18). The Queen of Sheba and Solomon talked at great length, but there is no indication of what language(s) were used (1 Kings 10).
>
> This long silence on the topic of languages lasted from Genesis 42:23 ("They did not know that Joseph understood them, for there was an interpreter between them") through to 2 Kings 18:26 ("Please speak to your servants in Aramaic, since we understand it. Don't speak to us in Hebrew in the hearing of the people on the wall"). We see monolingual Jews (those sitting on the wall) confronted by a multilingual enemy. At that time, only the rulers in Jerusalem were bilingual, knowing both Hebrew and Aramaic.

> This story in 2 Kings 18 and 2 Chronicles 32 foreshadows the change the Israelites would experience moving from a monolingual to a multilingual nation. After the exile, the Jewish people as a whole were bilingual in the two languages. (2022:85–87)

In the course of this "long silence" is a notable reference to dialect, demonstrating that the people of Israel were linguistically aware, and could make use of this awareness. This is the *Shibboleth* discussion in Judges 12. The Gileadites wanted a way to identify an Ephraimite, and to do this, they turned to linguistics:

> The Gileadites captured the fords of the Jordan leading to Ephraim, and whenever a survivor of Ephraim said, "Let me cross over," the men of Gilead asked him, "Are you an Ephraimite?" If he replied, "No," they said, "All right, say 'Shibboleth.'" If he said, "Sibboleth," because he could not pronounce the word correctly, they seized him and killed him at the fords of the Jordan. Forty-two thousand Ephraimites were killed at that time. (Judg 12:5–6)

Ezra and Nehemiah

Clear evidence of the move to bilingualism is found in the book of Ezra, which itself is bilingual. Ezra 4 contains the transcript of a letter written to King Artaxerxes by Rehum and his associates, who opposed the rebuilding of the temple. Ezra notes, "The letter was written in Aramaic script and in the Aramaic language" (Ezra 4:7). The Aramaic text of the letter follows. Rehum and his associates chose to write in Aramaic presumably because it was the lingua franca, not because it was a language Artaxerxes used, for when Artaxerxes replies, he begins by saying, "The letter you sent us has been read and translated in my presence" (v. 18). Suddenly language and translation are in focus in the narrative.

The book of Ezra records the letter in its original Aramaic, and the text of the book continues to be in Aramaic after Rehum's letter, after Artaxerxes' reply, right through until chapter 6 verse 18, where it switches back to Hebrew.

Not for long though. In chapter 7 there is another letter, this time from Artaxerxes to Ezra and it is presumably written in Aramaic for that is the language in which it is recorded, in Ezra 7:12–26. Ezra 7:27 reverts back to Hebrew, and the rest of the book continues in Hebrew.

In the book of Nehemiah, Ezra performs a public reading of the Law. Nehemiah 8:8 records, "They read from the Book of the Law of God, making it clear and giving the meaning so that the people understood what was being read."

The phrase "making it clear" could also be translated, "with interpretation" (NRSVUE) or "translating it" (NASB). Were the Levites translating the Law of Moses from Hebrew into Aramaic because the people no longer understood Hebrew, or were they explaining the meaning of the Law? Both are possible interpretations of the Hebrew, but most English translations of the Bible favor explaining rather than translating (see also chapter 20).

Daniel and Esther

Looking at the Jewish diaspora in the Babylonian and Persian empires, Paul Frank notes,

> The books of Daniel and Esther paint a picture of the Babylonian and Persian empires as highly multiethnic and multilingual. Even though Aramaic was the common language of these empires, apparently the successive rulers did not try to eradicate the languages of the various nations they conquered.
>
> The book of Daniel provides multiple examples of kings Nebuchadnezzar and Darius issuing decrees to "all peoples, nations, and languages" (Dan 4:1). The "peoples, nations, and languages" (Dan 4:1) wording is virtually identical in all cases ...[1]
>
> In the book of Esther there are three instances of decrees being issued in the name of King Ahasuerus to "every province in its own script[2] and to every people in its own language". (2022:87–88)

Frank (2022:89) proceeds to observe that "Daniel 7:13–14 presents a vision of God that is strikingly similar to John's visions recorded in Revelation", including reference to "all peoples, nations, and languages" serving the Ancient of Days. "In very few other places does the Bible contain references to people of all languages in the Kingdom of God."

We have already seen that parts of the book of Ezra are written in Aramaic. The same phenomenon occurs in Daniel. Daniel 2:4 states, "Then the astrologers answered the king, 'May the king live forever! Tell your servants the dream, and we will interpret it.'"

The translators of the NIV have omitted one word at this point. Other translations, as well as older editions of the NIV read, "Then the astrologers

---

[1] Note that all of these passages are in Aramaic, not Hebrew.
[2] The other Old Testament instances of the word translated here as "script" refer to a document rather than a type of writing. This appears to be the only reference in the Bible to scripts as ways of writing.

answered the king *in Aramaic*, 'May the king live forever! Tell your servants the dream, and we will interpret it'" (NIV 1988 [emphasis added]).

The text of the book of Daniel switches to Aramaic here, and continues to be in Aramaic until the end of chapter 7.

The intertestamental period

During the intertestamental period, there was significant change in the language people preferred to use, especially amongst the Jewish diaspora. As a result of this language shift, the Hebrew Scriptures were translated into Greek, a translation known as the Septuagint, so called because, according to tradition, it was translated by seventy scholars. This translation project was begun in Alexandria in Egypt during the reign of Ptolemy II Philadelphus (285–247 BC) when the Torah was translated. The rest of the Jewish Scriptures followed, at various times and in various places and with varying styles of translation. The project was completed by 132 BC (Jobes and Silva 2015).

At the same time, oral translations of the Scriptures were being made into Aramaic. These were known as *targums*, and often included explanation and elaboration as well as translation. The process of documenting targums began in the first century AD.

When the Septuagint was translated, a number of other works were also translated or added, a collection of books known as the Apocrypha. While only the Greek text of these books remain, an underlying Hebrew or Aramaic original is evident in many.[3]

With the exception of Nehemiah's response when confronted with children of mixed marriages who struggled to speak Hebrew (Neh 13:23–24), no preference is shown in the Old Testament with regard to choice of language for general usage. As was expedient, the Hebrew text was translated into Aramaic and Greek. Further, parts of the Scriptures were in all likelihood never written in Hebrew, the original text being written in Aramaic, or, in the case of parts of the Apocrypha, in Greek. This might suggest that choice of language has no role in the mission of God. Language is merely a vehicle for conveying the word or revelation of God. However, that is only half the story.

Chapter 2 of this volume argues that it is God's mission to be known. Hebrew, Aramaic, or Greek were chosen because they were well known. Translation gave access to those otherwise denied access to the Scriptures. Diaspora Greek-speaking Jews who were forgetting their Hebrew were not forced to study Hebrew in order to read the Scriptures. God's word was revealed to them in their adopted heart language.

---

[3] For further discussion on the Septuagint, see Jobes and Silva 2015.

Language in the New Testament

"By New Testament times, the vernacular of Galilee at least had shifted to Aramaic, and the vernacular of many diasporic Jewish communities had also shifted to one of the languages spoken in the region," writes Maik Gibson in chapter 20 of this book. Palestine at the time of Jesus and the early church was a linguistic melting pot, as different languages came into contact with one another, imperial and local. Jesus and his disciples were multilingual (see chapter 12). The New Testament is written in Koine Greek, the lingua franca of much of the region (see chapter 13).

This linguistic melting pot is illustrated in John 1, where John provides alternative translations of three words:

- They said, "Rabbi" (which means "Teacher"), "where are you staying?" (v. 38)
- The first thing Andrew did was to find his brother Simon and tell him, "We have found the Messiah" (that is, the Christ). (v. 41)
- Jesus looked at him and said, "You are Simon son of John. You will be called Cephas" (which, when translated, is Peter). (v. 42)

"Rabbi" (v. 38) and "Messiah" (v. 41) are based on the Hebrew, while "Cephas" (v. 42) is Aramaic. The three translations John provides are all Greek. See also John 20:24 and 21:1 where John specifies "Thomas (also known as Didymus)"—*Thomas* (Aramaic) and *Didymus* (Greek) both mean "twin"—and John 20:16 where John retains Mary Magdalene's Aramaic:

> Jesus said to her, "Mary."
>
> She turned toward him and cried out in Aramaic, "Rabboni!" (which means "Teacher").

Whereas our exploration of the Old Testament provided a chronological survey of language use, our exploration of the New Testament is focused on five illustrative case studies provided by the theologian Mamy Raharimanantsoa.

Jesus and Pontius Pilate

Mamy Raharimanantsoa provides a number of helpful case studies of the use of different languages in the New Testament. First of all he examines the interview between Pontius Pilate and Jesus, where he looks at the question of which language Pilate and Jesus used when speaking with one another. Raharimanantsoa (2022:94–95) aligns himself with Tresham and Macfarlane: "As a Roman, Pilate spoke Latin, but this language was probably not spoken by Jesus, the priests, or the crowd. It also seems unlikely that Pilate had learned Aramaic or Hebrew. Greek would be the natural medium of communication for Pilate to use with the people of

Judea" (Tresham 2009:83). "Roman prefects and governors communicated in Latin with their peers on issues of military administration ... Latin was also the official language of the Roman troops among the occupying force ... Communication between Romans and the inhabitants of Palestine was conducted, pragmatically, in Greek" (Macfarlane 1996:229).

Peter's northern accent

Raharimanantsoa (2022:96) turns next to the issue of dialect or regional accent in the account of Peter's denial. The servant girl addresses Peter three times:

- You also were with Jesus of Galilee. (Matt 26:69)
- This fellow was with Jesus of Nazareth. (Matt 26:71)
- Surely you are one of them; your accent gives you away. (Matt 26:73)

Jesus' identity is linked to the northern province of Galilee, and Peter's northern accent reveals his Galilean origins. Raharimanantsoa cites Leon Morris (1992:689) who explains that Galilean speech was noticeably different from Judean speech, although we do not have detailed knowledge of these differences. But "Peter, like the Ephraimites who were made to say 'shibboleth' (Judg 12:5–6), is given away by his speech" (Davies and Allison 2004:548).

Pentecost

Raharimanantsoa's third case study is the highly multilingual situation on the day of Pentecost, recorded in Acts 2. Writing of how the Festival of Pentecost brought together Jewish people from the diaspora to the city of Jerusalem, he cites Paul Wright (2019:111–112): "The list covers the longitudinal dimension of the world of the Bible, linking the ancient Near East with the Mediterranean basin ... The list of nations in Acts 2 is representative and not exhaustive of the diaspora of the first century."

Raharimanantsoa (2022:96–98) explains that the disciples were all Galileans like Jesus (Acts 2:7), but by the work of the Holy Spirit "began to speak in other tongues, as the Spirit gave them utterance" (2:4). Those who listened recognized their own language, the mother tongue or the language of the heart (2:8). He quotes Yves-Marie Blanchard (2013:17):

> *Ainsi, au jour de la Pentecôte, les Juifs et prosélytes, issus de tout le pourtour de la Méditerranée et censés comprendre le grec ... n'en sont pas moins émerveillés d'entendre l'évangile, « chacun dans son propre idiome (dialektos) » (ac 2,6), autrement dit dans « leurs propres langues » (glôssai: 2,11) ce qui suppose que les apôtres parlent des langues étrangères (heterai glôssai: 2,4).*

("Thus on the day of Pentecost, the Jews and proselytes from all around the Mediterranean, who are supposed to understand Greek ... are nonetheless amazed to hear the gospel, 'each in their own idiom' (*dialektos*) (Acts 2:6), in other words in 'their own languages' (*glôssai*: 2:11) which supposes that the apostles speak foreign languages (*heterai glôssai*: 2:4).")

Raharimanantsoa (2022:97–98) quotes Bruce to say,

"On that day, even if we stick to the idea of one region, one language, there were many languages represented. But one can imagine that behind the mention of residents of Mesopotamia (Acts 2:9) or Egypt (2:10), there would have been a number of other languages present. The incident was understood by the multitude gathered in Jerusalem as a sign from God, and 'all were amazed and perplexed' (2:12), for these Galilean disciples appeared for the moment to share among them a command of most of the tongues spoken throughout the known world." (Bruce 1988:54)

Pentecost is a clear affirmation of linguistic diversity, created by God in the beginning and affirmed at Babel (see chapter 9). It was a glimpse into an ideal world, where no one had to learn another language in order to understand what God was saying. No one even had to rely on a language of wider communication in order to understand what God was saying; at Pentecost, God spoke to the heart (see also chapter 19).

Raharimanantsoa writes, "If there is any allusion in Acts 2 to the events that transpired at the Tower of Babel (Gen 11), it is perhaps to be found here in verse 6, for here we are told that, on hearing these Galilean Jews speaking in their own native tongues, the crowds were confused (*synechythē* in Greek)" (2022:98). At Babel the unintelligibility factor caused by many tongues caused confusion; here the intelligibility factor does (Witherington 2006:136).

The arrest of Paul

Raharimanantsoa's fourth case study is Paul's testimony before his countrymen and the Roman authorities in Acts 21:37–22:29. Paul is speaking an unspecified language to the crowds in the temple, a riot erupts and he is arrested. As the soldiers are taking Paul off to the barracks, he turns to the arresting officer and says, "May I say something to you?" Luke (the narrator) does not indicate a change of language, but the arresting officer replies, "Do you speak Greek?" (Acts 21:37). This indicates either that Paul has switched language, from Aramaic or Hebrew to Greek, or that the commander was not present when Paul was arrested. The text continues, "After receiving the commander's permission, Paul stood on the steps and motioned to the crowd. When they were all silent, he said to them in Aramaic: 'Brothers and fathers, listen now to my defense.' When they heard him speak to them in Aramaic, they became very quiet" (Acts 21:40–22:2). There is a footnote on the word Aramaic: "or Hebrew".

Scholars are not in agreement as to whether Paul spoke Hebrew or Aramaic. Raharimanantsoa concludes,

> Regardless of whether this refers to Hebrew or Aramaic, it is clear that Paul addresses the crowd, not in Greek, but in a Semitic language. Paul's use of the language referred to in *tē Hebraidi dialektō* is pragmatic and tactical (Poirier 2003), in order to defuse a tense situation and to defend himself by testimony against the facts of which he is accused (cf. Acts 21:27–31). (2022:101)

The book of Revelation

Raharimanantsoa's final case study is the vision of God's people on earth and in heaven in Revelation 7:1–17. Following Erwin Morales (2007), Raharimanantsoa views the 144,000 and the "great multitude" as two distinct groups of people. Of the 144,000 Raharimanantsoa writes, "What interests us here is the ethnic character of the 144,000, who are described as a group of Jewish believers, originating from the tribes of Israel. This list of tribes assumes this is a monocultural context. They are "servants of God" (cf. 1:1, 6:11), therefore believers, yet faith in Christ has not erased their ethnicity" (2022:103). Raharimanantsoa then quotes Ian Paul, who writes, "The list portrays God's people as a community of the Messiah who have kept themselves pure in worship and thus stayed true to their calling as a priestly nation equipped for the holy war that they are to face" (2018:160).

The great multitude mentioned in Revelation 7:9–17, on the other hand are "those who have come through the tribulation by staying faithful to God. Their cultural identity (9a) and their moral identity (9b, 13–14 [see below]) are presented, as well as their activity of praising God (15–16) and their state in the presence of God (15–17). Paige Patterson (2012:200) rightly asserts that 'John is making the point that this group is ethnically distinct from the Jews who are sealed in the first part of the chapter, and they are further ethnically, tribally, and linguistically diverse from one another—indicating the extent to which the gospel of Jesus Christ has permeated the entire earth'" (Raharimanantsoa 2022:101).

Raharimanantsoa (2022:103) follows David Aune's suggestion (1998:466) that the multitude of believers can be interpreted as the fulfillment of YHWH's promise to Abraham that his descendants would be "like the dust of the earth" (Gen 13:16), "like the stars of the sky" (Gen 15:5), "like the sand of the sea" (Gen 32:12), and the promise that he would be the father of many nations (Gen 17:4–6, 16).

Raharimanantsoa (2022:103–104) continues, "Unlike the first monoethnic group mentioned above, the multitude is described as coming from a diversity of nations, ethnic groups, and peoples, representing great linguistic diversity (*ek pantos ethnous kai phylōn kai laōn kai glōssōn*: 'From every nation, from all tribes and peoples and languages' Rev 7:9). As part of their moral identity, they are dressed in white robes (9b, 13–14), carrying 'palm branches in their hands' (an allusion to the Feast of Tabernacles, e.g., Lev 23:40 and 43, Neh 8:15, cf. Ulfgard 1989). The multiethnic multitude is characterized by diversity, and 'the universality of the multitude is stressed by the fourfold division into nations, tribes, peoples, and languages' (Mounce 1997:162)."

Conclusion

Paul Frank writes, "The first biblical references to people of all languages being in the kingdom of God are in the Old Testament. John's vision on the Island of Patmos of a multilingual host in heaven was not a new revelation but testifies anew to what God had already revealed to the prophets of old. *God had announced his intention, years before the church was founded, that people of all languages would hear about him and enter the kingdom*" (2022:91 [emphasis added]).

Mamy Raharimanantsoa continues, "Although the New Testament is written in Greek, a number of other languages are also present. Jesus, Paul, and others selected specific languages in multilingual situations to communicate effectively, to worship God, and to talk about God. This suggests that within the mission of God no one language is more important than any other. Language, even dialect as we saw in the case of Peter, is part of our identity. But as a means of communication, language is a tool, not an end in itself" (2022:104–105).

In our journey from Genesis to Revelation, we have seen that while there is an awareness of language in the Scriptures, it is seldom the focus of the narrative. Throughout most of the Old Testament period, the people of Israel spoke Hebrew. This, however, changed around the time of the exile. John Edwards (1994 39) suggests that there are two primary ways of communicating with understanding in a multilingual context: a lingua franca and translation. We have seen how Aramaic was used as a lingua franca in the Assyrian, Babylonian, and Persian empires. We then noted the translation of the Hebrew Scriptures into Greek. In New Testament times, Greek was the primary lingua franca, and we saw how Pilate and Jesus would have almost certainly used Greek when conversing with one another. Thus, while both Edwards' methods work, his first method (lingua franca) is predominant. We also observed in Paul's choice of language when arrested that language is more than just a means of communication: his choice of language was part of his message.

Finally, there is another strand that must not be overlooked. The importance God places on linguistic diversity and "each of us hear[ing] in our native language" (Acts 2:8) was reaffirmed at Pentecost and further reaffirmed in John's vision of a great multitude drawn from "every ... language" (Rev 7:9) worshipping before the throne and before the Lamb. Linguae francae have a key role in the mission of God, but the more excellent way is to use the language of those we are addressing. In the mission of God, each language has value.

References

Aune, David. E. 1998. Revelation 6–16. *Word Biblical Commentary*. Vol. 52B. Dallas, TX: Word Books.

Benner, Jeff A. 1999. *The Paleo-Hebrew alphabet*. Online. Magnolia, MS: Ancient Hebrew Research Center. https://www.ancient-hebrew.org/ancient-alphabet/paleo-hebrew-alphabet.htm.

Blanchard, Yves-Marie. 2013. Transmission, tradition, traduction : Aux sources de l'herméneutique chrétienne. *Institut Catholique de Paris. Transversalités* 3(127):9–29.

Bruce, F. F. 1988. *The book of the Acts*. Grand Rapids, MI: Eerdmans.

Carson, D. A., ed. 2015. *The NIV Zondervan Study Bible*. Grand Rapids, MI: Zondervan.

Davies, W. D., and Dale C. Allison, Jr. 2004. *A critical and exegetical commentary on the Gospel according to Saint Matthew*. International Critical Commentary. Vol. 3. London: T&T Clark.

Edwards, John. 1994. *Multilingualism*. New York: Routledge.

Fernandez, Miguel Pérez. 1999. *An introductory grammar of Rabbinic Hebrew*. Translated by John Ewolde. Leiden, Netherlands: Brill. https://www.amazon.com/Introductory-Grammar-Rabbinic-Hebrew/dp/9004109048.

Frank, Paul. 2022. Multilingualism in the Old Testament. In Greed and Kruger, 81–91.

Jobes, Karen H., and Moisés Silva. 2015. *Invitation to the Septuagint*. Second edition. Grand Rapids, MI: Baker Academic.

Macfarlane, Roger T. 1996. Hebrew, Aramaic, Greek, and Latin: Languages of New Testament Judea. *Brigham Young University Studies* 36(3):228–238. https://www.jstor.org/stable/43044128.

Morales, Erwin T. 2007. Discourse analysis of the book of Revelation. MA thesis. Talbot School of Theology, Biola University, CA.

Morris, Leon. 1992. *The Gospel according to Matthew*. The Pillar New Testament Commentary. Grand Rapids, MI: Eerdmans.

Mounce, Robert. H. 1997. *The book of Revelation.* The New International Commentary on the New Testament. Revised edition. Grand Rapids, MI: Eerdmans.
Patterson, Paige. 2012. Revelation. In E. Ray Clendenen and David S. Dockery (eds.), *The New American Commentary.* Vol. 39. Nashville, TN: Broadman & Holman.
Paul, Ian. 2018. *Revelation: An introduction and commentary.* Tyndale New Testament Commentaries. Vol. 20. London: Inter-Varsity Press.
Poirier, John C. 2003. The narrative role of Semitic languages in the book of Acts. *Filología Neotestamentaria* XVI:107–116. http://www.biblicalstudy.ru/NT/01.pdf.
Raharimanantsoa, Mamy. 2022. Multilingualism in the New Testament. In Greed and Kruger, 92–109.
Tresham, Aaron. 2009. The languages spoken by Jesus. *The Master's Seminary Journal* 20(1):71–94.
Ulfgard, Håkan. 1989. *Feast and future: Revelation 7: 9–17 and the Feast of Tabernacles.* Coniectanea Biblica. New Testament Series. Stockholm: Almqvist & Wiksell International.
Witherington, Ben III. 2006. *Matthew.* Smyth & Helwys Bible Commentary. Vol. 19. Macon, GA: Smyth & Helwys.
Wright, Paul. H. 2019. Geography of the Nations in Jerusalem for Pentecost (Acts 2:7–11). In Barry J. Beitzel, Jessica Parks, and Douglas Mangum (eds.), *Lexham geographic commentary on Acts through Revelation,* 105–114. Bellingham, WA: Lexham Press.

Lamedh

*If your law had not been my delight,
I would have perished in my affliction.
(Psalm 119:92)*

12

The Languages of Jesus

Michael Greed

In Mark's Gospel Jesus begins his ministry by announcing that the time has come, that the kingdom of heaven is near, and that his listeners should repent (Mark 1:15).

Did Jesus say this in English (King James, of course)?

> The time is fulfilled, and the Kingdom of God is at hand: repent ye, and believe the gospel.

Or did he speak in Latin (as quoted by Jerome in his Vulgate)?

> *Quoniam impletum est tempus, et appropinquavit regnum Dei: poenitemini, et credite Evangelio.*

Or in Greek?

> ὅτι πεπλήρωται ὁ καιρὸς καὶ ἤγγικεν ἡ βασιλεία τοῦ θεοῦ· μετανοεῖτε καὶ πιστεύετε ἐν τῷ εὐαγγελίῳ.

Or in Hebrew?

הנה מלאו הימים ומלכות האלהים קלבה לבא שובו מדרכיכם
והאמינו בבשורה

Or in Aramaic?

ܐܠܐ ܠܡ ܘܗܐ ܐܬܡܠܝ ܙܒܢܐ ܘܩܪܒܬ ܡܠܟܘܬܗ ܕܐܠܗܐ ܬܘܒܘ ܘܗܝܡܢܘ ܒܣܒܪܬܐ

Latin was the language of the imperial Roman conquerors, and Latin loan words can be found throughout the Gospels: *centurion* and other military words, for example, and *denarius* and other financial words.

Greek was the lingua franca of Palestine and the Roman empire, and the whole of the New Testament is written in Koine Greek, the dialect that evolved from the conquests of Alexander the Great (356–323 BC).

Hebrew was the language of the Scriptures and faith; those educated within the faith tradition would have known it, and it may also have been a regional village language.

Aramaic was the everyday language of the home and society in Palestine, and it would have been Jesus' home language and mother tongue.

Multilingual Jesus

Contemporary scholarship suggests that Jesus was at least trilingual, in Aramaic, Hebrew, and Greek. He would have known a little Latin, too, a few words at least. Jesus was not an illiterate peasant: see, for example, Luke 2:41–50, where the child Jesus interacts with the teachers in the temple. When presented with the scroll of the prophet Isaiah at Nazareth, he read the Hebrew text and "all spoke well of him and were amazed at the gracious words that came from his lips" (Luke 4:22). Thus Jesus could clearly read Hebrew, and read it well. However this does not necessarily mean he used it in teaching or in everyday life.

The Gospels are written in Greek (see chapter 13 for a full discussion on Koine Greek). Thus, the words of Jesus are preserved in Greek. But that does not necessarily mean Jesus taught in Greek. His words may have been translated before they were preserved in writing.

Writing in 1970, James Barr rejected the possibility that Jesus taught in Greek, saying that he is "following the opinion which has been held by the vast majority of competent scholars in the field" (p. 9). The question in Barr's mind was the extent to which Jesus may have used Mishnaic (early Rabbinic) Hebrew alongside Aramaic.

Writing thirty-seven years after Barr, John Poirier thoroughly sifts the evidence and concludes:

> The best thesis is that Jesus could read and speak Aramaic and Hebrew (and perhaps also Greek), but that, when he

taught the multitudes or healed someone's child, he relied mainly upon Aramaic. (2007:133)

Contra Crossan (1991) and others who argue that Jesus was an illiterate Jewish peasant, Poirier, citing Flusser, demonstrates that Jesus "was educated beyond his peers (including his pharisaic interlocutors)" (2007:131). Amongst Poirier's data is the fact that Jesus could read and speak Hebrew (see, for example, Luke 4:16–30 where he reads the scroll of Isaiah). However, Poirier continues, "Does [this] mean that he regularly *taught* in Hebrew? Hardly" (p. 133).

Randall Buth, founder and director of the Biblical Language Center in Jerusalem, suggests otherwise. Buth demonstrates that Hebrew was not restricted to educated religious teachers but could also be used for speaking parables to peasants. "Specialists working in the field of Mishnaic Hebrew have proven that three languages, Hebrew, Aramaic, and Greek, were in common use" (Buth and Notley 2014:1).

Which brings us to Greek.

Building on the works of Stanley Porter, and applying insights drawn from sociolinguistics and multilingualism, Hughson Ong, himself multilingual in four languages, states that Greek was both the lingua franca and the language of prestige. Competency in Greek would have been essential, even for humble fishermen, especially in an area like Galilee, with Syro-Phoenicia to the north and west, the Decapolis to the east, and Samaria to the south. Ong sees Jesus and his contemporaries as multilingual and diglossic, that is, they used different languages or language varieties for different social situations—for example, one language for the home, another for public life. With regard to Jesus, Ong posits that while he would have spoken Aramaic at home,

> In Jesus' public conversations ... especially in the regions of Galilee and the Decapolis, his language with his conversation partners and the various groups of crowds would most likely have been Greek (e.g., Matt 5–7, Luke 6:20–49). (2015:339–340)

Supporting this is linguistic evidence that Jesus may have sometimes taught in Greek. In the Sermon on the Mount, delivered in Galilee, the first three beatitudes all begin with begin with π (after μακαριοι οι):

- Μακάριοι οἱ πτωχοί (*makarioi hoi ptochoi* [blessed are the poor])
- Μακάριοι οἱ πενθοῦντες (*makarioi hoi penthountes* [blessed are those who mourn])
- Μακάριοι οἱ πραεῖς (*makarioi hoi praeis* [blessed are the meek])

Furthermore, in John 7, Jesus tells his interlocutors that he is going away and that they will not find him. Their response: "Where does this man intend to go that we cannot find him? Will he go where our people live scattered among the Greeks, and teach the Greeks?" (John 7:35). This strongly suggests that Jesus was known to teach in Greek, and may have been doing so at the Festival of Tabernacles in the preceding verses.

In a 2012 paper, Ong uses Mark 14:32–65 as a case study, suggesting where Jesus might have used Aramaic and where he might have used Greek.

This is not the place to try to work out where Jesus might have used his various languages. Suffice to state that Jesus was multilingual, and parts of the gospel tradition may have had their origin in Hebrew, other parts in Aramaic, other parts in Greek. Most contemporary scholars agree that Jesus would have normally used Aramaic when teaching the crowds and ministering to them. An example of wordplay that only works in Aramaic can be found in Matthew 23:24 where *qalma* "gnat" is collocated with *gamla* "camel". At times Greek would have been the logical language to use—for example, when speaking with Pilate. It is likely that Pilate spoke Latin and Greek, but not much Aramaic, if any at all. Jesus spoke Aramaic and Greek, with perhaps a smattering of Latin. Therefore, they almost certainly spoke to one another in Greek (e.g., John 18:33–38, 19:8–11) (see chapter 11).[1]

It is interesting to note that, although Jesus grew up as a Jew, Hebrew was not his first language. His first language was that of a previously ruling empire.

Two missiological questions

Mark, Matthew, Luke, and John chose to write their Gospels and present what Jesus said in Greek. However, Mark has inserted four Aramaic phrases:

- *Talitha koum* (5:41)
- *Ephphatha* (7:34)
- *Abba* (14:36)
- *Eloi, Eloi, lema sabachthani* (15:34)

This serves to highlight the fact that, apart from those occasions where he may have spoken Greek, we do not have Jesus' actual words recorded.[2] What we have is a Greek translation. Barr (1970:9) writes:

> One of the peculiarities of Christianity is that the words of Jesus have not been preserved in the language in which they were originally spoken. Even from the earliest days there was no great effort—perhaps there was no effort at all—to ensure that his sayings should be kept alive in the original tongue. The tradition of his teaching was carefully

---

[1] For further reading on Jesus' possible use of Greek, see Stanley E. Porter (1993), *Did Jesus Ever Teach in Greek?* and Peter J. Williams (2018), *Can We Trust the Gospels?*

[2] And even if he were speaking Greek, the words recorded by the Evangelists may be a summary, not a verbatim record.

cultivated and was set forth in the various versions of the different Gospels, but it was a tradition in translation.

Lamin Sanneh expresses this idea succinctly: "Translation is the original language of religion in Christianity" (2009:116).

Focusing our attention on Mark, two key missiological questions confront us:

1. Why did Mark choose not to record Jesus' actual words, but rather to translate them?
2. Why did he choose to preserve the Aramaic on four particular occasions?

Why did Mark translate Jesus' words?

According to tradition, Mark was Peter's interpreter (or translator), he wrote his Gospel in Rome, and he is to be identified with the Mark or John Mark of Acts and a number of New Testament epistles. Much of this tradition finds its origin in a lost work of Papias, bishop of Hierapolis (c. AD 120–130) which is known to us through quotations by Eusebius (c. AD 260–340). Within this tradition it is suggested that Mark himself may be the young man carrying the water pot in 14:13, and who runs away naked in 14:51–52. Eusebius also comments that Mark was the first to announce the gospel in Egypt, using the Gospel which he had written. Ben Chenoweth (2017) proposes that Mark, while resident in Rome, wrote down the oral tradition in preparation for proclaiming the gospel in Egypt.

Richard Bauckham (2006) presents evidence that the oral tradition which existed before Mark put reed to papyrus was derived directly from eyewitnesses. In Mark's Gospel the primary eyewitness is Peter, but other eyewitnesses would include Bartimaeus (10:46–52) and Simon of Cyrene (15:21). Bauckham (p. 258) argues that "Peter grew up fully bilingual" but "when it came to having his words recorded he preferred to express himself in his native Aramaic and allow Mark to translate into more accurate and readable Greek". The Gospel writers and the early church felt no qualms about translating the Aramaic words of Jesus. Alfredo Delgado Gómez demonstrates that Mark chose his language with his audience in mind.

> For Mark, the function of his choice of Koine Greek with its low register and simple style was to address his Christian community and maybe the Hellenistic Jewish community (God-fearing Jews of the diaspora) who in the first century could be part of the lower classes of society and not part of the elite. (2020:401)[3]

---

[3] Alfredo Delgado Gómez's original Spanish article, ¡Levántate! ¡Ábrete! El idiolecto de Marcos a la luz de la sociolingüística, was written in 2017. Three years later he published an English translation of it under the title, Get up! Be opened! Code-switching and loanwords in the Gospel of Mark.

The data indicate that right from the very beginning of the Christian faith, followers of the Way recognised that the important thing was not the words or language used to represent the substance of their faith; what mattered was that very substance, an unchanging core of belief that God was revealing himself, making himself known, and putting the world to rights, and that Jesus of Nazareth was central to this mission that God was pursuing.

This mission that God was pursuing—the mission of God—is not a matter of particular words or particular language; it is the action of God—action that is communicated, amongst other means, with words and language. It is not the words or the language that are of central importance (which is why, in the end, it is not so important to identify exactly which language Jesus spoke when) but the essential, intrinsic substance, the unchanging core, the mission of God, which the words (in a given language) are conveying. "How beautiful on the mountains are the feet of those who bring good news," proclaimed the prophet (Isa 52:7a). The messenger's words present the substance and this message can and should be conveyed in any and every language.

But the messenger's words should not be confused with the substance which the messenger presents, just as the invitation should not be confused with the banquet to which one is invited, or the biography confused with the person about whom it is written. The words of the invitation or the biography are important since their purpose is to represent the reality of the banquet or the person. But in the end they are disposable, for they are a mere representation. They are like the reflection in a mirror and the partial knowledge in Paul's famous metaphor:

> For now we see only a reflection as in a mirror; then we shall
> see face to face. Now I know in part; then I shall know fully,
> even as I am fully known. (1 Cor 13:12)

The substance is the mission of God, which anticipates the time when we will know fully and face to face, when the light of the knowledge of God's glory shines in our hearts (2 Cor 4:6), when the earth will be full of the knowledge of the glory of God, as the waters cover the sea (Hab 2:14).

The substance, the mission of God, is vulnerable because the communication of it is dependent on words, translated words. Translation accepts this vulnerability, but translators, from those who translated the Septuagint onwards, recognise that the reality of the mission of God is too important to be left secret, hidden, or obscure. The substance is never changed by the translation, but each translation adjusts the representation of the substance and affects the understanding of it.

This is in direct contrast to the Qur'an where the language itself is considered inspired, and, as such, it is an untranslatable tradition. Comparing the Bible with the Qur'an, Sanneh understands why the comparison is "unflattering to Christianity, for translation concedes that an original text does not exist for Christianity, at least not in terms of Jesus' original words" (2009:223–224).

Mark and the other re-tellers and recorders of the tradition were not simply pragmatists, writing to be understood. Rather, they recognised that what mattered was not the words or language but the substance, the reality to which the words and language pointed. It is not simply acceptable to translate the good news of Jesus, it is mandatory, for it is the mission of God to be known.

Why did Mark preserve Jesus' words?

Having investigated why Mark chose not to use Aramaic, we now turn to the question of why he did in fact choose to use Aramaic. Mark makes generous use of Aramaic loanwords—for example, *pascha* (14:1) and *sabbaton* (1:21), and Aramaic proper names—for example, *Geenna* (9:43) and *Barabbas* ("son of the father" 15:7). There are two occasions when Mark translates an Aramaic name:

- "to them he gave the name Boanerges, which means 'sons of thunder'" (3:17b, where there is also a play on words)
- "Bartimaeus (which means 'son of Timaeus')" (10:46)

As noted in chapter 8, there are four occasions where Mark inserts an Aramaic word or phrase, which he then translates into Greek. We examined two of these Aramaic phrases in that chapter. We turn now to the other two.

- '*Abba*, Father,' he said, 'everything is possible for you. Take this cup from me. Yet not what I will, but what you will.' (Mark 14:36)
- And at three in the afternoon Jesus cried out in a loud voice, '*Eloi, Eloi, lema sabachthani*?' (which means 'My God, my God, why have you forsaken me?'). (Mark 15:34)

Jesus' home language

Jesus directly addresses God twice in Mark's Gospel. The first is the gut-wrenching prayer in the Garden of Gethsemane where Jesus addresses God, "*Abba*, Father". The second is Jesus' cry of lament and abandonment from the cross, *Eloi, Eloi, lema sabachthani*.

Matthew and Luke both record Jesus' prayer in Gethsemane but do not include the Aramaic *Abba*. Matthew, like Mark, records Jesus' cry of dereliction from the cross and then translates it into Greek. However, in Matthew's Gospel Jesus cries out in Hebrew (Buth 2014). The insertion of key phrases in Aramaic is unique to Mark.

Aramaic is Jesus' home language, the language of his heart. Mark arguably shows greater linguistic awareness and sensitivity than any of the other Gospel writers, for whenever Jesus speaks with his Father in prayer in Mark's Gospel he uses his "home language", Aramaic. Such is the power and intimacy of the language which one hears during one's formative childhood years! It is the testimony of the Bible translation movement that when a person relates to God in their own home language, something deep and transformative happens. Consider the following example from a Tatar pastor who was reading the story of the prodigal son to another Tatar man.

> As soon as I reached the place where the forgiving father addresses his elder son with the word *ulym* ("my son") in Tatar, tears gushed from his eyes and he wept for a long time. This single Tatar word touched some of the innermost strings of his soul. (IBT 2016)

Moreover, these two cries of Jesus are the rock-bottom moments of his life's path, when he came to terms with the inevitability of the cross and when he suffered divine dereliction on the cross. Both of them Mark preserves in the original Aramaic and we see into the innermost stirrings of Jesus' soul.

Conclusion

In this chapter we have seen how Jesus interacts with different languages. He was almost certainly multilingual in Aramaic, Greek, and Hebrew, but in the end it doesn't really matter, for no one language holds a place of special prominence in the Christian tradition; the original language of Christianity is translation (Sanneh 2009). What matters is the substance of God's mission, not the language used to express it. The choice of language is not important.

At the same time, the choice of language can be crucial. Jesus' mother tongue was Aramaic, and on the two occasions when Mark preserves something of the words of Jesus' prayers, he records his Aramaic words. He thereby demonstrates the role of the mother tongue in Jesus' prayer life.

Language does not matter, and language matters.

References

Barr, James. 1970. *Which language did Jesus speak? Some remarks of a semitist.* Bulletin of the John Rylands Library 51(1):929. https://www.manchesterhive.com/view/journals/bjrl/53/1/article-p9.xml.

Bauckham, Richard. 2006. *Jesus and the eyewitnesses: The Gospels as eyewitness testimony.* Grand Rapids, MI: Eerdmans.

Buth, Randall. 2014. The riddle of Jesus' cry from the cross: The meaning of ηλι ηλι λαμα σαβαχθανι (Matthew 27:46) and the literary function of ελωι ελωι λειμα σαβαχθανι (Mark 15:34). In Randall Buth and R. Steven Notley, (eds.), *The language environment of first century Judaea,* 395–422. Leiden, Netherlands: Brill.

Buth, Randall, and R. Steven Notley, eds. 2014. *The language environment of first century Judaea.* Jerusalem Studies in the Synoptic Gospels. Vol. 2. (Jewish and Christian Perspectives. Vol. 26.) Leiden, Netherlands: Brill.

Chenoweth, Ben. 2017. *The Rome Gospel.* Exegetical Histories Book 3. Kindle Edition. https://www.amazon.com/Rome-Gospel-Exegetical-Histories-Book-ebook/dp/B073P1TR5D.

Crossan, John Dominic. 1991. *The historical Jesus: The life of a Mediterranean Jewish peasant.* San Francisco, CA: HarperSanFrancisco. https://en.wikipedia.org/wiki/John_Dominic_Crossan#Books.

Delgado Gómez, Alfredo. 2020. Get up! Be opened!: Code-switching and loanwords in the Gospel of Mark. *Journal for the Study of the New Testament* 42(3):390–427.

IBT (Institute for Bible Translation). 2016. What is a true "heart language"? Summer 2016 Newsletter. ibtrussia.org/en/newsletter-0616.

Ong, Hughson T. 2012. An evaluation of the Aramaic and Greek language criteria in historical Jesus research: A sociological study of Mark 14:32–65. *Filologia Neotestamentaria* Vol. XXV:37–55.

Ong, Hughson T. 2015. Ancient Palestine is multilingual and diglossic: Introducing multilingualism theories to New Testament studies. *Currents in Biblical Research* 13(3):330–350.

Poirier, John C. 2007. The linguistic situation in Jewish Palestine in late antiquity. *Journal of Greco-Roman Christianity and Judaism* 4:55–134.

Porter, Stanley E. 1993. Did Jesus ever teach in Greek? *Tyndale Bulletin* 44(2):199–235.

Sanneh, Lamin. 2009. *Translating the Message: The missionary impact on culture.* Revised and expanded edition. Maryknoll, NY: Orbis Books.

Williams, Peter J. 2018. *Can We Trust the Gospels?* 107–109. Wheaton, IL: Crossway.

Mem

*I have kept my feet from every evil path
so that I might obey your word.
(Psalm 119:101)*

13

Koine Greek and the Mission of God

Eddie Arthur

Introduction

The New Testament arose in a multicultural and multilingual context in which Aramaic and Greek were widely spoken alongside local languages[1] including Hebrew and Latin (the language of Rome). In his providence, God could have inspired the New Testament to be written in any of these other languages, or indeed in a combination of different languages. The fact that he chose to use Koine Greek indicates that this language was equipped to play a particular role that other languages could not fulfil.

This chapter explores the role of Koine Greek in God's mission and develops lessons for the contemporary Church from God's actions in inspiring the New Testament.

The first section explores the historical and sociolinguistic contexts of the New Testament. The way language is used in the New Testament is then examined; this allows some tentative conclusions to be drawn both about

---

[1] Acts 2 gives an insight into the number of languages spoken in the Jewish diaspora, with people from fifteen different regions with distinct languages being listed.

the languages that Jesus and Paul used in their life and ministry and about the significance of Koine Greek as a vehicle of God's revelation.

The second section considers the concept of the mission of God or *missio Dei* and explores the role of Koine Greek in this context.

The conclusion draws some recommendations for the contemporary Church regarding the use of languages of wider communication and their relationship to minority languages.

The New Testament in its context

The books of the New Testament were written in the second half of the first century in the eastern portion of the Roman Empire. The books were written in a mainly Jewish context, building on and referring to the Old Testament and dealing with the realities of Jewish life in the Roman Empire. The stories of the Gospels play out in Palestine, while the other books of the New Testament have a broader geographical scope. The society in which the New Testament was written was highly diverse (Ehrensperger 2012:14). Even though the narrative of the Gospels takes place almost entirely within the boundaries of Jewish Palestine, it contains multiple references to other peoples and cultures such as Greeks, Syrophoenicians, Samaritans, and Romans. In the book of Acts and in Paul's Epistles, there are numerous mentions of different people and language groups. While commentators and theologians tend to concentrate on the theological implications of the role of law and grace during the encounters between Jews and Gentiles in Acts and the Pauline Epistles, there is also a sense in which they reflect cross-cultural conflicts as Jews, who were inwardly focused on their own nation and culture, were forced, by the reality of Christ's death and resurrection, to engage with the wider world.

Language in Palestine

At the time of Jesus and the New Testament, four languages were spoken in Palestine: Hebrew, Aramaic, Greek, and Latin.[2]

Hebrew

Hebrew was the historic language of the Jewish people. However, at the time of the New Testament the language profile of Palestine was dominated by the languages of various conquering peoples who had imposed their language and culture on the region. Hebrew was preserved in the Scriptures of the Old Testament and would have been used in the temple and possibly in local synagogues. Authorities differ as to the amount of Hebrew that would have been spoken on a daily basis, but it seems possible that it

---

[2] For an overview of the scholarly discussion on this topic see Ong 2016:165ff.

would have been spoken in the villages of Judea where contact with other languages would have been less frequent than in other parts of Palestine.

Aramaic

Aramaic, like Hebrew, is a Semitic language; it was a prominent language in the Persian Empire, which had dominated the region 300–500 years earlier. The books of Ezra and Nehemiah record the Jews' post-exilic return to Palestine under the authority of the Persian Emperor. In Nehemiah 8:8, during the public reading of the Torah, it was necessary for the Levites to explain or, perhaps, translate the text for their hearers (see chapter 11). This is possibly an indication that facility in Hebrew had declined during the exile and many people were already more familiar with Aramaic.

Latin

Latin was the language of the Roman Empire. It had a place in official life but was little used in day-to-day discourse. Where Latin terms occur in the New Testament, they tend to be referring to Roman objects or practices.

Koine Greek

The Greek[3] language spread throughout the Near East as a result of Alexander the Great's conquests and took root wherever populations of Greeks settled. By the time of the New Testament, it was the lingua franca of much of the region (Ong 2016:166).

Again, by the time of the New Testament, the invading Greeks had been displaced by the Romans and Koine was no longer the language of a politically dominant Empire. Such status as it had was derived from its use in trade and culture. However, it was still widely used in Palestine and elsewhere in the eastern Mediterranean at this time.

Shortly before the time of the New Testament, a revival of a more classical Greek led to the slow decline of Koine Greek. Most of the literature of the 300 years before Christ has been lost, and we are fortunate that the Koine translation of the Old Testament, the Septuagint, remains as a significant example of literature from this period. By the second century AD, the move away from Koine was complete, and Attic Greek dominated both pagan philosophy and Christian theology (Rydbeck 1998:363), and the Koine Greek of the New Testament was viewed as a debased form of the language (De Villiers 1990:248).

---

[3] The term Koine arose from the description of the form of Greek that developed in the wake of Greek conquests as ἡ κοινή διάλεκτος, the common dialect. This term is first attested in a text by the philosopher Kolotes who was born around 325 BC (Rydbeck 1998:362).

Summary

At the time of the New Testament, there were three languages spoken on a day-to-day basis in Palestine, with Latin used in some official circles. Different areas had different language profiles. For example, Caesarea was an area of significant Roman influence, and so it is likely that more Latin was spoken there than in other areas of the region. Based on what is known about patterns of occupation, trade, and religious activity, Bernard Spolsky (1985:41) describes the prevalence of languages in the different areas of Palestine, as adapted in table 13.1.

Table 13.1. Languages of Palestine

Location	Language(s)
Judean villages	Hebrew
Galilee	Aramaic, Hebrew, Greek
Coastal cities	Greek, Aramaic, Hebrew
Jerusalem, upper class	Greek, Aramaic, Hebrew
Jerusalem, lower class	Aramaic, Hebrew, Greek

Spolsky's contention is that those who were more likely to be in contact with traders would prioritize Greek, while Galileans, by virtue of their closeness to Syria, would prefer Aramaic. Likewise, the more cosmopolitan Jerusalem upper classes and coastal dwellers would have less use for Hebrew.

What language did Jesus speak?

The language spoken by the incarnate Son of God is clearly of some importance in any consideration of language and the mission of God. Lamin Sanneh suggests that Christianity seems unique "in being the only world religion that is transmitted without the language or originating culture of its founder" (2003:98). However, neither Scripture nor such historical and cultural evidence that exists allow us to make definitive statements about Jesus' preference for one language over another. If Spolsky's position outlined in the previous section is correct, then the Galilean Jesus would have spoken Aramaic, Hebrew, and Greek in that order, in which case it is likely that he taught in Aramaic (see chapter 12 for more on the languages Jesus spoke). However, others suggest that Jesus preferentially taught in Koine. This would explain why Mark includes the Aramaic phrase *Talitha koum* when Jesus was speaking to Jairus's daughter, the assumption being that Jesus was speaking Greek, but broke into the vernacular to address a young girl who would speak less Greek (Mark 5:41) (see chapter 8 for another possibility).

However, rather than trying to isolate one preferred language, it would seem wise to take a step back and consider the nature of the society in which Jesus grew up and ministered. A significant proportion of the world's population today is born into multilingual societies. These people learn to master more than one language, adapting the language they use to the context in which they find themselves. Given the experience of contemporary multilinguals, it would not seem unreasonable to assume that Jesus was multilingual, switching between Aramaic, Hebrew, and Greek according to the context. It is feasible that he could have taught in Hebrew in the Judean villages, in Aramaic in Galilee, and in Greek in Jerusalem (see discussion in Ong 2016:172). In passing, it is fascinating to note that Jesus had disciples who were named in all three common languages (Aramaic: Thomas and Thaddaeus; Greek: Andrew and Philip; Hebrew: John and Matthew).

What language did Paul speak?

Paul is the central character of the book of Acts and also the author of the majority of the New Testament Epistles. Given his prominence, it is worth briefly considering the way in which Paul used languages. Ehrensperger describes Paul in this way: "Paul used a Latin name, wrote in Greek and described himself as a Hebrew of the Hebrews" (2012:9). As a Roman citizen from the town of Tarsus, Paul probably grew up speaking Greek, though he may have known some Latin and perhaps something of a local language, too. It is possible that during his rabbinical training with Gamaliel he acquired some Hebrew or even Aramaic; however, it would have been equally possible for him to have studied the Old Testament in Greek.

Given the extent to which he travelled across the eastern Mediterranean, it is almost certain that Paul did most of his teaching in the lingua franca, Koine Greek. However, the "diversity of cultures under specific political circumstances is at the heart of Paul's theology" (Ehrensperger 2012:10).

Language in the New Testament

The New Testament is written in Koine, or New Testament, Greek. However, there are traces of other languages within the text that should be noted. There are suggestions by various authors that some of the New Testament books were written originally in Aramaic and that what we have today are translations from Aramaic into Greek (Nikolakopolous 1997:263). Others suggest that although the texts were originally written in Greek, they bear witness to the Semitic environment in which they were developed through traces of Aramaic and Hebrew syntax and semantics which are found in the text (1997:264). These considerations are beyond the scope of this chapter other than to remark that any text that is developed in a context where multiple languages are in common use is bound to show some traces of the other languages.

As has been mentioned, a number of Latin terms are found throughout the New Testament. These occur when referring to functions of the Roman Empire, such as *centurion, praetorium,* or *denarius.*

There are a number of Aramaic phrases included in the New Testament narrative, such as Jesus' cry of desolation on the cross (Mark 15:34). I suggest that these expressions retain the original and have not been translated into Greek in order to give emotional weight to the text (see chapter 12).

Although the documentation of the incident on the day of Pentecost in Acts 2 does not actually use any languages other than Greek, it does demonstrate that multiple languages can be used as a vehicle of God's revelation.

The role of Koine Greek

This brief overview of the New Testament in its language context has revealed three important points with regard to Koine Greek which need to be considered further in the context of the mission of God.

- Koine Greek was widely spoken across the eastern Roman Empire. The fact that the New Testament was written in this language means that it could be read and understood by a large number of people from different language backgrounds.
- While Koine was widely spoken, it was no longer imposed by political and military force. The official language of the Roman Empire was Latin. Greek maintained its position as a lingua franca through soft cultural and economic forces. However, at the time of the New Testament, Koine was losing ground to the more favored Attic Greek, and within a short time it would come to be viewed as an inferior form of the language.
- Although the New Testament is written in Koine Greek, the way in which other languages feature in the text for a variety of reasons shows that Koine is in no sense a sacred language and that other languages can therefore serve as vehicles for God's revelation of himself.

In the next section of this chapter, we will consider how these three factors about Koine Greek align with what we know about the mission of God.

Koine and the mission of God

The mission of God

Mission has been understood in various ways throughout history. It has been considered as saving people from eternal damnation, sharing the benefits of Christendom with the wider world, or as the extension of the Church into new territories. However, in 1991, David Bosch wrote, "During the past half a century or so there has been a subtle but nevertheless decisive shift toward understanding mission as God's mission" (1991:389). This concept, and the Latin phrase associated with it, missio Dei, first came to prominence at the conference of the International Missionary Council in Willingen, Germany, in 1952 (Bosch 1991:390).[4]

Timothy Tennent defines the mission in these terms:

> Mission is first and foremost about God and His redemptive purposes and initiatives in the world, quite apart from any actions or tasks or strategies or initiatives the church may undertake. To put it plainly, mission is far more about God and who He is than about us and what we do. (2010:54–55)

The mission of God involves actions of the triune God reaching out to redeem and reconcile. The nature of the mission of God is wide-ranging and is discerned by observing God's actions and priorities through the whole canon of Scripture. This chapter focuses on three specific aspects of the mission of God.

Unity

Chapter 2 of this book argues that a key feature of God's mission is the reconciliation of all things in heaven and earth to himself. A central part of this process is drawing together a reconciled community of people. This unity is not a social construct or a subjective feeling, but it is achieved through the death of Christ on the cross. God's people are forgiven and reconciled to him, and it is on this basis that they can be reconciled to one another. This unity involves the action of the triune God; it comes from the will of the Father, is made possible by the death and resurrection of the Son, and is established through the work of the Spirit.

Given humanity's place as God's image-bearers, the unity of his forgiven people is a central feature of God's mission. This importance is expressed in John 17 where the unity of Jesus' people is described in terms of the unity which exists within the Godhead and is pictured as a vindication and proof that Jesus was sent into the world by the Father.

Paul underlined this picture of a real unity that has been achieved through the death of Christ, which has broken down the wall of hostility (Eph 2:14) but which needs to be protected by people making every effort to keep the unity of the Spirit through the bond of peace (Eph 4:3). The theme of unity runs through all of Paul's letters. For example, the elevated theology of Romans emerges from a consideration of the integration of Jew

---

[4] For more on the development of the concept of *missio Dei*, see Arthur 2010, and chapter 7 of this book.

and Gentile into God's people and the tensions that exist between those of strong and weak faith.

In a multicultural, multilingual body such as the Church, tensions between different ethnic and cultural groups pose a particular threat to unity. This is illustrated by the difficulties between Hellenistic and Hebraic believers in Acts 6:1. This division continued to bubble under the surface throughout the period of Acts and the Pauline letters and has reappeared in various forms throughout the history of the Church.

Koine Greek provided a medium through which these cultural differences could be addressed. People from different linguistic and cultural backgrounds could read and understand the same message and be brought into a living experience of life in Christ. Neither Hebrew nor Aramaic, with their more limited local base, could have served this purpose. Throughout history, languages of wider communication such as Latin or Spanish have served to unite a disparate and fractious multicultural, multilingual Church.[5] Advocates of minority language Bible translation may downplay the significance of languages of wider communication in their desire to advocate for local, less prominent languages. However, God's use of Koine Greek shows that such languages have an important role to play in his mission. In situations of high language diversity, translations of the Bible such as the *Français fondamental* or *Today's English Version,* produced for those who are not native speakers of the languages, can help Christians from different language communities interact and share a common experience of God at work across natural boundaries.

Issues of power and influence

The reconciliation that lies at the heart of the mission of God is achieved through the death of Christ on the cross, and his resurrection. As Philippians 2 shows, Jesus' death was the culmination of a process of humility and submission. There will be a final day when Christ returns in triumph, but this is derived from his first being willing to empty himself of all claims to divinity and status.

As the Son achieved his triumph through humility and submission, so his people are called to a humble lifestyle in which submission to the secular authorities and church leadership, within family and work contexts, and to one another (Eph 5:21–6:9) are present. Humility and grace, rather than the exercise of power and authority, are to typify the spread of the Christian message.

God's choice of Koine Greek as the language for the New Testament reflects this principle. Koine was no longer the language of a powerful

---

[5] This is not to downplay the fact that these languages, and other languages of wider communication, have been used for control, colonialism, cultural assimilation and forced conversation, and that therefore the "unity" may sometimes be more a vision or desire than a reality. See also chapter 17.

imperial power; its influence and status were waning at the time that the New Testament Scriptures were inspired. The use of Koine made it possible for the Scriptures to be widely understood, while not endowing them with the secular cachet of a powerful imperium. Things would have been very different had the New Testament been written in Latin rather than Greek. Though Latin was less widely understood in the east of the Empire than it was in the west, it carried the notions of power and influence that came from imperial authority. The reception of the New Testament and the position of other languages would have been very different if Latin had been the language of inspiration, something that was demonstrated when Latin became the *de facto* language of the western church, and the use of other languages was suppressed.

The previous section demonstrated that it is important for Christians to have access to the Bible in languages of wider communication which provide for unity across ethnic and cultural divides. However, the principle of humility and submission, which lies at the heart of the mission of God, applies to the use of these languages. Majority language communities should recognize the importance of their language as a vehicle of unity, but they should not seek to impose the use of their language on others. In the Middle Ages, the use of Latin ensured the unity of the church across Europe, but also restricted the church's call to make disciples because so few people were able to understand the message.

On the day of Pentecost, the Spirit allowed people to hear and understand the apostles' message in their own languages. In the same way today, speakers of majority languages have a difficult balance to achieve in recognizing the place of their language as a vehicle for unity while also recognizing that others need the Scriptures in their own tongue. At the time of the New Testament, Koine was not the language of an empire; it was chosen for utility, not prestige. The perceived value of a language is of no consideration next to its value in communicating effectively. Likewise, there should be no place for linguistic imperialism in the church today.

"Sentness" and Bible translation

At the heart of the mission of God lies the concept of "sentness". The Father sent the Son and the Spirit proceeds from the Father and the Son. In John 20:21, the Son sent the Church into the world in the same fashion that the Father had sent him.

God is proactive in his mission; he does not wait for creation to move towards reconciliation before intervening, and Christ died for people who were his enemies, not his friends. This sent, outward-focused nature of the mission of God should compel God's people to break new ground in their proclamation of the message of reconciliation, reaching out to their metaphorical Jerusalem, Judea, Samaria, and ends of the earth. In the early life of the church, the use of a widely understood language aided the outward spread of the message. However, implicit in this barrier-breaking, forward momentum is the notion that Koine Greek would not be able to serve the church in all places and at all times. Just as the Hebrew of the Old Testament did not meet the needs of the Jewish diaspora community in Alexandria, leading to the translation of the Septuagint, so Koine Greek would be inadequate for a church spreading into Asia, North Africa, and Europe, necessitating the translation of the Bible into multiple languages.

Languages of wider communication facilitate God's mission, but they cannot fulfill all the needs of a growing and advancing Church.

Conclusion

This chapter shows that God's action in using Koine Greek as the medium for the inspiration of the New Testament is consistent with the revelation of the mission of God in Scripture. Trade languages and languages of wider communication can have an important role in enabling unity in the mission of God, but there is no place for linguistic imperialism. God can (and does) use any language, as all languages have their advantages as well as their limitations, for there is no single sacred language in God's mission. The use of Koine Greek shows a consistency between the content and mechanism of God's revelation, and its role in the New Testament gives us a vision for how different languages and language communities may interact.

References

Arthur, Eddie D. 2010. Missio Dei. In James Butare-Kiyovu (ed.), *International development from a kingdom perspective*, 49–66. Pasadena, CA: William Carey International University Press.

Bosch, David J. 1991. *Transforming mission: Paradigm shifts in theology of mission.* American Society of Missiology Series 16. Maryknoll, NY: Orbis Books.

De Villiers, Pieter G. R. 1990. The medium is the message: Luke and the language of the New Testament against a Graeco-Roman background. *Neotestamentica* 24(2):247–256.

Ehrensperger, Kathy. 2012. Speaking Greek under Rome: Paul, the power of language and the language of power. *Neotestamentica* 46(1):9–28.

Nikolakopolous, Konstantine. 1997. The language of the New Testament as an example for the historical unity of the Greek language. *The Greek Orthodox Theological Review* 42(3/4):259–271.

Ong, Hughson T. 2016. The language of the New Testament from a sociolinguistic perspective. *Journal of Greco-Roman Christianity and Judaism* 12:163–190.

Rydbeck, Lars. 1998. The language of the New Testament. *Tyndale Bulletin* 49(2):361–368.
Sanneh, Lamin. 2003. *Whose religion is Christianity?: The gospel beyond the West.* Grand Rapids, MI: Eerdmans.
Spolsky, Bernard. 1985. Jewish multilingualism in the first century: An essay in historical sociolinguistics. In Joshua A. Fishman (ed.), *Readings in the sociology of Jewish languages,* 35–50. Leiden, Netherlands: Brill.
Tennent, Timothy C. 2010. *Invitation to world missions: A trinitarian missiology for the twenty-first century.* Invitation to Theological Studies 9. Grand Rapids, MI: Kregel Publications.

Nun

Your word is a lamp for my feet,
a light on my path.
(Psalm 119:105)

14

The Way from Babel: The Role of Language and Translation in Advancing God's Mission

Paul Kimbi

Introduction

The account of creation in Genesis 1 concludes with the creation of humankind:

> So God created humans in his image,
>   in the image of God he created them;
>   male and female he created them. (Gen 1:27, NRSVUE)

Bruce Ware argues that "we are created to reflect [God's] own nature so that we may represent him in our dealings with others and over the world he has made ... God's image is reflected in our relation to one another and to God" (2002:21). D. J. A. Clines (1968:86) talks about the integrated nature of humankind—our bodies are not just a mere dwelling place for the soul nor a prison house for it, but both body and soul form a unit. Bryan

Harmelink writes that all we know "depends on our being in a world that is inseparable from our bodies, our language and our social history—in short, from our embodiment ... The very ability to use language is a gift from the one who created us" (2019:3).

Communication, then, is a core component of the image of God in humankind. "We communicate because he communicates" (Harmelink 2019:3). Communication helps us galvanize ourselves to respond to the responsibilities we have towards God, towards one another, and towards the environment. God uses language as a key instrument to advance his mission in the world, and we in turn use language to respond to God's invitation to participate in his mission.

From creation to Abraham: God's commission and missional intent

When God made humankind in his image and placed them in the world he had created, he commissioned them to "be fruitful and increase in number; fill the earth and subdue it" (Gen 1:28a). This charge was intended to accompany the unfolding plan of God making himself known amongst the nations. After the fall in Genesis 3 and the consequent destruction of the world in Genesis 6, God refashioned the world through Noah and his family and again charged Noah and his sons: "Be fruitful and increase in number and fill the earth" (Gen 9:1b). God later chose Abram (Abraham) (Gen 12) and repeated this charge to him. In Genesis 17, he says to Abram: "As for me, this is my covenant with you: You will be the father of many nations. No longer will you be called Abram; your name will be Abraham, for I have made you a father of many nations" (Gen 17:4–5). God is "totally covenantal and eternally committed to the mission of blessing the nations through the agency of the people of Abraham" (Wright 2006:63) and invites believers to make him known amongst the nations (Ps 2:8).

When the descendants of Noah spread out across the earth in Genesis 10, they did so "by their clans and languages, in their territories and nations" (Gen 10:31, see also vv. 5 and 20) (see also chapter 10 in this book). The Hebrew word *goy*, translated in the NIV as "nations," is rendered *ethne* in the Septuagint (the Greek translation of the Hebrew Scriptures). This Greek word *ethne* is almost synonymous with *ethnic* or *ethnic groups* and is used in parallel with "languages". I, therefore, submit that, building on the argument of Genesis 10, when God talks about nations, he sees different language communities.

Babel: God empowers us through languages

The story of the Tower of Babel is discussed thoroughly in chapter 9, so I will simply highlight a few salient points here. When people began to multiply, they came up with the idea of building a city and a tower in order to make a name for themselves. Their mission was in opposition to God's mission. Rather than make God known, they wanted to make themselves known. This was facilitated by the use of a single language (Gen 11:1). The single language they spoke served as leverage to resist the command to fill the earth. But God equally used language to disempower a rebellious people. Genesis 11:7 states that God confused their language. One way we can read "confused their language" would be to disempower them by differentiating the languages they speak. The multiplication of languages at Babel disempowered the people against their resistance to filling the earth, but at the same time it also acted as a centrifugal force, causing them to spread out. God initially used languages to cause the people to move out to different parts of the world. In this way, God took the power away from the powerful and affirmed the value of language diversity over uniformity.

The languages of the world are a tool for propagating God's word. In addition, language conveys culture. "When [some of] the missionaries came to Africa, they did not simply bring the gospel message, they also brought western culture" (Prill 2018:161) which nuanced the gospel. Thorston Prill recounts a story about a Christian parachurch organization in South Africa and observes that the organization's leaders were both expatriates and nationals, but that, during meetings, the nationals tended to stay quiet (2018). Their silence was sometimes interpreted as ignorance but this was not the case. They simply felt inferior when using the English language. "By using the English language the way they did, the missionaries not only exercised power over their Indigenous co-leaders but also sent out a message of communicative superiority. This message was emphasized even more by the missionaries' refusal to learn the local language" (2018:169). Language use can be an exercise of power. God sometimes empowers us with language for effective mission, and underestimating the role of language in our ministry can lead to very negative repercussions or counterproductivity.

Language axis: A potential tower of disenfranchisement

A language axis is a grouping of nations and peoples based on a common lingua franca. Examples are the Francophonie and the Commonwealth of Nations. The Francophonie (fifty-four member states) developed from "a cultural and linguistic association mainly aimed at the maintenance of the position of French in the world to a political entity active in promoting the defense of language and cultural diversity in a global world" (Véronique 2013).

One question we have been asked in many communities in Cameroon during mobilization for Scripture translation is why the Scriptures should be translated into the local language when almost every member of the community understands English or French, both of which have multiple versions of the Bible. This often leads us to think about Babel, the place where people, united by one language, decided to build a tower to make a name for themselves. "It was man's first initiative at globalization ... and the globalists are speaking the same language as they spoke then: let us make a name for ourselves" (Tofibam 2020:4). Language axis has the potential to lure people into an insidious form of Babel. In chapter 9 of this book, Gary Simons argues that "one speech" is the power of empire and domination. "By scattering the people in Genesis 11 God was affirming minority identity and opposing imperial identity" (Greed 2016:4). Over the ages, language has been used for centralization and for building a culture around a common language, leading to the marginalization of minority languages. The Greeks and Romans of classical antiquity, for example, sought to centralize the world and enforce the use of language and culture to make a name for themselves (Tofibam 2020).

Anna Dillon (2016) observes that language policies (see chapter 19) can lead to linguistic neo-colonialism, thus to centralization. She cites the example of Ireland. "Colonized by British rulers for over six centuries since 1366 ... the use of the Irish language was considered disloyal to the crown and also, at times, was seen as an infection of the purity of Britishness. In many cases, the language was considered something to be extinguished along with the religion of the Irish people" (Dillon 2016). Language shift (see chapter 20) and, worse still, language extinction leads to a disenfranchisement or sheer annihilation of the identity of a people. In contrast, when the early missionaries went out, they generally sought to learn the language of the people and translate the Bible into these languages.

What language will we speak before the throne and before the Lamb (Rev 7:9)? A lingua franca? Shall we appear in blocs such as Francophonie or the Commonwealth? I write this article in English, but my first language is called Kom, a language spoken in Cameroon. I believe I will represent my ethnic group, the Kom people, before the throne amongst the great community of saints and not appear in heaven as a proselyte of English.

Pentecost: With the Holy Spirit come languages

At Pentecost, God chose to accompany the coming of the Holy Spirit with the ability to "speak in other tongues" (Acts 2:4), and the disciples were empowered to become witnesses of Christ in Jerusalem, Judea, Samaria, and to the ends of the earth (Acts 1:8), echoing God's creation mandate for people to fill the earth. God chose to show the coming of the Holy Spirit with the sign of languages. Pentecost was a reminder of Babel, empowering the disciples to scatter in diverse directions to different language communities (different nations) and become witnesses of Christ. The speaking in tongues in Acts 2 demonstrates "God's acceptance of all languages and the importance he places on them as a means of communicating his truths" (Prill 2018:168–169). In this regard, Pentecost is thus a continuation of Babel. Human empires tend to impose one language, but God had intended a world of diversity from the beginning.

The road from Pentecost to Bible translation

Many of the early missionaries who came to Africa understood the importance of the word of God in the local language and many engaged in study of the local languages and translation of the Bible into them. For example, Alfred Saker, the Baptist missionary who came to Cameroon, arrived in the country in 1842 and had the Gospel of Matthew translated into the Douala language barely four years after his arrival. By 1862 he had the whole New Testament translated into Douala (Slageren 1969:59). Similarly, Presbyterian missionaries arrived in Cameroon in 1890, and "their leader Rev. A. C. Good studied the local language called Bulu. He produced a Bulu dictionary and also translated the Four Gospels of the New Testament into the Bulu language" (Babalola 1988:158).

Language is inexorably linked to mission, and the success of the missionaries in communicating the gospel in the early days of Christianity in Africa significantly depended on their ability to learn and use the local language in their communication. Christianity and colonization came to many African nations almost at the same time. It is said that, while many of the missionaries thought it necessary to learn the local languages to communicate the word of God, the colonial staff never did.

"Christian faith is intrinsically missionary ... The entire Christian existence is to be characterized as missionary existence" (Bosch 1991:9–10). Bosch further notes that mission now can go in every direction, by all and sundry. Bible translation nurtures and matures many believers so that they can be involved in missional activities and helps believers to communicate their faith using their own language—believers who had hitherto been unable to do so.

African language communities are embedded with different layers of culture and religions. I grew up in a community with different expressions of African traditional religion and Christianity and, to a limited extent, Islam, all cohabiting in the same community. The challenge that has stopped many in such communities from being involved in mission within their own community has been the absence of Scriptures in the mother tongue, the only language they understand. Christianity remains vulnerable in communities without mother-tongue Scriptures. African traditional religion, for example, thrives on the use of the local language where it is practiced.

Accounts of Scripture engagement after the publication of the Kom New Testament show that Scriptures available in a language people understand promotes mission in a very significant way. Two short anecdotes substantiate this.

Miriam is a woman of advanced years in the Kom tribe of northwest Cameroon. Her dreams to read the word of God were cut short because she realized she could not go to school at a mature age to learn English, the only language in which the Scriptures existed for the Kom people. Her hopes were rekindled in 1998 when the New Testament was being translated into the Kom language, accompanied by literacy classes in the language. Finally, she became literate in her language and could read the Bible. She quickly began reading the Bible to many of the elderly women in the community. The inability of these elderly women in her church to read the Bible in the only language they understood had been to them like a stone at the tomb of the word of God. Their worry had always been, "Who will roll away the stone for us?" Miriam is now the answer to that prayer. She reads for the women; she shares the good news with her peers in the community. Miriam, empowered by the availability of Scriptures in Kom, is making God known to many around her.

Margaret helped her husband get to know Jesus because she read the Scriptures in her own language. Like Miriam, Margaret was illiterate in her mature age, but with the translation of the New Testament, she enrolled in the literacy classes and learned to read and write the Kom language. Her husband was mesmerized to hear his wife read (from the Kom New Testament). On Christmas Eve, 2006, she read the Christmas story from Luke 2 to her husband and her co-wives with their many children. Like the Pentecost experience in Acts 2, her husband watched her in awe and not long afterwards began to follow Christ, and was baptized (see chapter 5 for more on oral language in the mission of God).

Conclusion

God speaks to be understood. We understand better when we hear a message in our preferred language. When Jesus explained the parable of the seed, he said, "But the seed falling on good soil refers to someone who hears the word and understands it. This is the one who produces a crop, yielding a hundred, sixty or thirty times what was sown" (Matt 13:23). Languages can be likened to the soil and the good soil is the language in which one understands a message best. When we hear God only through another language, God is mediated to us, that is, he comes to us through an intermediary. The word of God is no longer mediated for the Kom people in Cameroon, and the impact is evident.

Scripture internalization is easier when it is in one's own language. There is a sense of dignity now that the Kom people have the word of God in their language. Many in the community, like Miriam and Margaret, have been empowered to share the good news and they are doing it confidently because they have the word in the language they understand best. Many have come to faith because they have understood the message of salvation presented to them. Church growth is visible in the community. Some of the former Kom translators are now serving in related language communities, and the Kom New Testament is being used to speed up the translation of other New Testaments in the cluster of related languages. Such is the impact as God uses the Kom language to advance his mission both inside and outside the Kom nation.

References

Babalola, E. O. 1988. *Christianity in West Africa: A historical analysis.* Ibadan, Nigeria: BRPC.

Bosch, David J. 1991. *Transforming mission: Paradigm shifts in theology of mission.* American Society of Missiology Series 16. Maryknoll, NY: Orbis Books.

Clines, D. J. A. 1968. The image of God in man. *Tyndale Bulletin* 19(1):53–103.

Dillon, Anna. 2016. An exploration of linguistic neo-colonialism through educational language policy: An Irish perspective. *Journal for Critical Education Policy Studies* 14(3):97–130. https://www.researchgate.net/publication/313402170.

Greed, Michael. 2016. Towards a theology of language diversity. https://www.academia.edu/24802794/Towards_a_Theology_of_Language_Diversity.

Harmelink, Bryan. 2019. A theology of embodied presence: God with us through translation. Paper presented at the 10th biennial Bible translation conference. Bible translation and embodiment: Incarnate Word and incarnational mission, 11–15 October 2019, Dallas, Texas. https://btconference.org/2019.

Prill, Thorsten. 2018. Cross-cultural stumbling blocks on the mission field – Yesterday and today. *Haddington House Journal* 20:161–178.

Slageren, Jaap van. 1969. *Histoire de l'Église en Afrique (Cameroon).* Yaoundé, Cameroon: Éditions CLÉ.

Tofibam, Alfred Fuka. 2020. God: The original master globalist. https://alftofibam.weebly.com/articles.html.

Véronique, Georges Daniel. 2013. Organisation Internationale de la Francophonie. Encyclopedia of Applied Linguistics. https://www.researchgate.net/publication/316017827_Organisation_Internationale_de_la_Francophonie.

Ware, Bruce A. 2002. Male and female complimentarity and the image of God. *Journal for Biblical Manhood and Womanhood*, JBMW 7(1):14–23.

Wright, Christopher J. H. 2006. *The mission of God: Unlocking the Bible's grand narrative.* Kindle edition. Downers Grove, IL: InterVarsity Press.

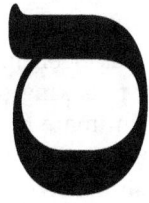

Samekh

*You are my refuge and my shield;
I have put my hope in your word.
(Psalm 119:114)*

15

The Continuum Between Language and the Mission of God

Sung Chan Kwon

Introduction

God is *Deus loquens*—the God who speaks. While the mission of God is much bigger than language, God uses language in his mission. This is evident in John 1 where the relationship between God and the Word is foundational. In this chapter we look at the connection between language and relationship, highlighting the visibility of the Word made flesh, and what it means for the Word to be not only heard but also seen. We then look at the relationship between language and the Spirit, concluding with an emphasis on the translatability of Christianity and of the Bible.

The divine relationship: The Word and God

One of the distinctive features of human beings is language. We are "speaking beings" (*homo loquens*). Since God is a speaking God (*Deus loquens*) and he created human beings in his image (Gen 1:27), the character and the role of language are to be traced back to God himself.

God created the whole world through the Word (Gen 1:1–31). John declares, "Through him [the Word] all things were made; without him [the Word] nothing was made that has been made" (John 1:3). The word of God is not just an instrument for making something but, since the Word has divine personality, it has an intimate relationship with God. God works through the Word. The Word has power to accomplish what God is doing.

John describes the relationship between God and the Word like this: "The Word was with God, and the Word was God" (John 1:1b). The phrase "was with God" shows the dynamic relationship of the Word with God, while the phrase "was God" shows the essence of the Word as God. The Greek preposition *pros* (here translated "with") is normally used with acting verbs and means "toward". Further, the preposition *pros* never occurs with the stative verb "to be" in John's Gospel except in John 1:1–2. By this means John reveals the dynamic oneness of the Word and God, and their intimate relationship and communication.

This divine relationship between God and the Word is the starting point of the mission of God, and the mission of God is the basis of the mission of the Church. The Church, then, should reflect the character of the triune God in her mission, the core characteristics of relationship and oneness. God created the world, including us, through the Word, so as to have the same relationship with us as he has with the Word. Since God is inviting the world, human beings in particular, into this holy relationship first through the Word Jesus Christ and now through the community of disciples, our language and our language-related ministry should focus on relationship.

After Jesus finished his mission on earth and rose again from the dead, he came to his disciples and said, "As the Father has sent me, I am sending you" (John 20:21b). The identity and ministry of the community of disciples is a reflection of the divine relationship and ministry. Jesus emphasized the manner and the foundation of the sending more than the action of sending itself. Based on the foundation of the relationship between God and the Word, God sent the Word into the world. Following the same relationship and manner, Jesus is sending his disciples out. That is why the incarnate Word, Jesus, entered an intimate relationship with his community of disciples before sending them into the world. Language is not just a tool for task-oriented mission. Whatever way we use our language, we need to develop relationships through it.

The Word became flesh, Jesus Christ

God created the world through the Word based on their relationship, and the triune God invites us, whom he created in his own image, into the divine community. However, the whole world lies under the power of darkness. To continue his mission, God sent the Word into the world: "The Word became flesh and made his dwelling among us" (John 1:14).

Let us examine two key features in this incarnation event that relate to the mission of God.

1. **The visibility of the Word.** Since the Word, Jesus Christ, became flesh, people around him could see the grace and truth of God. Everything of Jesus, including his life, death, and resurrection, is the exact expression of the Word of God. John confesses, "We have seen his glory, the glory of the one and only Son, who came from the Father, full of grace and truth" (John 1:14b).

   The Word should be seen as well as heard. This means that the Bible should be translated first through the lives of the translators. Words that are heard without being seen (words without love) are nothing more than sound. The Apostle Paul says, "If I speak in the tongues of humans and of angels but do not have love, I am a noisy gong or a clanging cymbal" (1 Cor 13:1, NRSVUE). In the mission of God, language and life should be integrated; our words need to be visible.

2. **The dwelling of the Word.** John uses a special word for "dwell". The Greek word *skēnoō* ("to dwell," John 1:14), which is used only this once in John's Gospel, contains the Old Testament concept of tabernacle: the Word Jesus Christ is the place where God and his creatures meet. God dwells in our culture and language first of all to draw us into his eternal place. The language of a people group is the place where outsiders meet them. Further, the Word of God is truth himself, nevertheless he resides in human language and culture. Today, we are so often involved in mission work without dwelling in the language and culture of those we are serving that we do not see language and culture as dwelling places, but simply as tools to use. In the mission of God, we need to see language as a dwelling place (see chapter 4).

The Bible testifies about Jesus Christ

What, then, is the relationship between Jesus and the Bible? If Jesus is the Word of God, in what sense can we say that the Bible is the word of God? Dr Lamin Sanneh compares the word of God and the Qur'an of Islam as follows: "For Christianity, the Word of God is Jesus, the Word 'made flesh who dwelt among us, full of grace and truth'. For Islam, the word became a holy book and dwelt among us, full of commandments and directives" (2007). Sanneh further notes that in Christianity, if we look for the word of God that is equivalent to the Qur'an, it is Jesus Christ himself rather than the Bible (2007). Karl Barth states that the Bible is not, itself and in itself, God's past revelation and that we do the Bible a dishonour when we directly identify it with revelation itself (2004:125–126). The Word of God is Jesus and the Bible testifies about him.

The Jews believed that the Scriptures were the word of God just as Muslims do with regard to the Qur'an. Jesus pointed out, "You study the Scriptures diligently because you think that in them you have eternal life. These are the very Scriptures that testify about me, yet you refuse to come to me to have life" (John 5:39–40). The Bible is the word of God because it testifies about Jesus.

At this point, the work of the Holy Spirit is necessary. Jesus told his disciples, "I will send you the Advocate—the Spirit of truth. He will come to you from the Father and will testify all about me" (John 15:26, NLT). The disciples were eyewitnesses and yet the Spirit of truth came upon them to testify about Jesus. Today, we rely on the Bible to know Jesus and to testify about him. The Bible is the word of God because it is God-breathed, and the Spirit of truth is within us as we use it to testify about Jesus. Thus, the language in God's mission is valid only within the work of the Spirit of truth, the Advocate.

The Bible is translatable

The Bible is translatable. To understand this proposition, we need to clarify three different concepts: changeability, non-translatability, and translatability. The difference between these concepts is in the degree to which each concept treats the relationship between meaning and form.

First, *changeability* allows for a change of meaning. It does not recognize one truth, rather, it insists on many truths. Syncretism is a form of changeability, relativism another form. In this case, there is no ultimate meaning, which means there is no ultimate truth.

On the other hand, *non-translatability* does not allow for a change of form. It locates itself on the opposite side of the spectrum from changeability. The Qur'an is a good example. Sanneh points out that "Muslims ascribe to Arabic the status of a revealed language, for it is the medium in which the Qur'an bears testimony to its own Arabic uniqueness" (1989:212). In this case, meaning and form are inseparable. The danger of non-translatability is that the form which contains a meaning gradually replaces the meaning itself. Sacrifice is a good example in the Old Testament, as are circumcision and Sabbath. The Jews replaced the meaning of these practices with the form of them. When the people of God lost the meaning of sacrifice, God said, "The multitude of your sacrifices—what are they to me? ... I have more than enough of burnt offerings, of rams and the fat of fattened animals" (Isa 1:11). Something similar happened with Latin, which was the only holy language in the Roman Catholic Church for more than a thousand years, until the Second Vatican Council. It was an act that went against the translatability of Christianity. A form is valid only while it contains the meaning which it represents.

Third, *translatability* denies both extremes. Translatability keeps the meaning but is open to a change of form. Christianity supports translatability. The key point of translatability is to discern meaning. When we say the Bible is translatable, we mean that the Bible keeps the meaning but is open to change of form, that is, different languages. It does not designate certain languages such as Hebrew, Greek, and Latin as non-translatable languages. Christianity is about the meaning and the essence, that is, Jesus Christ, rather than the form of translation. Sanneh (2007) lists three characteristics of Christianity regarding translatability:

- Christianity is propagated without the language of its founder
- Christians are unique in almost forgetting the birthplace of Jesus in Bethlehem
- The language of Christianity should be simple, everyday workaday language

Let us think for a moment about the meaning of this translatable character of Christianity. If we agree that Jesus mostly used Aramaic in his everyday life even though he probably spoke Greek in certain contexts (see chapter 12), we may ask why the disciples did not record what Jesus exactly said in Aramaic. Was it just for speaking to people in a language everyone knew? If it were just for facilitating communication, Islam's insistence on the non-translatable holy language would be difficult to explain. The reason for changing the form of what Jesus said is deeper than just the surface level purpose of spreading religion; it touches upon the essence of our faith.

I would like to highlight two aspects here.

First, *all languages are worthy of containing the essence*. The truth can be expressed through any language. God has no preference among languages to express his truth. As John declares, "There before me was a great multitude that no one could count, from every nation, tribe, people and language, standing before the throne and before the Lamb" (Rev 7:9). The translatable character of Christianity reveals that we value all languages.

The second aspect is the other way around. Paradoxically, *changing the form prevents any single form from replacing the essence*, and as such, emphasizes the importance of the essence. The essence is God himself, the Word of God, Jesus Christ. Not to give a specific meaning to Jesus' place of birth and his language means giving meaning only to Jesus. The danger of fixing Jesus in one locality, language, and culture is far greater than the danger of any distortion that would arise from translating Jesus into different languages and cultures.

Conclusion

The mission of God is much bigger than a language, yet language reveals critical characteristics of the mission of God. God is *Deus loquens* (the God who speaks) and that means God uses languages. Some implications of this are:

First, relationship is foundational since the Word of God has an intimate relationship with God, as opposed to being merely an instrument. Even learning a new language should be a matter of building a relationship with the people who speak the language rather than just a goal to gain new linguistic knowledge.

Second, an important feature is the visibility of the word. The meaning communicated through the use of language should be seen through the life of the speaker, in the same way as the Word became flesh. When the Word became flesh, the Word was not only heard but also seen. Unless the language we speak is also demonstrated in our lives and interpersonal interactions it is just an empty sound.

Third, language, even the written Bible, does not have power in itself. Language has power, and the Bible as the word of God in particular has power, only when the Spirit works through it and when it testifies about Jesus.

Finally, all languages, or to be more precise, the people who speak those languages, are precious. The translatability of Christianity emphasizes the value of all languages and the value of the essence which needs to be translated. It is important that we keep focusing on the essence, Jesus himself. If our goal is to adhere to a form we will miss Jesus. Changing the form through translation enables people to meet the essence of God's Word—Jesus.

References

Barth, Karl. 2004. *Church dogmatics: The doctrine of the word of God*, Vol. 1, Part 1. Translated by G. W. Bromiley, G. T. Thomson, and Harold Knight. London: T&T Clark.

Sanneh, Lamin. 1989. *Translating the message: The missionary impact on culture*. Maryknoll, NY: Orbis.

Sanneh, Lamin. 2007. Reflections on the comparative history of translation in Islam and Christianity. Lecture in Andrew Walls' Seminar, Wycliffe Hall, UK, June 2007.

Ayin

*Deal with your servant according to your love
and teach me your decrees.
(Psalm 119:124)*

16

Mission as Translation: A Case Study in Contextualization

Michael Greed, with Kividi Kikama

Editor's introduction

The previous two chapters traced language through the Scriptures, concluding that translation is essential as we participate in God's mission to make himself known. The greater part of the present chapter is a case study from the Yansi people in the Democratic Republic of Congo, where Kividi Kikama, himself a Yansi Christian, examines the choice of one particular word in the translation of the Scriptures. Kikama's case study is preceded by some remarks on the translatability of the Scriptures and the impact of Bible translation. The chapter concludes with some insights based on the writings of Lamin Sanneh.

The translatability of the Scriptures

To help guide our thinking in this spiritual, missional, and sociological space, Dick Kroneman (2022:382–383) presents the following questions relating to the Bible and Bible translation. These are not presented as guiding questions that will be answered in the following text; rather they are here for consideration before plunging into the deeply theological implications of Bible translation and contextualized theologies.

1. **What is the Bible?** Is the Bible God's direct revelation or is it a witness of God's revelation, in a more indirect sense?
2. **What is the nature of God's self-revelation in the Bible?** Is the Bible primarily a book of propositional truths regarding God and man, sin and salvation? Or is the Bible primarily a story about the mission of God in this world, and an invitation to people in the church and outside the church to repent and participate in God's mission?
3. **What is Bible translation?** Are Bible translations a direct representation of the Bible as God's main form of self-revelation (mirror metaphor)? Or are Bible translations an attempt to communicate the meaning of the Bible across a threefold gap of history, language, and culture (bridge metaphor)?
4. **Where is meaning located?** Is meaning located in the biblical text and its translations? Or is meaning located in the interaction between the text and the readers or hearers?
5. **How is accuracy in translation defined?** Is accuracy defined in terms of words in the translation corresponding with words in the source text, or in terms of the reader's accurate understanding of the intended meaning of the text?
6. **What is the task of the translator?** To move the reader toward the text or to move the text toward the reader? Preservation of the "objective meaning" of the text or communication of the intended meaning of the text?

Kroneman goes on to explain that none of the apostles, as far as we know, used local languages when sharing the gospel.

> Koine Greek (the language of wider communication) was the main vehicle for the rapid ... expansion of the church during its formative years [see also chapter 13]. The availability of the Septuagint, the Greek translation of the Hebrew Bible, was no doubt an important factor in facilitating the spread of the gospel in the Hellenistic world beyond the borders of Jerusalem and Judea. When the authors of the New Testament quote the Old Testament, they usually quote the Greek Septuagint. There is no indication whatsoever that they considered the Septuagint as an inferior (translated) version of the Holy Scriptures that were originally written in Hebrew and Aramaic. (Kroneman 2022:384–385)

16 Mission as Translation: Contextualization (Greed and Kikamba)

Lamin Sanneh writes,

> Bible translation has marked the history of Christianity from its very origins: the Gospels are a translated version of the preaching and message of Jesus, and the epistles are a further interpretation and application of that preaching and message. Christianity is unique in being promoted outside the language of the founder of the religion. (2002:71)

Within 500 years of the life of Jesus, the Bible had been translated into Syriac, Coptic, Gothic, Latin, Ge'ez, Armenian, Georgian, and Old Nubian. The Venerable Bede translated John's Gospel into (Old) English c. 735, while Cyril and Methodius completed their translation of the Bible into Church Slavonic in 865.

A new era of Bible translation was inaugurated by Martin Luther, who, translating from the original texts, published his German translation of the New Testament in 1522 and the complete Bible in 1534. During the sixteenth century the Bible was translated into a number of other European languages, and in the nineteenth century into a number of Asian languages.

In the twentieth century, a key figure in the Bible translation story was William Cameron Townsend, founder of SIL and Wycliffe Bible Translators. In 1934, he established a training school in the USA, Camp Wycliffe, to train candidates in descriptive linguistics and to prepare them physically for the rugged conditions they would encounter in Mexico. This "linguistic approach" to Bible translation became an essential feature of SIL (Aldridge 2017:25). Bible translation is multiplying exponentially in the twenty-first century, as figure 16.1 (Wycliffe 2022:4) shows.

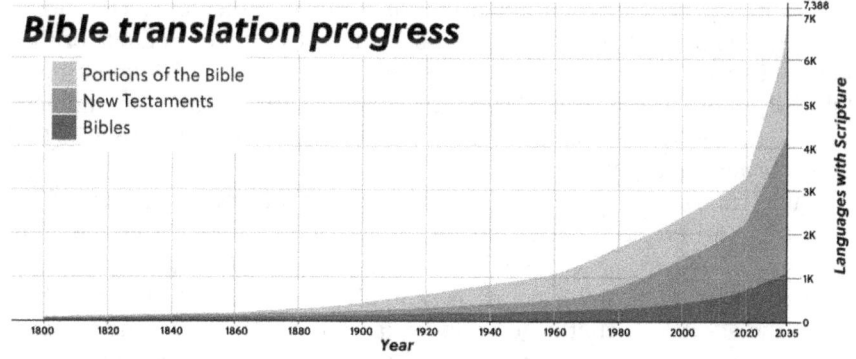

Figure 16.1. Bible translation progress.

The contextual nature of theology and the impact of Bible translation

Describing the contextual nature of theology, Victor I. Ezigbo writes,

> Theology emerges and indeed finds its voice within the matrix of different, albeit mutually complementary sources. Theologians who attend to the contextual affairs of their community are confronted by theology's contextual face: its invitation to theologians to explore how the context of a Christian community is an essential *locus theologicus* (source of theology). Theologies profoundly reveal (or betray) theologians' particularities in terms of their choice of hermeneutical approaches, choice of theological data, and selective appropriation of theological data. All theologies have what may be described as a contextual accent: an identity marker that points to the historical, social, political, and religious currents of the context from and for which they are produced. (2021:4)

Bryan Harmelink (2020) draws attention to research that shows how Bible translation paves the way for the establishment of local churches and contextual theology, as the people of God attempt to understand their faith in terms of their particular context. Mark Noll writes, "Over the course of the last century, the Christian entrance into local cultures has accelerated as never before. Many factors have contributed to this acceleration, but the most important is translation" (2012:23). Sanneh picks up the theme: "The flowering of Christian activity in modern Africa took place in ground suitably worked by vernacular translation" (2009:5). The Scriptures in the local language provide the foundation for contextual theology. Tite Tiénou writes, "We have learned that all Christian theologies are products of their social, historical, and cultural environments" (1993:246). Commenting on this discussion, Harmelink observes, "Theologizing or thinking theologically is vital to the life of the Church as the people of God grow in *faith seeking understanding* in their various contexts" (2020).

Bible translation is a core element of God's mission. God himself has both used and blessed translations of his word(s) to achieve his missional purposes. However, when the Bible is translated into languages whose speakers differ from the original Old and New Testament audiences, there comes the additional challenge of understanding and internalizing the message, because of the often enormous cultural differences between the original audiences and the new audience. A translation of the Scriptures into a local language, therefore, is key to enabling contextualized theologies to develop. In the following case study, Kividi Kikama, a Yansi missiologist and pastor involved in translating the Scriptures into his own language, Iyansi,[1]

---

[1] Note: the Yansi are the people; Iyansi is the language.

helps us understand the critical need for Bible translation coupled with the delicate challenge of local theologizing.

Kikama's case study: The urgency of contextualization

African theologians and church leaders have perceived that the contextualization of the gospel message and the church is both an urgent need and an ongoing task in God's mission in post-colonial Africa. Researching the identification of Jesus as the Yansi's *Mwol* (King and Lord), as a translation of the Greek *Kyrios*, is an attempt by the Yansi Christians to make a modest contribution to this urgent need. The missiological task is to strive for a meaningful and effective communication of the gospel message in the mission of God in Africa and indeed among all peoples of the world.

The African theologian Bolaji Idowu wrote, "The difficult and urgent problem which preoccupies the church today in Africa is the apparent foreign character of Christianity. The God preached by the church was identified with the God of the white man." (1969:12). At the Fourth World Bishops Synod (Rome, October 1974), African bishops followed the same line of thought, stressing the importance of building "African churches, having within them all the means of salvation, rooted in the local structures and cultures and fully responsible for the spiritual destiny of their peoples" (Ngindu Mushete 1977:41).

In a recent study entitled *From 'Ubuntu' to Koinōnia: The Spirit-formed Community and Indigenous African Compassion,* Jerry Ireland argues that rapid church growth in Africa did not produce a genuine ethical and moral transformation of the sort that would be expected from God's people according to the Scriptures. He attributes this lack to what he calls "the imposition of western-style, materialistic, and individualistic forms of compassion that bypass the deeply rooted, tightly linked notions of community and spirituality" (2019:2). He suggests that this can be addressed by

> giving greater attention to the ways in which the African concept of 'ubuntu' and the biblical concept of *koinonia* intersect. By maximizing the biblical framework of the church as the Spirit-formed people of God ... local pastors can help foster forms of compassion that are truly indigenous and therefore offer the greatest hope for lasting change. (2019:2)

This approach of embodying the gospel message in local African languages, images, symbols, rituals, and practices was used effectively by the writers of the eleven Christological essays included in the book *Faces of Jesus in Africa*, edited by Robert J. Schreiter (1991). These essays were a serious attempt to respond to the same fundamental Christological question, Who is Jesus for African Christians and how can they relate to him?

The emphasis in these essays is on Africans experiencing meaningful and transforming relationships with Jesus in their respective socio-cultural contexts. The authors acknowledge the similarities, the divergences, as well as the limitations of these local concepts in their application to Jesus.

François Kabasélé wrote two essays in this collection of works in an attempt to explain three possible ways the Luba people identify Jesus and relate to him: Jesus as Chief, Jesus as Ancestor, and Jesus as Elder Brother. Despite the wider identification of Jesus Christ with the African image of chief, this view has its shortcomings, which Schreiter sums up as follows:

> Some have noted that this image has become outdated and obsolete in some areas of Africa where this position of leadership has lost its power. Others cautioned against negative implications of this symbol, especially the domineering aspects that sometimes accompany being a chief. But as Kabasélé points out, this does not disqualify the possible inclusion of this symbol as a way of identifying the face of Jesus. It simply reminds us that chief does not mean the same thing in every culture ... that no human symbol is without negative as well as positive connotations. One only needs to think of the Mediterranean correlate of chief: *kyrios* or Lord, with its imperial overtones. (1991:xii)

Learning about God and about culturally appropriate language for embodying the gospel in the local context is an ongoing process.

A case study from the Democratic Republic of Congo: Communicating Jesus Christ as *Mwol* to the Yansi people

When I discovered that the Yansi Christians used the word *mwol* in the translation of the Iyansi catechism and in their prayers, and also in the Yansi Bible translation project, my interest was stimulated and I wanted to research this term. I wanted to find out whether its use was both culturally relevant and biblically grounded.

Definition of the term *mwol* in the Yansi socio-cultural context

The term *mwol* has many meanings in Iyansi. It designates the clan of the chief, *amwol*, in plural form, and the chief himself, *mwol*, in the singular. *Mwol* is used in society, especially by older generations, as a title of respect given to some people because of their social rank, role, and good conduct. There are other meanings too, but our focus here is on the *mwol* (chief), and *amwol* (his clan).

The source and nature of the *mwol's* authority

The authority of the *mwol* is legal, temporal, and spiritual. He claims the legitimacy of his legal authority from being born in the matrilineal *mwol* clan, *amwol*. The power of the *mwol* comes from his status as a true representative of the living-dead ancestors. Since the Yansi believe that the Creator God, *Nkier Mpung*, distanced himself from his creation and that life continues after death, the Yansi, like other Bantu people, have to keep good relationships and maintain regular communication with their living-dead ancestors. This is why they continue to practice what has been described as ancestor worship.[2] Generally, the *mwol*, as spiritual leader, exercises the role of a priest or collaborates with the priesthood clan in the village by officiating the community service at the tomb of a great ancestor such as the founder of the village. The transfer of power in *mwol* succession is regulated by a spiritual ceremony.[3]

The *mwol*, as the representative of the living-dead ancestors, is also accountable to the communities under his leadership through the council of elders, and the representatives of their respective constituencies. He functions as the political, military, and religious leader with responsibilities to take care of the people, maintaining unity and peace, and resolving conflicts.

Since the *mwol* can only be fined and not dismissed in case of wrongdoing, he is expected to be a man[4] of good character with qualities of fairness in conflict resolution, integrity, generosity, good conduct, respectfulness (especially to wives), not a practitioner of witchcraft, and approved by the living-dead ancestors as indicated by a successful hunting test, to name but a few criteria. Any public offense they commit requires a public admission and reparations.

Evaluation and integration of the concept of *mwol* into Christianity by the Yansi Christians

Certain requirements need to be met before elements of *mwol* can be integrated into Christianity. Tshibangu Tshishiku states, "One of the tasks

---

[2] This issue has been extensively studied by others. My interest here is in the role the chief, *mwol*, plays as spiritual leader, especially during a crisis.

[3] The transition of power to a new chief requires a period of seclusion and initiation into ancestral traditions and wisdom. There is a grand public ceremony of enthronement including an official presentation to the public as their new *mwol*, reminding the *mwol* of their obligations, responsibilities, and rights. The following symbols of authority are conferred upon the *mwol*: a bracelet, a necklace, a powder, leopard teeth, leopard skin for the throne, royal caps, a royal staff, and attire in the royal color red. For more information on the rites of succession and enthronement of a new chief *mwol*, see Malembé, "La Société Politique Yansi" (1967:221–235) and Kabasélé, "Christ as Chief" (1991:103–115).

[4] In the Yansi tradition the *mwol* is normally a man. Exceptionally, there were two female *mwol* in my village, because there were no men who met the requirements.

of African theology consists of appreciating the ancestors' animistic beliefs by approving those deemed acceptable and rejecting those not valid, not failing to give theological reasons for those rejected" (1974:36–37). For the evaluation to be biblically grounded, Alphonse Ngindu Mushete argues it must have a foundation built on a life of faith, with the Bible and the traditions as major sources of revelation (1977:56–57).

Mavumilusa Makanzu strongly affirms the Bible as the only source for an authentic Christianity. He states that the Bible should be the only guide for the churches to decide what to accept from the Christian religious system imported from Europe and America, and what to reject or to keep from their own cultural heritage (1973).

The different uses of the word *mwol* in the Iyansi language and sociocultural context have revealed the traditional Yansi understanding of the nature and source of the authority, power, and legitimacy of the *mwol* (chief). Today the word is used for political, military, or religious leaders, to show the utmost respect for political and religious dignitaries.

And so I propose that, linguistically, *mwol* is a highly suitable word for Yansi Christians to use in their faith response to Jesus Christ. However, is it also acceptable in the light of the Scriptures? To address that, I need to answer two questions:

1. What negative elements in Yansi traditional assumptions and practices regarding the use of the word *mwol* are in conflict with faith in Jesus Christ?
2. What are the positive elements in Yansi cultural assumptions and practices regarding the use of the word *mwol* that can be refined, elevated, and filled with biblical meaning, and also be integrated into Christians' understanding and experience of who Jesus is as their *Mwol* (Lord)?

Negative elements

According to my findings, the legitimacy of the *mwol's* power and authority comes from belonging to the *amwol* clan and from the approval of the living-dead ancestors. By contrast, the Lord Jesus clearly told his disciples, "All authority in heaven and on earth has been given to me" (Matt 28:18b). In his final prayer to God his Father, Jesus also said, "Glorify your Son, that your Son may glorify you. For you granted him authority over all people that he might give eternal life to all those you have given him" (John 17:1–2).

The Yansi traditional belief in a distant Creator God (*Nkier Mpung*) and in the living-dead as mediators with him is in conflict with the teachings of the Scriptures. The Yansi Christians now believe that Jesus Christ, their true *Mwol*, is the only mediator between them and God, according to the Apostle Paul's teaching. "For there is one God and one mediator between God and mankind, the man Christ Jesus, who gave himself as a ransom for all people" (1 Tim 2:5-6). However, some Yansi Christians, as well as the *mwol* from their area, have been known to continue to address their needs to the living-dead ancestors, especially in times of crisis when they believe their prayers to the God of the Bible are not answered and their problems not solved (Kikama 1978).

There is one further negative element that has not yet been examined. The Iyansi term *amwol*, in the plural, is used for twins. This is not because they are chiefs, but because they are considered to possess spiritual power, and are therefore venerated. They are distinguished at birth by different colored wristbands, treated as special children, and taken care of like kings and queens, their lives—from birth to death—filled with many celebrations, rituals, symbols, special songs, and regulations. In light of the Scriptures, the Yansi Christians have been rejecting the ambivalent, selfish, and burdensome expressions of twins' *amwol* power. In contrast, Yansi Christians experience God's unconditional love, grace, and forgiveness in Jesus Christ, their true *Mwol*.

Positive elements

In my study for a model of the local church for the Bantu that is theologically Christian and culturally Bantu, I benefitted from the Apostle Paul's use of metaphors. Paul wanted to make a clear distinction between Christian churches and both the Jewish synagogues and mystical cults (Banks 1980:33-79). This is why he did not use the religious terms existing in that society. He used secular or ordinary local terms but gave them theological content. For example, the word *ekklesia* "church" is a secular term used for a regular assembly meeting or gathering of citizens in a city to decide matters affecting their welfare. But Paul gave this ordinary word a new Christian meaning by adding to *ekklesia* "in God the Father and the Lord Jesus Christ" (1 Thess 1:1). He did the same with the terms "family," "body," and "gift". He gave them new meanings by adding new content to them: "the family of God," "the Body of Christ," and "the gift of the Holy Spirit" (see Kikama 2000:137-138).

The early Christians used the Greek term *Kyrios* (Lord) when the text of the Scriptures said YHWH, following the practice of the Jews who used the Hebrew term *Adonai*, out of reverence for God's holy name. This practise followed the Septuagint, the Greek Old Testament, where *Adonai* is translated as *Kyrios*. The Greek term, *Kyrios*, was used to identify the Roman emperor. Paul and the early Christians took it and gave it new Christian content, that is, the risen Christ is our Lord, our *Kyrios*. In his sermon on the day of Pentecost, Peter said, "Let all Israel be assured of this: God has made this Jesus, whom you crucified, both Lord and Messiah" (Acts 2:36).

I suggest the term *Mwol* can function in a similar way.

Conclusion: Challenges and opportunities

The use of the title *Lord* by the Apostle Paul evokes the idea of total consecration and absolute obedience to Jesus Christ. Jesus Christ was well established as the foundation of the Yansi Christian faith, and the first-generation Yansi Christians made many sacrifices as a result of their new-found faith in Jesus Christ as their Savior and Lord.

The great challenge today is to unite the second and third generations of Yansi Christians, in the region and in the diaspora, under the Lordship of Jesus Christ through contextualized connections between Christian faith and Yansi culture. The hope of the Yansi church is that it would faithfully revive, restore, and rebuild the churches. I believe the ongoing Bible translation in Iyansi will remove the language barriers and facilitate contextually interactive discipleship in villages, churches, and schools as Iyansi people deal with issues from both the traditional worldview and modern culture.

Editor's conclusion: Mission as translation

With Kikama's case study fresh in our minds, we turn to the Gambian missiologist and theologian Lamin Sanneh to bring this chapter to a close.

Sanneh (2009) differentiates between mission by *diffusion* and mission by *translation*. In "diffusion" the culture that brings the message is part of the message and "it is implanted in other societies primarily as a matter of cultural adoption. Islam ... exemplifies this mode of mission" (p. 33). Mission by translation, on the other hand, sees "the recipient culture as a valid and necessary locus of the proclamation, allowing the religion to arrive without the requirement of deference to the originating culture" (p. 33). "Mission as translation," Sanneh continues, "is the vintage mark of Christianity" (p. 34):

> [Translation forces a separation] between the truth of the message and its accompanying mode of cultural conveyance ... By drawing a distinction between the message and its cultural carriage, mission as translation affirms the *missio Dei* as the hidden light of its work. It is the *missio Dei* that allowed translation to enlarge the boundaries of the new Christian audience. (pp. 36–37)

Sanneh continues,

> Christianity is remarkable for the relative ease with which it encounters living cultures. It renders itself as a translatable religion, compatible with all cultures. It may be imposed or resisted in its Western form, but it is not uncongenial in any garb. Christianity broke free from its exclusive Judaic frame

and, taking a radical turn, adopted Hellenic culture to the point of complete assimilation. (p. 56)

Translation means that one central, governing ecclesiastical authority cannot be maintained. Translation opens the floodgates to local, contextual theologizing. This is a risky but essential process. Andrew Walls writes,

> It was necessary to explore the sense of the Scriptures using the indigenous vocabulary, the indigenous methods of debate, the indigenous patterns of thought. It was a risky business. There's no such thing as safe theology. Theology is an act of adoration fraught with a risk of blasphemy, but an act of adoration, of worship, nevertheless. (2002:8)

Kikama and the Yansi translators took this risk as they wrestled with the question of whether *Mwol* was the best way to render *Kyrios* in their language. Every translation team, from those who translated the Septuagint in the second and third centuries before Christ to the Iyansi translation team in the Democratic Republic of Congo today, enables the faith to break free and take root in another local soil, working with God, empowered by his Spirit, in his mission.

References

Aldridge, Fredrick A. (Boone). 2017. The Summer Institute of Linguistics and the 'linguistic approach'. In Gary F. Simons (ed.), *A threefold purpose: Rediscovering the heart of SIL*. Dallas, TX: Pike Center for Integrative Scholarship. Leanpub.

Banks, Robert. 1980. *Paul's idea of community: The early house churches in their historical setting*. Grand Rapids, MI: Eerdmans.

Ezigbo, Victor I. 2021. *The art of contextual theology: Doing theology in the era of world Christianity*. Eugene, OR: Cascade Books.

Harmelink, Bryan. 2020. Exploring a theology of translation as revelation. Ms. https://www.sil.org/system/files/reapdata/10/94/76/109476956115773748713527122988738133260/Harmelink_Theology_of_Translation_as_Revelation.pdf.

Idowu, E. Bolaji. 1969. Introduction. In Kwesi A. Dickson and Paul Ellingworth (eds.), *Pour une théologie Africaine : Rencontre de théologiens Africains, Ibadan*. Yaoundé, Cameroon: Éditions Clé.

Ireland, Jerry M. 2019. From 'Ubuntu' to Koinōnia: The Spirit-formed community and indigenous African compassion. *Journal of African Missiology* 4(1):1–20. https://missioafricanus.com/wp-content/uploads/2019/05/From-Ubuntu-to-Koinonia-Jerry-Ireland.pdf.

Kabasélé, François. 1991. Christ as chief. In Robert J. Schreiter (ed.), *Faces of Jesus in Africa*. Maryknoll, NY: Orbis Books.

Kikama, Kividi. 1978. Interview with Nameneya Bonga, Pastor Walusayi, Pastor Mansuku, and Pastor Lupungani. Busala and Nianga, Zaïre, 17 September 1978. Ms.

Kikama, Kividi. 2000. Toward a Bantu Christian theology of the local church as new clan in Jesus Christ: Identity, mission, structures, and leadership as perceived by Baptist laity in Kinshasa, Democratic Republic of Congo. PhD dissertation. Trinity International University, Deerfield, IL.

Kroneman, Dick. 2022. Different paradigms relating to God, language and translation. In Greed and Kruger, 380–395.

Makanzu, Mavulimusa Jean-Perce. 1973. Recours à la Bible pour un Christianisme authentique [Back to the Bible for an authentic Christianity]. Sermons and themes at the Synode national de l'Église du Christ au Zaïre [National Assembly of the Church of Christ in Zaire].

Malembé, Paul. 1967. La société politique Yansi [Societal politics of the Yansi]. *Cahiers Économiques et Sociaux* 5(2):221–235.

Ngindu Mushete, Alphonse. 1977. La Théologie en Afrique, d'hier à aujourd'hui [Theology in Africa, from yesterday to today]. Documents of the 20th anniversary of the Catholic Faculty of Theology of Kinshasa. Kinshasa, DRC: Science et Sagesse (Science and Wisdom).

Noll, Mark. 2012. *Turning points: Decisive moments in the history of Christianity*. Third Edition. Grand Rapids, IL: Baker Academic.

Sanneh, Lamin. 2002. Domesticating the transcendent. In Athalya Brenner and Jan Willem Van Henten (eds.), *Bible translation on the threshold of the twenty-first century: Authority, reception, culture and religion*. New York, NY: Sheffield Academic.

Sanneh, Lamin. 2009. *Translating the message: The missionary impact on culture*. Revised and expanded edition. Maryknoll, NY: Orbis Books.

Schreiter, Robert J., ed. 1991. *Faces of Jesus in Africa*. Maryknoll, NY: Orbis Books.

Tiénou, Tite. 1993. Forming indigenous theologies. In James M. Phillips and Robert T. Coote (eds.), *Toward the 21st century in Christian mission*. Grand Rapids, MI: Eerdmans-Lightning Source.

Tshibangu Tshishiku, Tharcisse. 1974. *Le propos d'une théologie Africaine* [A description of an African theology]. Kinshasa, DRC: Presses Universitaires de Zaïre.

Walls, Andrew. 2002. Demographics, power and the gospel in the 21st Century. Paper presented at the SIL International Conference and WBTI Convention, 6 June 2002. Waxhaw, NC. https://www.wycliffe.net/wp-content/uploads/2020/01/Demographics-Power-the-Gospel-A-Walls_EN.pdf.

Wycliffe. 2022. State of the Bible 2022. Oxford: Wycliffe Bible Translators UK & Ireland. https://cfbecdc18044a5f9a723.b-cdn.net/wp-content/uploads/2022/09/State-of-the-Bible-2022.pdf.

Part Three

Language and Flourishing Life Today

"Theology ought to be able to show, in broad contours, how the vision of flourishing life it is commending ought to be lived in different stages and under different conditions of life" (Volf and Croasmun 2019:81).

As we investigate the role of language in the mission of God, are we able to show how the vision that we are commending, of language in the flourishing life of the mission of God, impacts different conditions of life? Is there a role for language in the flourishing life that the Creator intends, that Jesus brings, and that the Spirit empowers? The SIL vision statement states, "We long to see people flourishing in community using the languages they value most." Part three explores **the role of language in five specific areas**.

"The LORD is righteous, he loves justice," sings the psalmist (Ps 11:7). The foundations of God's throne are righteousness and justice (Ps 89:14, 97:2), and he secures justice for the poor and oppressed (Ps 103:6, 140:12). Yet what role, if any, does language play in **issues of justice**? **Chapter 17** explores the relationship between language, justice, and mission.

Poverty is broader than simply the lack of material goods. **Chapter 18** examines the five faces of poverty (Duncan 2008), and suggests a sixth face: **linguistic poverty**. The author then proceeds to suggest how language can itself become a doorway out of social poverty.

Language policy and planning includes the choice of a language variety for specific purposes, and the stabilization, implementation, and expansion of that usage. This further involves the selection of a writing system, the acceptance of one variety of a language throughout the speech community, and a process by which the language becomes a normal medium of communication. **Chapter 19** investigates intersections of language purposes with the purposes of God.

Languages are not static. As generations come and go, and as language communities interact with one another, **languages are discarded and others adopted**; the old language withers and the new one flourishes. Does it matter if a language is discarded? If so, to whom? How does this impact the role of language in God's mission? **Chapter 20** explores these issues.

With more than seven thousand languages spoken in the world today, and mobility being more common than ever in our "global village," languages (or their speakers) are always running into one another. Does this have to lead to exclusion, or can it lead to **"linguistic hospitality"**, where space is made for all, whatever languages they speak? **Chapter 21** discusses linguistic hospitality, particularly in church life.

References

Duncan, Malcolm. 2008. Poverty: What does it look like and can we rise to the challenge? In Marijke Hoek and Justin Thacker (eds.), *Micah's challenge: The Church's response to the global poor*, 151–163. Milton Keynes, UK: Paternoster.

Volf, Miroslav, and Matthew Croasmun. 2019. *For the life of the world: Theology that makes a difference*. Grand Rapids, MI: Brazos Press.

Pe

*Make your face shine on your servant
and teach me your decrees.*
(Psalm 119:135)

17

Language, Justice, and Mission

Evan Falk

Introduction

Justice is a theme woven throughout the Scriptures, aimed at community and wholeness, at *shalom* (Gorman 2015:214). God himself is righteous; God is just. The twin terms of *ṣĕdāqāh* and *mišpāt* (righteousness and justice) of the Old Testament became the *dikaiosynē* (righteousness) of the New Testament (Swartley 2006:33). This righteousness is not simply blamelessness, but "right relationships" (Grieb 2006:59–60). It is rightness, unbroken by the *un*rightness of injustice. Justice, then, is "an extension of God's own identity onto and into the people of God" (Gorman 2015:214).

For the people of God, then, justice is not merely a normative standard by which we judge policies; it is part of our identity as kingdom people living in a broken world, becoming, as in 2 Corinthians, the righteousness (the *dikaiosynē*) of God (Grieb 2006:78).

Unfortunately, Christian theology has historically predisposed many to think of justice only as "retributive", with a perpetrator, a victim, and a judge. It is often a leap to move from justice as retribution to justice as the unbroken state of rightness that *injustice* disrupts (Wolterstorff 2006:23).

Missiologically, we must make that leap in our understanding of justice if we are to live as God's people, participating in God's mission. If this kind of justice is, as we have suggested, part of God's identity, then we must seek to make it part of our own, as well. This means that justice is not merely a matter of policy, but of incarnation.

Justice, especially understood in this holistic sense, impacts our lives in a myriad of ways, leading to a variety of subdisciplines, including the focus of this paper: linguistic justice. In its broadest sense, we might say that a state of linguistic justice is one in which, in any area where language plays a role, all needs are cared for. For some, this may mean seeing that language presents no additional barriers, while for others it may involve safeguarding linguistic diversity (Alcalde 2015:34); there is a rich, ongoing conversation to which we are invited.

For God's people participating in God's mission, linguistic justice means learning to recognize those needs, listening to the value that people place on their languages, and seeking to understand both the struggles and joys that language brings. It means adjusting our postures, our mental models, and our hearts, as much as our strategies. It means living out our God-bestowed justice identity in a world that is richly blessed with linguistic diversity.

Speakers[1] of non-dominant languages[2] face significant justice issues arising from a fundamental inequality in the status of their languages. Examples include limited access to services, vulnerability to exploitation, and pressure to make decisions about their languages with long-lasting social repercussions (see also chapter 3).

Beginning with an overview of the disparity between languages that creates these issues, this chapter will explore justice concerns that arise surrounding language, as well as existing responses to these justice issues. While these approaches have merit, I propose a holistic orientation that also recognizes language not only as a tool we use, but as part of how we process and experience the world around us.

It is within this holistic view of both language and the person that, I believe, a missiological approach to language and justice must begin. As we seek to see people flourishing in community, we must strive to understand not only how their languages function and interact but how these dynamics affect the people who use them, addressing or exacerbating the issues of justice they face.

Bias and locatedness

As the missiologist Michael Barram observes, we cannot separate ourselves from our locatedness; we must acknowledge it rather than feign neutrality

---

[1] "Speakers" here references any form of language use, whether spoken, signed, written, or thought. See p. 3.

[2] This is the term Benson and Kosonen (2013:6) opt for, since it avoids the ambiguity of "minority" or "Indigenous" and highlights "the oppressed status of these languages relative to dominant languages of power". For this reason, and because it reflects the *relative* status of a language, it is my preferred term.

(2018:29–30). As a native English speaker from a predominantly anglophone region of Canada, I myself could well be a case study in linguistic justice. My privilege as an English speaker has allowed me to function comfortably without fluency in any other languages when living in Asia and in Europe. Even as I compose this chapter, I am keenly aware of the benefits I enjoy in access to materials and in the ability to express myself in the dominant language of academia (Altbach 2007:2).

My work with SIL, while not in a linguistic capacity, also impacts how I see language. My views are heavily influenced by both the exceptional people with whom I work and the situations I encounter through my work. These circumstances will naturally bias some of my thinking, but they also, I hope, offer me some insight.

Justice issues in language

Justice is about people, so the relatively young field of *linguistic justice* has come into existence to study and address the important human justice issues that arise surrounding language. As such, linguistic justice *can* be defined very broadly; this chapter will focus particularly on issues facing speakers of non-dominant languages.

The "global language system"

To understand the justice issues facing people, we must understand the disparity in status between their *languages*. Dutch sociologist Abram De Swaan has written extensively about the "global language system," a hierarchy in which local languages are each "satellites" of another more "central" language, which is generally adopted as a mutual second language by neighboring language groups, allowing them to communicate with each other and with native speakers of the central language (2001:1–6).

Each of the approximately one hundred central languages orbits one of twelve "supercentral" languages, which each orbit a single "hypercentral" language—English. Thus, the world, "divided by a multitude of languages", is "connected by a lattice of multilingual speakers" (2001:2).

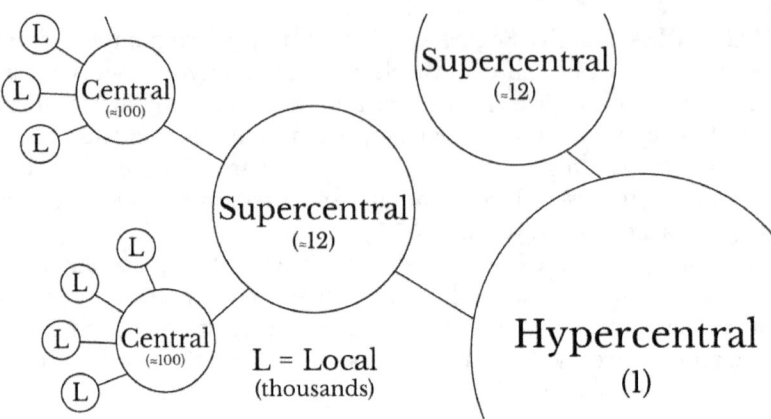

Figure 17.1. Representation of De Swaan's "global language system".

De Swaan's model (2001:1–6) oversimplifies the complexity of linguistic relationships in important ways, but is nonetheless a foundational model in the current linguistic justice conversation and is helpful in recognizing the disparity in status that leads to many of the issues we will explore. The examples detailed here, while not by any means exhaustive, are illustrative of the issues which arise within this imbalance.

Access to services

Many of the critical issues facing speakers of non-dominant satellite languages are encompassed by the question of access to services and opportunities only available via a "central language" or "common communications network" (Gazzola and Grin 2007:98–99). This includes access to healthcare, education, the justice system, and a voice in government.

The type and quality of services varies tremendously from context to context—a justice issue in itself. Within any given context, however, the principle of distributive justice "specifies a fair allocation of a society's income, resources and power" (Mott and Sider 2000:51). Yet, systems that administer this distribution cannot help but be discriminatory: governments "must *use*, and thus *choose*, languages" (Pool 1991:496).

Observing a phenomenon within healthcare which may easily be applied to any service, Emmanuel Scheppers et al. note that a person's lack of proficiency in the language in which a service is offered "inevitably leads to discrimination" and a struggle to "ask questions or to represent themselves or their families" (2006:339).

Discrimination, exploitation, and suppression

While many of the justice issues surrounding language are a natural product of linguistic diversity, some are the acts of those who would take advantage of the vulnerability that a language's status imparts to its speakers. These justice issues are closely related to those which occur naturally but take on a different character through their intentional nature.

Discrimination:
While a lack of access to shared resources may be a regrettable but unintentional effect of a multilingual society, it may also be specifically *targeted* at speakers of non-dominant languages, denying them basic services, housing, or employment opportunities (Alim 2019:188). Language here may be cited either as the rationale for such acts or as the *means* by which this discriminatory behavior is enacted.

Exploitation:
Speakers of non-dominant languages, lacking access to reliable information, are often exploited for their *naïveté*. As an example, during the COVID-19 pandemic some dangerous misinformation had been particularly targeted toward speakers of non-dominant languages (Broderick and Dixit 2020:para. 7, Burke 2020:paras. 17–26).

Vulnerable people are also exploited by relocation to a place where they cannot function in the dominant language—whatever their previous language repertoire. This is particularly conspicuous in human trafficking, where victims' silence is assured by their inability to communicate effectively with authorities (Guilbert 2015:paras. 5–6).

Suppression:
Language suppression has continued to be an issue throughout the world, including within wealthier nations. Notable examples include Spanish suppression of Euskera in the Basque region (Clark 1981:93), American suppression of Spanish in California (Bucholtz et al. 2019:166–167), and Canadian suppression of indigenous languages in residential schools (Truth and Reconciliation Commission of Canada 2015:140).

What is remarkable about each of the above instances is that their stated purposes were for the benefit of the non-dominant language communities, that they could become more proficient in the common tongue. Whether well-meaning or disingenuous, this highlights one of the ways in which our *orientation* to language directs our approaches to linguistic justice.

Orientations and responses

Influential language scholar Richard Ruíz identifies three helpful "orientations" (1984:18–28) to language into which most responses fall: language as a *problem*, as a *right*, and as a *resource*.

Language as problem

Ruíz suggests that the majority of the work in the field sees language as a problem to be overcome (1984:18). Belgian philosopher and economist Philippe Van Parijs, one of the most prolific contributors to the fledgling field of linguistic justice, has written extensively concerning economics-based approaches which exemplify the "language as problem" orientation.

Van Parijs uses De Swaan's model to explain the justice issue as a problem of "asymmetric bilingualism" (2002:72): one language group bears the cost of learning the language of another group, but both groups share the benefit (p. 59).

Seeking a model that provides not only "linguistic efficiency" but "linguistic justice" (Van Parijs 2002:66), Van Parijs advocates for a just distribution of costs, recognizing both the explicit financial cost and the "implicit opportunity cost" of time spent learning a language rather than other learning activities (p. 72).

This approach sees the non-dominant language as the problem and offers as the solution a more equitable cost-sharing for the non-dominant language speakers to learn the dominant language. In cases where it is economically feasible (rare, considering the greatest concentrations of languages are usually in the smallest economies), this cost-sharing could address some of the justice issues faced by language communities. Yet, it reduces the value of language to a "communication technology" (Church and King 1993:338)—essentially, a tool.

Language as right

The most prominent approach to linguistic justice in a rights framework lies in the declaration from the 1996 UNESCO World Conference on Linguistic Rights, which outlines rights for individuals, languages, and "language communities" (1996:5–15).

These rights are ambitious and powerful, but there is little evidence this declaration has been effective (Milambiling 2019:212), and it was never formally adopted by the United Nations (p. 214).

The rights-based approach to linguistic justice has been criticized for its overreach, weakening "potential rights" through unenforceable "claimed rights" (Paulston 1997:82). Ruíz notes that when "the rights of the few are affirmed over those of the many" (1984:24), non-compliance frequently results.

As with the economic approach, a rights-based approach is often not feasible given the means of a society relative to its concentration of languages.

Language as resource

Ruíz advocates for a "resource orientation" (1984:28–29) towards language, recognizing the value that non-dominant languages can add to society. For example, with increasing globalization, languages spoken by immigrants may be of economic or political benefit to societies in relationships with foreign powers where that language is dominant. This orientation dramatically increases the value of some languages but excludes languages that offer no such benefit. Language as a resource still reduces language to a tool.

Limitations of these orientations

The problem and resource orientations both see language in terms of its practical benefit. Though not wrong, this is incomplete. The approaches above could doubtless have significant benefit, but despite Van Parijs' protestations (2002:63), within these models a language is only valuable if it is useful to the dominant population.

The rights orientation assigns inherent value to language for individuals and communities, but with broad strokes that fail to recognize what that value actually is. Clumsy and nearly impossible to implement, the rights approach may have some value in applying political pressure to address justice issues, but has yet to bear significant fruit.

Reorientation

Ruíz's orientations (1984:18–28) remain helpful in identifying justice responses, but I believe we must move beyond choosing a single orientation and seek a more holistic appreciation for what language is and does. For this, we turn to the issue of language death and the question of what is lost.

Language death

Language death has been occurring naturally throughout history (Hale et al. 1992:1), but in recent decades has accelerated at an alarming rate (Romaine 2007:115). Trends in globalization, regionalization, and nationalism have put tremendous pressure on non-dominant language groups to adapt to global, regional, or nationally dominant languages, rather than maintaining their own (Kosonen 2008:171).

Linguist and political commentator John McWhorter questions whether it would be "inherently evil" if the world was reduced to a single spoken language. He suggests that language death is really just "a symptom of people coming together" (2009:67–68). While McWhorter represents a minority position, his question forces us to critically evaluate the value of language.

Some, like Hale et al. (1992:8), see language death on par with the extinction of an animal species. Fellow linguist Peter Ladefoged disagrees, calling the extinction metaphor an appeal "to our emotions, not to our reason" (1992:809–10). If a language community has accepted that the cost of being part of the larger society in which they now find themselves is to give up their language, Ladefoged argues, then "this is a view to which they are entitled", and it would be "paternalistic" (1992) to persuade them otherwise.

Ladefoged (1992) does not confront the justice issues that might force a community to make that choice, nor the consequences they may face as a result. Van Parijs (2000:227) does attempt to address this, but suggests that "injustice is limited to the transition period" and has no long-term effects. Citing the Bretons in France as an example, Van Parijs further argues that "they could not expect the rest of the French population to subsidize forever their learning of French as a second language" (2002:62).

Working among the modern Breton people, Pamela Serota Cote found, through the positive results of the reintroduction of their language, that something *had been* lost (see also chapter 3). Though only a small number were learning the language, high rates of alcoholism and depression declined, and people described the restoration of their language as helping to "complete the whole" (Cote, cited in Wallace 2009:para. 15).

In identifying what is lost with language, Cote drives us to consider what language is.

Language as mediator of experience

The concept of identity is often linked with language, but it is a fuzzy concept with no agreed definition (Joseph 2004:9). Yet, something about language's relationship to the self *does* appear to drive behavior, leading linguists to seek a clearer understanding of this dynamic (Eberhard 2021:11–12).

South African statesman and writer Jan Smuts was one of the first to link language and identity (Joseph 2004:7). Smuts writes that it is through "language that I rise above the mere immediacy of experience … Language gives names to the terms of my experience, and thus through language they are first isolated and abstracted" (1926:254). Smuts imagined that the "apparatus of thought" with which he experienced *everything* was a product of language shared with those with whom he shared the history and development of that language.

Cote's observations among the Bretons over 80 years later echo Smuts. We experience the world, notes Cote, "through a process of interpretation, which occurs in language … The diversity of our languages represents the richness of our expressiveness of Being" (cited in Wallace 2009:para. 12).

If we imagine language to form at a basic level within a community as people interpret their reality, we begin to understand how language loss means losing the space for ways of thinking "which are idiomatic to that language" (Shank Lauwo 2019:88). That is a loss for society as a whole, but far more so for the language community.

As George Steiner observed, every "language maps the world differently," thus when "a language dies, a possible world dies with it" (1998:xiv).

Taking the Bretons as an example, it could be said to be even worse. Upon losing the language which developed alongside them, *forming* and *being formed* by their experiences (Joseph 2004:13), a people may become unmoored from their own experience of the world.

A holistic orientation to language and justice

I believe we need an orientation that recognizes that language is at times a tool and at other times the very means by which we experience reality. Our view of justice must recognize that language is not only one thing, and not always sacred, though sometimes it is. Language is sometimes about utility and sometimes about poetry.

When I attempt to speak Thai, I am limited to very simple phrases, like "Is the durian fruit ripe?" As I eat the durian, though, I moderate the experience through English, with thoughts about the texture, the flavor, and that slight tingle on my tongue that comes from eating a perfectly ripe durian.

For me, Thai is a tool that allows me to complete the *transaction*—much as English is a tool for the fruit seller when my Thai inevitably fails. The *experience*, however, is interpreted entirely through English, much as a wine-taster's experience is interpreted through the terminology they have learned and developed.

I wonder, sometimes, what durian tastes like in Thai.

Missiological implications

As demonstrated by the responses to justice, our orientation has significant implications for our praxis. Given that so much of modern mission happens within both domestic and international contexts where multiple languages are at play, our missiology and praxis must account for the justice implications of the work we do in and around language.

Despite the scarcity of published missiological materials, mission has a long history in this area. Existing missiological frameworks for justice, whether formal or informal, have led individuals and agencies alike to recognize the justice issues faced by speakers of non-dominant languages and act accordingly. SIL's own history owes much to founder Cameron Townsend's encounter with the injustice faced by the Cakchiquel (Kaqchikel) people of Guatemala due to the status of their language (Hefley and Hefley 1984:39–40).

Reframing Babel

There is an underlying default bias against linguistic diversity that comes out of our reading of the Babel story (Hayashi 2017:64). Even beloved theologians casually refer to Babel in negative terms, as a curse that divided humanity (Peterson 2005:25, 242). This narrative is so pervasive that it serves as an archetype even in entirely non-religious sources which reference, for example, "the Babel fiasco" (Van Parijs 2002:63). In this, we have done a tremendous disservice to our fellow believers, to our society, and to the speakers of non-dominant languages who suffer because we have for generations seen their linguistic diversity as a curse and a problem (see chapter 9 for more on reframing Babel).

A re-examination of the Genesis story exposes the falseness of this interpretation. Firstly, in Genesis 2:19, God brought all the animals "to the man to see *what he would name them*" (emphasis added). Allowing humanity to name what God had created based upon our experience of it speaks of a gracious God who does not *impose* language but wishes to see it form naturally.

This natural formation continued and diversified in Genesis 10 prior to the Babel story (Greed 2016:2–3). The disobedience of Babel was, therefore, humanity's *resistance* to the created order wherein language was spreading out and diversifying. Church historian Neal Blough argues convincingly that in the context of the imperial project of Babel, the common language was *not* about communication, but was "an attempt to impose a universal point of view and way of speech upon humanity" (2002:para. 10).

God's response, rather than inflicting linguistic diversity upon humanity as a curse, may rather be seen as a gracious restoration of the right order (Yoder 1997:62–63). In the context of the natural formation and diversification of language in Genesis, the "enforced uniformity" of Babel is an anomaly. It is a linguistic majority imposing itself upon all others. God's intervention set language free once again, allowing it to form and be formed by our unique experiences, just as it was in Eden, and as it was in Genesis 10. God did not impose uniformity upon creation, and would not suffer human empires to do so either.

Thus, Babel is of the order of justice we see in the *ṣĕdāqāh* and *mišpāṭ* of the Old Testament. Such justice is not punitive, but rather restores right order and relationship (Grieb 2006:59–60). By recognizing God's desire for linguistic development and diversity from Genesis 2 and 10, along with the gracious justice dispensed at Babel to restore that order, we not only reframe a story we have long misused but also lay the first stones of a strong theological foundation for a missiology of linguistic justice.

Implications for praxis

Though mission has been responsible for considerable good in the area of language, we must also recognize problematic aspects of our heritage.

Much missional motivation has historically emerged from a questionable interpretation of Matthew 24:14, understanding it as a promise that we may hasten Christ's return through "fulfilling" the Great Commission by communicating the gospel to the entire world (Bosch 2011:323–24).

This motivation not only gives us a clear *language as problem* orientation, but a *people as problem* orientation as well; languages and their speakers stand in the way of Christ's return. Local languages may be engaged, but this motivation leads us to act for expediency, not justice.

Similarly, in the quest for expediency, linguistic mission practitioners have been accused of perpetuating injustices by uncritically engaging in English-language teaching as a means for proselytism (Pennycook and Coutand-Marin 2003:341). The criticism here is twofold: that of luring potential converts in by the promise of English, only to be taught by unqualified evangelists, and of perpetuating the questionable idea that "access to English can be a solution to global inequalities" (p. 347). Even where the motivation *may* include justice, the approach shows little regard for the languages of those reached.

To correct these missteps, we must reorient ourselves to recognize both the justice implications of the work we do and the many roles language plays in our experience of the world. Coupled with a reimagining of Babel, we can build a fresh missiology of language and justice that recognizes a broader picture of how language forms and is formed within communities.

Margaret Doll (2022) writes, "It is on the edges or margins of societies that we find the disenfranchised, and those with weak or compromised ties to the larger group," and mission—not least linguistic mission, as Doll has in mind here—has a long history of engaging with the marginalized. We also have a rich missiology of contextualization, which recognizes that the gospel is not transmitted but rather reincarnated within cultures (Aram I 1999:32).

It is through this incarnation that our holistic approach to language as an integral part of the person will bear fruit. While we may have opportunities for advocacy among governments, our quest for righteousness and justice, for *şĕdāqāh* and *mišpāt*, leads us to look behind the languages to see the people who value them. Our concern is not for language preservation simply to preserve knowledge, but for the wholeness of people, communities, and relationships.

Conclusion

This chapter provides an overview of the disparity in status between languages and the justice issues that have resulted. It explores responses to these issues through the framework of Ruíz's three orientations, before offering an alternative orientation that accounts for the *multiple* ways in which language is part of our lives, whether as a simple tool or as the mediator of our existential experience.

It concludes by exploring the missiological implications of these findings and proposing at least the beginnings of a missiology of linguistic justice based on a reframing of the Genesis accounts of language leading up to and including Babel.

In this reading of Genesis, we can see that linguistic justice is not a new fad or concern, but something which has always been part of God's good design. People's languages impact their lives in ways we do not yet fully understand, but which we can measure. Through language, we experience the world and assign meaning to our experiences. By intentionally and critically engaging with a missiology of language and justice that recognizes the justice implications of work in and around language, we can inform and reform mission praxis to cultivate a world in which none are forced to choose between their survival and their languages.

References

Alcade, Javier. 2015. Linguistic justice: An interdisciplinary overview of the literature. *Amsterdam working papers in multilingualism* 3:27–96. SSRN Electronic Journal. https://doi.org/10.2139/ssrn.2630104.

Alim, H. Samy. 2019. (De)Occupying language. In Netta Avineri, Laura R. Graham, Eric J. Johnson, Robin Conley Riner, and Jonathan Rosa (eds.), *Language and social justice in practice*, 184–192. New York, NY: Routledge.

Altbach, Philip G. 2007. The imperial tongue: English as the dominating academic language. *International Higher Education* 49:2–4. https://ejournals.bc.edu/index.php/ihe/article/view/7986.

Aram I. 1999. The incarnation of the gospel in cultures: A missionary event. In James A. Scherer and Stephen B. Bevans (eds.), *New directions in mission and evangelization 3: Faith and culture*, 29–41. Maryknoll, NY: Orbis Books.

Barram, Michael D. 2018. *Missional economics: Biblical justice and Christian formation.* The Gospel and Our Culture Series. Grand Rapids, MI: Eerdmans.

Benson, Carol, and Kimmo Kosonen, eds. 2013. *Language issues in comparative education: Inclusive teaching and learning in non-dominant languages and cultures.* Comparative and International Education: A Diversity of Voices 24. Rotterdam: Sense Publishers.

Blough, Neal. 2002. From the Tower of Babel to the peace of Jesus Christ: Christological, ecclesiological and missiological foundations for peacemaking. *Mennonite Quarterly Review* 76(1):7+.

Bosch, David J. 2011. *Transforming mission: Paradigm shifts in theology of mission.* Twentieth anniversary edition. American Society of Missiology Series 16. Maryknoll, NY: Orbis Books.

Broderick, Ryan, and Pranav Dixit. 2020. India is in the middle of a coronavirus YouTube frenzy, and it's going to get people killed. BuzzFeed News, 19

February 2020. https://www.buzzfeednews.com/article/ryanhatesthis/the-most-popular-youtube-videos-about-the-coronavirus-are.

Bucholtz, Mary, Dolores Inés Casillas, and Jin Sook Lee. 2019. California Latinx youth as agents of sociolinguistic justice. In Netta Avineri, Laura R. Graham, Eric J. Johnson, Robin Conley Riner, and Jonathan Rosa (eds.), *Language and social justice in practice*, 166–175. New York, NY: Routledge.

Burke, Fintan. 2020. The dangers of misinformation and neglecting linguistic minorities during a pandemic. *Horizon: The EU Research & Innovation Magazine*, 16 April 2020. https://projects.research-and-innovation.ec.europa.eu/en/horizon-magazine/dangers-misinformation-and-neglecting-linguistic-minorities-during-pandemic.

Church, Jeffrey, and Ian King. 1993. Bilingualism and network externalities. *The Canadian Journal of Economics* 26(2):337–345. https://doi.org/10.2307/135911.

Clark, Robert P. 1981. Language and politics in Spain's Basque provinces. *West European Politics* 4(1):85–103. https://doi.org/10.1080/01402388108424307.

De Swaan, Abram. 2001. *Words of the world: The global language system*. Cambridge, UK: Polity.

Doll, Margaret. 2022. Language and the redemptive word of God. In Greed and Kruger, 139–149.

Eberhard, David. 2021. Identity choices of minoritized communities: Testing the identity construction factors. In J. Stephen Quakenbush and Gary F. Simons, (eds.), *Language and identity in a multilingual, migrating world*, 11–33. Dallas, TX: SIL International.

Gazzola, Michele, and François Grin. 2007. Assessing efficiency and fairness in multilingual communication: Towards a general analytical framework. *AILA Review* 20(1):87–105. https://doi.org/10.1075/aila.20.08gaz.

Gorman, Michael J. 2015. *Becoming the gospel: Paul, participation, and mission*. The Gospel and Our Culture Series. Grand Rapids, MI: Eerdmans.

Greed, Michael P. 2016. Towards a theology of language diversity. https://www.academia.edu/24802794/Towards_a_Theology_of_Language_Diversity.

Grieb, A. Katherine. 2006. "So that in him we might become the righteousness of God" (2 Cor 5:21): Some theological reflections on the Church becoming justice. *Ex Auditu* 22:58–80.

Guilbert, Kieran. 2015. App aims to help trafficking victims break the language barrier. *Reuters*, 21 May 2015. https://www.reuters.com/article/usa-trafficking-apps-idUSL5N0YC25B20150521.

Hale, Ken, Michael Krauss, Lucille J. Watahomigie, Akira Y. Yamamoto, Colette Craig, LaVerne Masayesva Jeanne, and Nora C. England. 1992. Endangered languages. *Language* 68(1):1–42. https://doi.org/10.2307/416368.

Hayashi, Larry S. 2017. The blessing of Babel: A theology of languages. CanIL Electronic Working Papers 3:64–76. https://www.canil.ca/wordpress/student-services/academic-resources/electronic-working-papers/.

Hefley, James, and Marti Hefley. 1984. *Uncle Cam: The story of William Cameron Townsend, founder of the Wycliffe Bible Translators and the Summer Institute of Linguistics.* Huntington Beach, CA: Wycliffe Bible Translators.

Joseph, John E. 2004. *Language and identity: National, ethnic, religious.* New York, NY: Palgrave Macmillan.

Kosonen, Kimmo. 2008. Literacy in local languages in Thailand: Language maintenance in a globalised world. *International Journal of Bilingual Education and Bilingualism* 11(2):170–188.

Ladefoged, Peter. 1992. Another view of endangered languages. *Language* 68(4):809–811.

McWhorter, John. 2009. The cosmopolitan tongue: The universality of English. *World Affairs* 172(2):61–68.

Milambiling, Joyce. 2019. The universal declaration of linguistic rights. In Netta Avineri, Laura R. Graham, Eric J. Johnson, Robin Conley Riner, and Jonathan Rosa (eds.), *Language and social justice in practice*, 208–216. New York, NY: Routledge.

Mott, Stephen, and Ronald J. Sider. 2000. Economic justice: A biblical paradigm. *Transformation: An International Journal of Holistic Mission Studies* 17(2):50–63. https://doi.org/10.1177/026537880001700202.

Paulston, Christina Bratt. 1997. Language policies and language rights. *Annual Review of Anthropology* 26:73–85. https://doi.org/10.1146/annurev.anthro.26.1.73.

Pennycook, Alastair, and Sophie Coutand-Marin. 2003. Teaching English as a missionary language. *Discourse: Studies in the Cultural Politics of Education* 24(3):337–353. https://doi.org/10.1080/0159630032000172524.

Peterson, Eugene H. 2005. *Christ plays in ten thousand places: A conversation in spiritual theology.* Grand Rapids, MI: Eerdmans.

Pool, Jonathan. 1991. The official language problem. *American Political Science Review* 85(2):495–514. https://doi.org/10.2307/1963171.

Romaine, Suzanne. 2007. Preserving endangered languages. *Language and Linguistics Compass* 1(1-2):115–132. https://doi.org/10.1111/j.1749-818X.2007.00004.x.

Ruíz, Richard. 1984. Orientations in language planning. *NABE Journal* 8(2):15–34. https://doi.org/10.1080/08855072.1984.10668464.

Scheppers, Emmanuel, Els van Dongen, Jos Dekker, Jan Geertzen, and Joost Dekker. 2006. Potential barriers to the use of health services among ethnic minorities: A review. *Family Practice* 23(3):325–348. https://doi.org/10.1093/fampra/cmi113.

Shank Lauwo, Monica. 2019. Ubuntu translanguaging and social justice: Negotiating power and identity through multilingual education in

Tanzania. In Netta Avineri, Laura R. Graham, Eric J. Johnson, Robin Conley Riner, and Jonathan Rosa (eds.), *Language and social justice in practice*, 88–96. New York, NY: Routledge.
Smuts, Jan Christiaan. 1926. *Holism and evolution*. London: Macmillan.
Steiner, George. 1998. *After Babel: Aspects of language and translation*. Third edition. Oxford: Oxford University Press.
Swartley, Willard M. 2006. The relation of justice/righteousness to *shalom/ eirēnē*. *Ex Auditu* 22:29–53.
Truth and Reconciliation Commission of Canada. 2015. *Canada's residential schools: The history, Part 1 Origins to 1939*. The Final Report of the Truth and Reconciliation Commission of Canada. Vol. 1. Montreal: McGill-Queen's University Press. https://archives.nctr.ca/NCTR-EDU-003-001-016.
UNESCO. 1996. World conference on linguistic rights: Barcelona declaration. Barcelona, Spain: United Nations Educational Scientific and Cultural Organization. https://unesdoc.unesco.org/ark:/48223/pf0000104267.
Van Parijs, Philippe. 2000. The ground floor of the world: On the socio-economic consequences of linguistic globalization. *International Political Science Review* 21(2):217–233. https://doi.org/10.1177/0192512100212006.
Van Parijs, Philippe. 2002. Linguistic justice. *Politics, Philosophy & Economics* 1(1):59–74. https://doi.org/10.1177/1470594X02001001003.
Wallace, Lane. 2009. What's lost when a language dies. *The Atlantic*, 10 November 2009. https://www.theatlantic.com/national/archive/2009/11/whats-lost-when-a-language-dies/29886/.
Wolterstorff, Nicholas. 2006. Teaching justly for justice. *International Journal of Christianity and Education* 10(2):23–37. https://journals.sagepub.com/doi/10.1177/205699710601000202.
Yoder, John H. 1997. *For the nations: Essays evangelical and public*. Grand Rapids, MI: Eerdmans.

Tsadhe

*Your statutes are always righteous;
give me understanding that I may live.
(Psalm 119:144)*

18

Language and Poverty

M. Paul Lewis[1]

Christians commonly accept the Scriptures as a record (and foretelling) of God's revelatory acts in time and space, of his communication of his nature, and of his restorative and redemptive acts in history, past and future. We very properly describe those collected writings as God's word. In this chapter I want to focus on that activity of restoration and the role given to human agents by the God who delighted in walking and talking with people in the cool of the day (Gen 3:8). God's mission, mediated through language, provides the opportunity to bless the nations. Alleviating poverty should be seen as an end in itself; Christ-followers should view themselves as instruments in God's mission to restore, reconcile, and bless. Rather than a deficit, poverty represents opportunity for growth, development, and blessing.

Christ himself highlighted this as the focus of his mission when he quoted from Isaiah, "The Spirit of the Lord is on me, because he has anointed me to proclaim good news to the poor. He has sent me to proclaim freedom for the prisoners and recovery of sight for the blind, to set the oppressed free" (Luke 4:18).

---

[1] My thanks to David Eberhard, Steve Echerd, and Donald Kidd for helpful comments and suggestions on earlier drafts of this paper. All remaining shortcomings are my own.

What is poverty?

The popular notion of poverty is that it is a deficit, a state of not having enough material goods nor the means to acquire them. Yet scholars of development have identified for us that poverty is a multi-dimensional phenomenon (Chambers 1983, Duncan 2008, Myers 1999, Samuel 1995). Robert Chambers (1983) identifies poverty as being more than material and speaks of poverty as a state of entanglement in a web of causes and reinforcement mechanisms. Vinay Samuel (1995) puts a face on poverty by focusing on it not so much as a status or condition but as the lived experience of human beings who deal with challenges of various kinds in their daily lives. Bryant Myers (1999) moves that perspective from the individual to the communal by focusing on the "household" as a primary center of poverty. And it bears pointing out that all of us as individuals, families, communities, societies, and cultures, in one way or another, are poor in some aspect of our lives. Henri Nouwen, a notable advocate for the poor in the Roman Catholic tradition, describes it in this way:

> Poverty has many forms. We have to ask ourselves: "What is my poverty?" Is it lack of money, lack of emotional stability, lack of a loving partner, lack of security, lack of safety, lack of self-confidence? Each human being has a place of poverty. (Nouwen 1997)

This should keep us from embracing the notion that there are those who have and those who have not and steer us away from a paternalistic or imperialist model of service and development. The notion of "walking with the poor" (Myers 1999) and incarnational ministry (that is, serving in and with communities) must be our starting point. As Immanuel himself entered our world and walked with us, offering life in abundance that we may flourish in his love, even so, believers are sent to walk with the poor in such a way that they, too, may experience the abundant life God desires for all people (see also chs. 2 and 3). In the development community, including language development practitioners, there has been a shift away from the deficit model to adopting a more positive approach of appreciative inquiry. This approach focuses not on what is lacking but on what is desired as well as on existing and potential resources (Bushe 1998, Marmor 2005).

Five faces of poverty

Malcolm Duncan (2008) identifies five "faces" of poverty. Three are the better-known deficits of material goods (hunger, health, economic and race-based deprivation), civic participation (social injustice, inequality, human trafficking, access to education), and, of particular interest to missiologists and Bible translation agencies, spiritual poverty, including what has more recently been termed "Bible poverty". The two other faces of poverty identified by Duncan, aspirational poverty and identity poverty, are often only referred to implicitly. Many of those who talk about development and addressing the issues of poverty tend to focus on feeding the hungry, healing the sick, educating the disenfranchised, working for justice, and, above all, providing access to the Bread of Life. Loss of identity and loss of the ability to foresee and aspire to a better future (the flourishing of all people) are rarely identified as issues that need special attention. It is to these faces of poverty that the discipline of linguistics has particular relevance.

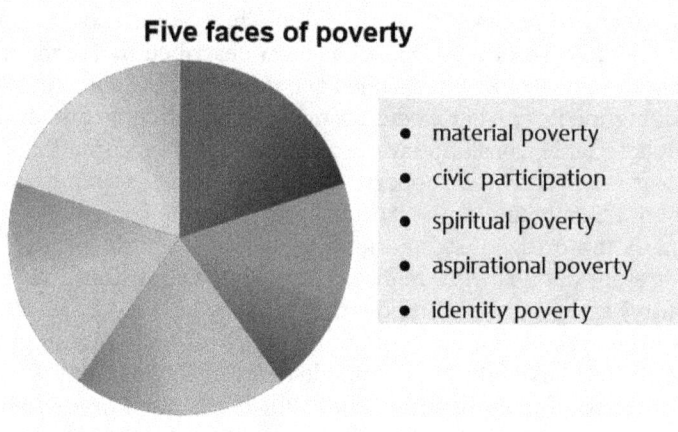

Figure 18.1. Duncan's five faces of poverty.

Identity poverty and aspirational poverty are inextricably connected with the role of language and its uses as a creator and marker of identity. Though all of the faces of poverty described by Duncan are societal in nature, for convenience, I will merge identity and aspirational poverty under the rubric of "social poverty" as a way to distinguish them from economic, civic, and spiritual poverty. This approach gives us a window into how "language work" extends beyond (without replacing) Bible translation and other areas of Christian ministry, yet remains within the contours of God's mission.

Identity poverty

Duncan describes identity poverty as "a poverty that is deeply embedded in the psyche of individuals, even whole communities throughout their history. It is a poverty that springs from being undervalued persistently. It is the sense that the community you are a part of is worthless" (2008:161).

Lewis (Lewis and Simons 2016) describes how the early roots of SIL's work were grounded in an understanding that, along with the beginnings of a Bible translation project (indeed, integral to that project), there were a variety of efforts aimed at appreciating and improving the self-image of the people of Tetelcingo, the rural town in Mexico where SIL finds its roots. Cameron Townsend encountered identity poverty and met it with vegetable and flower gardens, piped-in water, and a clock in the town square, all demonstrating a profound interest in the evident needs of the people of that "miserable little town" (Svelmoe 2008). It seems that, for Townsend, this approach was more instinct than pre-planned strategy. Based on his own comments, Townsend may have understood those development activities as more of a means to achieve his ends, rather than as an end in themselves (cf. Pittman and Townsend 1987). It has been described by Harmelink et al. (2016) as a "see-do" strategy: see a need and do something about it. Whatever the underlying ideology, that *modus operandi* set an example and established a pattern where Bible translation was not divorced from incarnational holistic development work and was supported by medical, educational, and policy advocacy both locally and at the national level in some contexts.

For many minoritized and marginalized communities, identity poverty is a very present and growing reality. It is a major contributor to language (and identity) endangerment and death.

It has been argued that if a community opts to abandon its language and identity, outsiders have no right to impede that desire. That may well be true in terms of decision making and agency, but it has been argued elsewhere (Lewis and Simons 2016) that outsiders do have a role to play in assisting those communities in making an informed decision about their own future by providing awareness of the options that are available to them and by offering perspective on the real costs and benefits of any decisions they may (fail to) make. Moreover, there are now calls among applied linguists to go beyond language preservation and to engage more deeply with minoritized communities, as abandonment of those communities rises to the level of an ethical issue in the academic world (Roche 2020). In many cases, identity can be sustained, oral use of the language for some functions can be secured, and, more rarely, written use of the language can be introduced, if not fully and securely established. In the worst-case scenario, informed and sensitive outsiders can assist those communities that choose to engage in language and identity shift in a kind of linguistic hospice care that eases the transition from one language and identity to another, walking with the identity poor through the valley of the shadow of death, in a manner of speaking.

Aspirational poverty

Where identity poverty speaks of a lost past, aspirational poverty, according to Malcolm Duncan (2008:161) is "aspirational poverty for the future". "This poverty exhibits itself in the conviction that an individual or community cannot change—that change itself is impossible." Duncan goes on to say: "It is perhaps the most harrowing thing to witness because it is the witnessing of the slow steady death of a person's or a community's hope" (2008:162).

Identity poverty and aspirational poverty often go hand-in-hand as the devaluation of a past identity seldom provides much motivation to carry that identity into the future, especially if there are no perceivable benefits to be gained. That poverty is multiplied when not only are there no perceivable benefits but when even the possibility of change is experienced as being far out of reach. Identity poverty and aspirational poverty are two sides of the same coin: social poverty.

Social scientists also speak of a deep-rooted hegemony where the dominant community's negative perceptions of the minoritized community, expressed verbally and enacted systemically, are adopted by the members of the minoritized community themselves. In those cases, community members actively work to shed their identity, including their language and any other markers of that identity, committing societal suicide (e.g., Denison 1977). Children raised in such an environment of self-loathing cannot avoid being scarred by what they don't see and when they are not allowed to hear about their heritage.

We need only look at Native American communities in the USA, First Nations in Canada, and Aboriginal communities in Australia to see the long-term effects of social poverty. There is evidence that social problems such as alcoholism, drug addiction, juvenile delinquency, and suicide occur with greater frequency in communities where there is a longstanding history of negative perceptions associated with the local identity and where the language of primary identity is disparaged and little used (Ball et al. 2013, Chandler and Lalonde 1998, Hallett et al. 2007, McIvor et al. 2009). Social problems often arise when community values can no longer be transmitted from elders to youth because of intergenerational language shift and the language barrier it creates within families (see chapter 20 for more on language shift). Young people then look to their peers as the source of their identity, and gangs and urban clans become the unit of social organization that is most salient in creating meaningful relationships and an affirming sense of identity. This correlation between social poverty and social disruption is even stronger when there is no evidence that there is any way out of that hopeless status. Remedial efforts often attempt to address these symptoms without addressing the underlying hopelessness of social poverty.

The sixth face of poverty: Linguistic poverty

In light of the above, we can add one more label to the taxonomy of poverty: linguistic poverty. This poverty is not the lack of proficiency in a particular language but rather the inability to fully access a linguistic repertoire that adequately meets the needs and aspirations of the community. In some cases a linguistically poor community is deprived of opportunities by being confined to a monolingual repertoire which is inadequately developed to meet their current needs and desires. There is a space for this heritage language, but it is small and cramped. When education in their language is unavailable, when life-crucial bodies of knowledge, both "traditional ecological knowledge" (Grenoble and Whitecloud 2014) and external Western scientific knowledge are only accessible in a language they do not speak or understand, when communication between the generations is disrupted, and when hope is only held out by means of language and identity shift, linguistic poverty becomes one of the facets of social poverty.

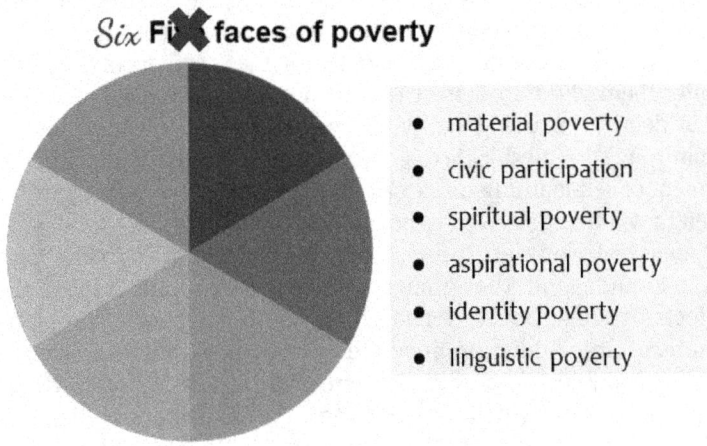

Figure 18.2. Six faces of poverty.

The role of language in addressing social poverty

In many cases, bilingualism becomes a doorway out of social poverty, with an associated decline in use of the heritage language. Aspirational goals are perceived to be achievable only through a different language and identity, and the heritage language is retained in fewer and fewer domains of use as increased levels of proficiency in the more useful dominant language are sought and achieved. In some cases, the link between language and identity is ultimately broken or only weakly retained as the distinctive heritage identity is clothed in a new set of linguistic and cultural markers.

Ethnographic self-examination is perhaps the most thorough way for a community to evaluate the status of social poverty through extensive interviewing and observation, but an assessment of intergenerational language transmission may be a useful proxy, as most parents want their children to flourish in every way possible, and language choice is one indicator of what the community's perception of the most beneficial identity might be.

Frequently those choices are based on popular misperceptions of how languages are acquired, and it takes only a few interviews to find out why parents are making those decisions on behalf of the next generation.

Gary Simons (2011) has proposed that language development can be understood as the reconfiguration of the languages and their functions within a community, adding or changing what the languages in a particular linguistic repertoire are used for. One way not to abandon minoritized communities and to walk with the linguistically poor is to focus holistically on all of the faces of poverty but especially on the social poverty that produces linguistic poverty. This can be accomplished by walking with those communities as they evaluate their identity and their aspirational goals and how best to adjust their linguistic repertoire to meet those goals.

Conclusion: Poverty makes a good host

The work of language development can be understood as an activity that missional linguists are uniquely equipped to carry out, but also particularly charged to carry out in the name of Immanuel, the God who not only speaks to us but who walks with us, whatever our condition and wherever we are. Rather than a deficit, poverty represents opportunity for growth, development, and blessing. Henri Nouwen speaks powerfully to this role for those of us who choose to walk with the linguistically poor.

> Poverty is the quality of the heart that makes us relate to life, not as a property to be defended but as a gift to be shared. Poverty is the constant willingness to say good-bye to yesterday and move forward to new, unknown experiences. Poverty is the inner understanding that the hours, days, weeks, and years do not belong to us but are the gentle reminders of our call to give, not only love and work, but life itself, to those who follow us and will take our place. He or she who cares is invited to be poor, to strip himself or herself from the illusions of ownership, and to create some room for the person looking for a place to rest. The paradox of care is that poverty makes a good host. When our hands, heads, and hearts are filled with worries, concerns, and preoccupations, there can hardly be any place left for the stranger to feel at home. (Nouwen 2024)

Hear again the words of Jesus: "Looking at his disciples, he said:

> 'Blessed are you who are poor,
>   for yours is the Kingdom of God.
> Blessed are you who hunger now,
>   for you will be satisfied.
> Blessed are you who weep now,
>   for you will laugh.' " (Luke 6:20–21)

References

Ball, Jessica, Ken Moselle, and Sarah Moselle. 2013. Contributions of culture and language in Aboriginal head start in urban and northern communities to children's health outcomes: A review of theory and research. Division of Children, Seniors and Healthy Development, Health Promotion and Chronic Disease Prevention Branch, Public Health Agency of Canada. https://ecdip.org/wp-content/uploads/2022/01/Language-Culture-Child-Health-Theory-Research-Ball-Moselle-Moselle.pdf.

Bushe, Gervase R. 1998. Five theories of change embedded in appreciative inquiry. Presented at the 18th Annual World Congress of Organization Development, Dublin, Ireland, July 14–18, 1998. Published in David L. Cooperrider, Peter F. Sorenson, Jr., Therese F. Yeager, and Diana Whitney (eds.), *Appreciative inquiry: An emerging direction for organization development*, 2001:117–127. Champaign, IL: Stipes, and in David L. Cooperrider, Peter F. Sorenson, Jr., Therese F. Yeager, and Diana Whitney (eds.), *Appreciative inquiry: Foundations in positive organization development*, 2005:121–132. Champaign, IL: Stipes. https://www.gervasebushe.ca/ai5.pdf.

Chambers, Robert. 1983. *Rural development: Putting the last first*. Essex, UK: Longman Scientific & Technical.

Chandler, Michael J., and Christopher Lalonde. 1998. Cultural continuity as a hedge against suicide in Canada's First Nations. *Transcultural Psychiatry* 35(2):191–219.

Denison, Norman. 1977. Language death or language suicide? *International Journal of the Sociology of Language* (IJSL) 12:13–22.

Duncan, Malcolm. 2008. Poverty: What does it look like and can we rise to the challenge? In Marijke Hoek and Justin Thacker (eds.), *Micah's challenge. The Church's response to the global poor*, 151–163. Milton Keynes, UK: Paternoster Press.

Grenoble, Lenore A., and Simone S. Whitecloud. 2014. Conflicting goals, ideologies and beliefs in the field. In Peter K. Austin and Julia Sallabank (eds.), *Endangered languages: Beliefs and ideologies in language endangerment, documentation and revitalisaton*, 337–354. Oxford: Oxford University Press.

Hallett, Darcy, Michael J. Chandler, and Christopher E. Lalonde. 2007. Aboriginal language knowledge and youth suicide. *Cognitive Development* 22(3):392–399.

Harmelink, Bryan, Francis Viscount, Andy Clark, Woza Olla Woyita, Grace Chou, Phil Smith, Larry Jones, David Ross, and Manna Mondal. 2016. How does God use language in what he's doing in the world? SIL International. https://drive.google.com/file/d/1u67XAAtdFjeEgt9xNPjsrcRtBU7ZDv5X/view?usp=sharing.

Lewis, M. Paul, and Gary F. Simons. 2016. *Sustaining language use: Perspectives on community-based language development*. Dallas, TX: SIL International.

Marmor, Thomas W. 2005. The added value of appreciative inquiry and results based management for language programs. Ms.

McIvor, Onowa, Art Napoleon, and Kerissa M. Dickie. 2009. Language and culture as protective factors for at-risk communities. *International Journal of Indigenous Health* 5(1):6–25.

Myers, Bryant L. 1999. *Walking with the poor: Principles and practices of transformational development*. New York, NY: Orbis Books.

Nouwen, Henri. 1997. Our poverty, God's dwelling place. In *Bread for the journey: A daybook of wisdom and faith*, 18 August 1997. New York: HarperCollins.

Nouwen, Henri. 2024. Poverty is a quality of the heart. Henri Nouwen Society, 19 August 2024. https://henrinouwen.org/meditation/poverty-is-a-quality-of-the-heart/.

Pittman, Richard S., and William Cameron Townsend. 1987. *One ship sails east*. Waxhaw, NC: Summer Institute of Linguistics.

Roche, Gerald. 2020. Abandoning endangered languages: Ethical loneliness, language oppression, and social justice. *American Anthropologist* 122(1):164–169. https://doi.org/10.1111/aman.13372.

Samuel, Vinay. 1995. A theological perspective. In Tetsunao Yamamori, Bryant L. Myers, and David Conner (eds.), *Serving with the poor in Asia: Case studies in holistic ministry*, 145–154. Monrovia, CA: MARC.

Simons, Gary F. 2011. On defining language development. Paper presented at the International Conference on Language Conservation and Documentation, University of Hawaii-Manoa, 11–13 February 2011.

Svelmoe, William Lawrence. 2008. *A new vision for missions: William Cameron Townsend, the Wycliffe Bible Translators, and the culture of early evangelical faith missions, 1896–1945*. Tuscaloosa, AL: The University of Alabama Press.

Qoph

*I rise before dawn and cry for help;
I have put my hope in your word.
(Psalm 119:147)*

19

Education and Language Policy Development as Components of Holistic Ministry in Multilingual Contexts

Catherine M. B. Young

Introduction

Using language to communicate is to engage in one of the most fascinating gifts of God. Communication is not limited to the human species, but the nuance and complexity of human languages is unique in its enabling interaction with others and with God himself. Language is embedded in the very act of creation when God spoke the universe into existence, and is identified throughout Scripture as the means of connection between God and the people he created.

Through the 1997 Lausanne consultation in Haslev, Denmark, the Theology and Strategy Working Group of the Lausanne Committee for World Evangelization encouraged the global Church to move from viewing the multiplicity of cultures (and, by association, languages) as a problem complicating the sharing of the gospel to a position where they celebrate the diversity of cultures as God's gift to the Church and a means by which the true fullness of his good news and the reality of his kingdom may be discerned (Lausanne Movement 1997). This chapter explores the role of language policy and planning (LPP) among people, churches, and organizations working in any given language community. The goal of approaching planning and policy development through language is to facilitate a context where individuals and groups are participating as legitimate decision makers and advocates about the future of their own language and culture. The desired outcome is to enable a linguistic and educational environment where people can live confidently in their identity in Christ as children of God.

This chapter begins with an overview of language policy and planning, that is, the assessment and actions related to language and development initiatives. Language policy and planning advocates recognize the validity and value of all languages and those who speak them. Often, those who speak lesser-known languages struggle or even suffer abuse or ostracism because of the languages they speak or the community to which they belong. They are marginalized, ignored, or oppressed, unable to flourish in their own communities or to engage with wider swathes of national and global populations, because of attitudes toward them based on their language and culture. Thus, language and development activities need to be embedded within a rigorous understanding of the social, political, and economic contexts in which language use occurs and the purposes for which the language repertoire is used.

With a clear understanding of the importance of LPP for the flourishing of people, this chapter then weaves together its significance within the mission of God. Holistic mission, including language development and Bible translation, is inextricably embedded in God's design for the world. The church cannot ignore its responsibility to engage in language development as part of its calling into God's mission.[1]

Language use: Different tools for different purposes

When we consider our daily lives, we use different tools for different purposes and wear different clothes on different occasions. Similarly, in each interaction we have, we need to think about the ways in which different languages or different varieties of a language are used for different purposes when we consider different contexts, different audiences, and different events. Our social and interpersonal competence directs us to make appropriate decisions on language use.

---

[1] Portions of this paper have been adapted from Catherine M. B. Young's 2011 PhD dissertation, "Enablers and constraints of an effective and sustainable mother tongue-based multilingual education policy in the Philippines".

On an individual level, we make decisions about the form—or register—to be used when speaking officially or in a public setting. Those choices may involve being more precise when we articulate words, choosing to select more formal vocabulary (father vs. dad, child vs. kid) or choosing standard forms rather than dialect. Even in a predominantly monolingual context where most participants share the same language, people are continually making choices—sometimes explicitly but often subconsciously—about how language can or should be used when they interact with one another. For example, in a church, there are often agreed but contrasting varieties of a language that are perceived to be appropriate for prayer or discussion in a formal church setting in contrast to a small group or individual context.

These challenges underpin the discipline of language policy and planning.

Language policy and planning

A brief overview of the development of language policy and planning as a sociolinguistic initiative may help in understanding its connection with the mission of God and the responsibility of the Church.

Einar Haugen is credited with developing one of the first models of language planning and the first recorded academic use of the term "language planning" (1966:922–935). He describes four major phases or steps in language planning.

- **Norm Selection:** the choice of a language variety for specific purposes associated with official status or national roles in status planning.
- **Codification:** related to the stabilization of the norm selected and the standardization process in corpus planning (described below).
- **Implementation:** the actions of government agencies, institutions, and writers in adopting and using the selected and codified norm involving (among other things) the production of newspapers, textbooks, and other publications, as well as adoption for mass media.
- **Elaboration:** the expansion of language functions and the adoption of new vocabulary, such as scientific and technical.

However, as Moshe Nahir notes, these steps are theoretical starting points ([1984] 2003:423). Challenges may arise when community members with different language experiences come together to make decisions about language use.

When a language is being written for the first time, decisions are made regarding orthography (agreement on a writing system and selection of a script) and grammatical standards and forms. Gibson Ferguson's (2006:21) three core actions of language planning are:

- **Graphization:** the adoption of a writing system for an oral language and the establishment of spelling and other orthographic conventions such as capitalization and punctuation.

- **Standardization:** the process of one variety of a language becoming widely accepted throughout the speech community.
- **Modernization:** the process of a language becoming the equal of other developed languages as a medium of communication.

Heinz Kloss described two categories of action relating to language planning (Ferguson 2006:28).

- **Status planning:** addressing the function of a language or varieties of a language in society and the rights and responsibilities of the people using the language. Status planning has the aim of changing the status of a language relative to other languages and would usually be done by governments or other officials. Status planning has the potential to either enhance or detract from the prestige of languages in relation to one another.
- **Corpus planning:** in contrast with status planning, corpus planning comprises actions relating to the language itself rather than actions about the use of the language. Thus, standardization of vocabulary and the linguistic forms such as grammatical and phonological alternatives are components of corpus planning. Outputs of corpus planning could potentially include graphization, the development of an agreed set of grammatical rules and the development and publication of dictionaries and literature in the language.

About twenty years after the work of Haugen, Ferguson, and Kloss, Robert Cooper added an additional dimension to these frameworks (or models) associated with language planning, asking eight analytical questions which Dennis E. Ager summarizes as:

> What actors attempt to influence what behaviours of which people for what ends under what conditions by what means through what decision-making process with what effect? (2001:6)

Cooper situates decisions relating to language planning in the domain of social change and planning. The goal is to see an increase in the numbers of people who are using a language, linking that with concepts associated with language maintenance and language revitalization. He refers to this approach as "acquisition planning" (Ferguson 2006:34). Colin Baker describes acquisition planning as the "bedrock of language planning" (2006:50).

Cooper maintains that language planning is most likely to succeed when influential stakeholders are at the core of a movement for change in the ways in which languages are used to enable communities to flourish. Thus, the goals of acquisition planning (Hornberger 2003:452) relate closely to domains such as education, organized religion, mass media, and the workplace.

Governments instruct and permit institutions such as the media and education systems to choose their medium of communication and instruction. Academic and development organizations such as SIL are uniquely positioned to offer an evidence-based contribution to such decision making.

Language policy and planning as a sociolinguistic discipline, then, among other things, advocates for and honors speakers of lesser-known languages, equipping them to determine and achieve their own linguistic, social, educational, and religious goals, thereby contributing to their well-being while strengthening their nation through better understanding and participation. The relative prestige of speakers of different languages affects power relations within nations and between nations. Language planning activities impact the present and are future focused, influencing the context that enables minority language communities to flourish, which, as noted in chapter 3 of this book, is God's desire for all people.

A missiological framework

As we consider the role of Christian agencies such as SIL Global in the domain of language policy and planning, it is critical to first situate such initiatives within a missiological framework. This will create an applied theological perspective that can guide the rationale for engagement.

Bryant Myers considers the impact of a modern worldview on the thinking and practice of Christian activity (1998:143–153). He notes that the separation of evangelism and development is a reflection of a worldview that understands the spiritual and the physical realms of life as being separate and distinct. Such a dichotomy then shapes how Christians understand development. Similarly, Daniel O'Neill notes,

> We must consider the long-range purposes of God to bless all tribes, tongues and nations through His people in whom His very presence dwells in unity. We must see the integral value in being children of God and in doing the works of service for the poor—of both demonstrating His love and proclaiming His greatness as one seamless action. (2020)

Indeed, the very use of the term *development* has potentially divisive implications that "imposes a narrow and linear economic model of development and fails to recognize the need for transformation in so-called developed countries. While we recognize the value of planning, organization, evaluation and other such tools, we believe they must be subservient to the process of building relationships, changing values and empowering the poor." (Chester 2002:20)

Language is one of the defining features of human experience. However, when we examine international development discourse and practices, language and cultural knowledge are often left on the periphery (Taylor-Leech and Benson 2017:339–355, Footitt et al. 2018). Within this statement is an echo of Todd Johnson and Gina Zurlo, who note that "many of the world's most pressing problems are out of sight from mainstream evangelicalism—urban poverty, slum settlements, addiction, slavery" (2014:56).

Christopher Wright summarizes well the theological paradigm that should challenge this disconnect:

> The whole gospel must be drawn from the whole Bible ... For centuries God revealed his passion against political tyranny, economic exploitation, judicial corruption, the suffering of the poor and oppressed, brutality and bloodshed. The laws God gave and the prophets God sent addressed these very matters more than any other issue except idolatry (they regarded such things as idolatry's manifestations). Meanwhile the psalmists regularly cried out in songs of social protest and lament that we tend to screen out of our Christian worship. (2009:23)

Language development, like these other social issues, needs to be brought back into focus as a concern of the worldwide Church.

In light of this, how is the church to understand and engage with language-related initiatives as part of its missional calling? And how do we act as field linguists, sociolinguists, and education specialists to employ our disciplines in a missional context to enable supportive language policies and practices as ministry to marginalized communities, aligning such actions with compassionate service, as described by Wright?

Language policy and planning in a missional context

Language is a cross-cutting issue, inextricably tied to human development.

Nancy Hornberger contends that the discipline of LPP experienced a "resurgence of interest" (2006:24) in the latter part of the twentieth century owing to an increased concern about the spread of English and other global languages, coercive relations due to their power, and issues of language endangerment. David Crystal (2000) describes the perilous status and potential death of many minority languages across the world as a matter of widespread concern, not only among linguists and anthropologists but among all concerned with issues of cultural identity in an increasingly globalized context.

While LPP involves purposeful actions to choose, codify, and promote the use of languages in selected domains (D. Johnson 2013), and education is often the key to enacting LPP decisions, Robert Kaplan contends that LPP barely registers on agendas to support marginalized, non-dominant language communities or, at a macro level, low-income countries (Taylor-Leech and Benson 2017:340). Prestigious languages are used by those in power as a standard against which other languages are assessed (see chapter

17 for more on language and justice). This impacts the access that speakers of local languages have to appropriately designed education and development initiatives. Such limitations stand in opposition to the purposes of God for the peoples of the earth.

Integral mission

Integral mission is now the *modus operandi* of the Lausanne Movement, expressed succinctly in the Cape Town Confession of Faith, which prioritizes the scriptural foundation of the mission of God's people while emphasizing the focus on both individual and societal transformation.

> The Bible declares God's redemptive purpose for creation itself. Integral mission means discerning, proclaiming, and living out the biblical truth that the gospel is God's good news, through the cross and resurrection of Jesus Christ, for individual persons, for society, and for creation. All three are broken and suffering because of sin; all three are included in the redeeming love and mission of God; all three must be part of the comprehensive mission of God's people. (Lausanne Movement 2011)

I believe this is well summarized further in the Cape Town Commitment document as "the salvation we proclaim should be transforming us in the totality of our personal and social responsibilities" (Lausanne Movement 2011:28) or, as described by Dietrich Bonhoeffer, "The church is the church only when it exists for others ... the church must share in the secular problems of ordinary human life, not dominating but helping and serving" (O'Neill 2020).

Participation in holistic mission and ministry can contribute in both top-down sectors and bottom-up domains—confronting injustices enacted upon the marginalized and enabling policymakers and others to recognize equitable policies and practices while journeying with others, including members of non-dominant language communities, to imagine a different world, assess the institutional spaces that work against justice, and work towards their legitimate participation in new structures. It causes us to consider a missiologically informed understanding of the design and delivery of education and development initiatives within multilingual contexts, particularly in relation to partnerships with and actions within national and international development networks. An understanding of such contextualization of education and development practices will empower those on the margins, the poor, the remote, and the less well known.

Global Bible translation efforts and the work of Christian researchers and academics have enabled significant contribution to data and the documentation of the world's languages. However, in some contexts, a move toward language and cultural preservation or revitalization may focus more on documenting the knowledge of the language itself rather than communicating outputs of such research, to impact the human flourishing of the people groups involved.

O'Neill emphasizes the importance of academic rigor and empirical research to produce both qualitative and quantitative data to persuade an "increasingly evidence-based constituency of donors, governments, and multilateral organizations" (2020). He aligns these activities to the scriptural mandate to advocate for the voiceless or the oppressed in the halls of power and shed light on injustices. This theme is also extensively explored by Walter Brueggemann (2018), who describes the ways in which maintaining silence allows the powerful to retain control, and contexts in which marginalized people themselves break repressive silence and speak out.

Post-colonial studies, as alluded to above, lead us to concerns about the ways by which the power dynamics of language use have come into focus. Urbanization and migration have highlighted issues associated with language and identity. These complex realities call for contextual and interdisciplinary approaches to the study of language use, language development efforts, and translation. At the same time, Jayakumar Christian (2014)[2] calls us to theological reflection. We need to recognize both our own identity in Christ and the importance of other people's identity. We need to address the concept of marred identity and poverty on multiple levels:

- **A poverty of being:** A broken sense of identity
- **A poverty of relationships:** Societal relationships working to maintain the entrapment of the marginalized rather than empowering them
- **A poverty of purpose:** A lack of vision for the future and lack of a powerful sense of vocation

Christians advocate for a holistic response to the powerlessness of the poor and for building a sense of self through reconnecting with their God-given identity (Seager 2018). Rigorous academic research, evidence-based advocacy on the potential of local languages for effective education, and development initiatives are not in tension with a compassionate biblical understanding of poverty and marginalization. Rather they complement each other.

As we consider the practical implications of an understanding of LPP in a missiological framework, we need to address issues such as those listed in and discussed by Philip Smith and Matt Wisbey (2013). The complexity of cultural change in an increasingly globalized world is exacerbated in the challenges of interaction between local language communities, supportive actors such as local, national, and international agencies, and policymakers

---

[2] See also https://www.arotahi.org.nz/project/following-the-god-of-the-empty-handed-by-jayakumar-christian/.

within those agencies—those who often dominate access to international development funding.

Participation, particularly in national and international environments, for the identification and framing of supportive policies for education and development has implications for our equipping of Christian workers. Foundationally, there remains a need to build capacity in working across cultures. We need to become reflective practitioners on the themes of cultural anthropology and intercultural communication strategies (Reimer 2017:81). We need to proactively share and implement evidence-based innovative change based on rigorous research. Practitioners in all domains of language and development activity need to develop confidence and competence in interaction with government officials and leadership of international agencies to discuss and demonstrate the viability of local language use in education and development initiatives. Similarly, both practitioners and local and global Christian institutions should have credibility through the development of effective partnerships built on tested principles (Butler 2006) of cooperation and collaboration. Such investment in seeking contextual change requires a commitment to dialogic learning (Vella 2002 and Vella et al. 1997) with foundational practices of healthy listening and reflection.[3]

Conclusion

Wright notes that holistic/integral ministry should be the defining feature of biblical Christian engagement with others (2005:9–12). He critiques the identification of holistic mission as one of the special issue groups at the 2004 Lausanne Forum in Pattaya and emphasizes that, rather than being a discrete issue, holistic ministry should be the foundational *modus operandi* on which all activities are built. Within Christian ministries focused on language and development initiatives, the same challenge exists. Do we identify as those involved in integral mission, where each contribution is seen as valuable in promoting the flourishing of others who are discovering more of their identity in Christ?

We need to carefully examine the multiple paradigms within which faith-based and other non-government organizations focused on minority language communities operate globally. How can our actions and relationships effectively influence government and institutional partnerships and

---

[3] A practical example of the contribution of rigorous research and academic excellence in ethnoarts, descriptive linguistics, mother tongue-based multilingual education, and other disciplines to national and local policy development is documented by UNICEF Thailand (2018). Interagency collaboration between national and local government, multilateral agencies, INGOs and academic institutions supported effective language and development initiatives among the Pattani Malay, a non-dominant language community in a conflict zone in southern Thailand.

opportunities with marginalized communities? Approaches to language planning and policy development need to ask and answer some critical, ideological questions about the ways in which language communities form a collective and invest in their languages with varying degrees of value. The complementary roles of insiders and outsiders (those who are users of a language and those who are not users of that language variety) as the decision makers in relation to the language in focus also need to be scrutinized. There is also a need for rigorous investigation of the implications of international workers operating within a post-colonial environment, as well as greater understanding of the impacts of globalization on language and education policy. This has implications for organizational approaches to increased localization of staffing and identification of appropriate management practices by national and international agencies.

In conclusion, I see a parallel with the work of Nehemiah, who was in a position of influence in the Persian court. He hears that people he cares about (his own people) are in "trouble and disgrace" (Neh 1:1–4) for the wall is broken down and the gates have been burned by fire. Nehemiah asks questions, he listens—and he mourns because of the pain that the people were experiencing. He fasts, prays, and calls on God.

How may the prayerfully guided contributions of our organizations and allies within the complex multilingual systems associated with non-dominant language communities (people who have often been marginalized by the economic and social power structures) enable holistic rather than fragmented interventions that support communities to flourish in the fullness of God's purposes?

References

Ager, Dennis Ernest. 2001. *Motivation in language planning and language policy*. Multilingual Matters 119. Bristol, UK: Multilingual Matters.

Baker, Colin. 2006. *Foundations of bilingualism and bilingual education*. Bilingual Education & Bilingualism 79. Bristol, UK: Multilingual Matters.

Brueggemann, Walter. 2018. *Interrupting silence: God's command to speak out*. Louisville, KY: Westminster John Knox Press.

Butler, Phill. 2006. *Well connected: Releasing power and restoring hope through kingdom partnerships*. Milton Keynes, UK: Authentic.

Chester, Timothy. 2002. *Justice, mercy and humility: The papers of the Micah Network International Consultation on Integral Mission and the Poor*. Milton Keynes, UK: Paternoster Press.

Christian, Jayakumar. 2014. *God of the empty-handed: Poverty, power and the kingdom of God*. Kindle edition. Swindon, UK: Acorn Press Ltd.

Crystal, David. 2000. *Language death*. Cambridge: Cambridge University Press.

Ferguson, Gibson. 2006. *Language planning and education*. Edinburgh Textbooks in Applied Linguistics. Edinburgh, UK: Edinburgh University Press.

Footitt, Hilary, Angela Crack, and Wine Tesseur. 2018. Respecting communities in international development: Languages and cultural understanding. *INTRAC/University of Reading.* http://doras.dcu.ie/23795/1/Listeningzonesreport-EN.pdf.

Haugen, Einar. 1966. Dialect, language, nation. *American Anthropologist* 68(4):922–935.

Hornberger, Nancy H., ed. 2003. *Continua of biliteracy: An ecological framework for educational policy, research, and practice in multilingual settings.* Bilingual Education and Bilingualism 41. Clevedon, UK: Multilingual Matters.

Hornberger, Nancy H. 2006. Frameworks and models in language policy and planning. In Thomas Ricento (ed.), *An introduction to language policy: Theory and method,* 24–41. Malden, MA: Blackwell Publishing.

Johnson, David Cassels. 2013. What is language policy? In David Cassels Johnson, *Language policy,* 3–25. London: Palgrave Macmillan.

Johnson, Todd M., and Gina A. Zurlo. 2014. Global Christianity and global diasporas. In Chandler Im and Amos Yong (eds.), *Global diasporas and mission,* 38–56. Oxford: Regnum Books International.

Lausanne Movement. 1997. Gospel contextualisation revisited. https://www.lausanne.org/content/gospel-contextualisation-revisited.

Lausanne Movement. 2011. The Cape Town Commitment. https://www.lausanne.org/content/ctcommitment#capetown.

Myers, Bryant L. 1998. What makes development Christian? Recovering from the impact of modernity. *Missiology* 26(2):143–153.

Nahir, Moshe. (1984) 2003. Language planning goals: A classification. *Language problems and language planning* 8(3):294-327. In Christina Bratt Paulston and G. Richard Tucker (eds.), *Sociolinguistics: The essential readings,* 423–448. Oxford: Blackwell.

O'Neill, Daniel. 2020. Integrating faith and global health: An applied theological framework. Christian Connection for International Health, 20 June 2020. https://www.ccih.org/integrating-faith-and-global-health-an-applied-theological-framework/.

Reimer, Johannes. 2017. *Missio politica: The mission of church and politics.* Carlisle, UK: Langham Global Library.

Seager, Greg. 2018. Poverty: A marred identity. Christian Health Service Corps, LinkedIn, 11 August 2018. https://www.linkedin.com/pulse/poverty-marred-identity-greg-seager.

Smith, Phil, and Matt Wisbey. 2013. Signposts to identity-based community development. LEAD Asia. https://www.leadimpact.org/ibcd.

Taylor-Leech, Kerry, and Carol Benson. 2017. Language planning and development aid: The (in) visibility of language in development aid discourse. *Current Issues in Language Planning* 18(4):339–355.

UNICEF. 2018. Bridge to a brighter tomorrow: The Patani Malay-Thai Multilingual Education Programme. Bangkok: UNICEF Thailand. https://www.unicef.org/thailand/sites/unicef.org.thailand/files/2018-09/unicef%20Bridge%20to%20Brighter%20Edu-EN-low%20Res.pdf.

Vella, Jane. 2002. *Learning to listen, learning to teach: The power of dialogue in educating adults.* Revised edition. Hoboken, NJ: John Wiley & Sons.

Vella, Jane, Paula Berardinelli, and Jim Burrow. 1997. *How do they know they know? Evaluating adult learning.* Jossey-Bass Higher and Adult Education Series. San Francisco, CA: Jossey-Bass.

Wright, Christopher J. H. 2005. Re-affirming holistic mission: A cross-centered approach in all areas of life. Lausanne World Pulse Archives. Issue 10-2005. https://www.lausanneworldpulse.com/themedarticles-php/61/10-2005.

Wright, Christopher J. H. 2009. Whole gospel, whole church, whole world. Lausanne Movement. https://lausanne.org/content/whole-gospel-whole-church-whole-world. See also Christianity Today 53(10):23. https://www.christianitytoday.com/2009/09/main/.

Young, Catherine M. B. 2011. Enablers and constraints of an effective and sustainable mother tongue-based multilingual education policy in the Philippines. PhD dissertation. Bangor University, Wales. https://research.bangor.ac.uk/portal/files/39864699/C_M_B_YOUNG_PhD_2011_OCR.pdf.

Further Reading

Haugen, Einar. 1987. *Blessings of Babel: Bilingualism and language planning: Problems and pleasures.* Contributions to the Sociology of Language 46. Berlin: Mouton de Gruyter.

Myers, Bryant L. 2011. *Walking with the poor: Principles and practices of transformational development.* Maryknoll, NY: Orbis Books.

Myers, Bryant L. 2017. *Engaging globalization: The poor, Christian mission, and our hyperconnected world.* Mission in global community. Grand Rapids, MI: Baker Academic.

Resh

Your compassion, LORD, is great;
preserve my life according to your laws.
(Psalm 119:156)

20

A Biblical Reflection on Language Shift and Identity

Maik Gibson[1]

Introduction

Once, when teaching in Kenya, I was asked by a Kenyan student, "Can you be a Kikuyu if you don't speak Kikuyu?" as if I, a foreign sociolinguist, would be able to settle the matter of who could be included as a Kikuyu and who couldn't. But the question demonstrates that language and identity are at least often related, and that the matter is complex: if language either determined identity, or had nothing to do with it, I doubt that the question would have been asked. It demonstrates that language and identity are linked, but that the relationship is not a simple one.

We in SIL often work with communities that are minorities in some sense, and are not treated with the same respect that other larger communities may

---

[1] This chapter grew out of material developed by myself and Angharad Evans for teaching Sociolinguistics, linking it to broader missiology, first at Redcliffe College, and now at Moorlands College. I must also acknowledge George and Mary Huttar for getting me started thinking about the sociolinguistics of biblical times.

be. This, of course, is variable. These communities find that other languages have more prestige and utility, which in some cases leads to these languages being adopted not just as means of communication with outsiders, but also within the community, which can lead to the traditional language not being learnt by younger generations—this is language shift.

This chapter questions the missiological response to such situations—where languages are either being lost or in danger of being lost. An associated question is whether this loss of language leads to a loss of identity. Should we therefore work with the community to do all we can to battle this shift? Or are languages just vehicles for self expression such that what language one speaks really has no bearing on one's true self, and therefore a shift of language is of no concern? Does the truth lie somewhere in between, or should the response be contextual?

Rather than trying to settle the question of how language and identity are linked once and for all (an impossible task, no doubt), what I seek to do here is to first examine what Scripture says, whether directly or indirectly, about language and identity. And then I reflect on what this means for those of us who seek to serve the minority communities of the world through their languages, which in many cases are under threat of language shift. I will then seek to set this briefly against the broader context of what is behind language shift, and its implications for communities today.

The Bible's narrative is not focused on language shift, nor even on language itself. Occasionally the biblical writer does draw attention to a difference of language (e.g., Gen 42:23, 2 Kings 18, many verses in Mark and Acts 22) whether because of a multilingual environment or a difference between the language of the narrative and the events. The gift of speech is one of the first things that God gives Adam, who has the right to name animals. The puzzle of linguistic diversity (whether stemming from language shift or accelerated language change) is a theme of the story of the Tower of Babel. But in general, languages are part of the backdrop of the drama, often assumed by the writer to be obvious, needing no comment, which makes interpretation more difficult for us today. I will attempt to document the main language shifts that occurred within the biblical period, and also examine the one case where there was active resistance to language shift.

The languages of the patriarchs

We read that Abraham was called out of Ur of the Chaldees, probably in what is now southern Iraq. What language he spoke we do not know, but given the time and location (both subject to some debate) it could well have been Akkadian, an Eastern Semitic language. It is very unlikely to have been Hebrew, even though Abram is referred to as a Hebrew (probably meaning foreigner) in Genesis 14:13. This is the first time the word *Hebrew* is used in the Bible, and it may surprise us that it is never used in the Hebrew Bible to refer to the language, but only to the people.

The Hebrew language of biblical times is closely related to other languages of Canaan, which belong to the northwestern group of Semitic languages, unlike Akkadian. So, what to make of this? It makes it very unlikely that Hebrew would have been the language that Abraham brought with him from Ur—Hebrew's characteristics fit with other languages of Canaan, not Iraq. So Abraham and his entourage probably arrived in Canaan speaking Akkadian, or something similar. This is consistent with the fact that Abraham's forebears have names which have no clear Hebrew etymology, and the fact that he was renamed while in Canaan. Two generations later we have the first evidence (outside of personal names) of the use of Hebrew in the covenant between Jacob and Laban. Referring to the witness stone, we read in Genesis 31:47 that "Laban called it Jegar Sahadutha, and Jacob called it Galeed"; Jacob named it in Hebrew, and Laban (who had settled in Aram rather than in Canaan) in Aramaic. It is interesting that it is Jacob, the father of the nation of Israel, who is first recorded as using a specific Hebrew word.[2] There is no doubt from this brief cameo of language that at least some of the patriarchs had changed their primary language.

A two-generation timescale for language shift to happen is common, especially when migration has taken place. Along with now being surrounded by people speaking Hebrew, or something like it, we may hypothesize that Abram's act of leaving Ur and its gods (an act of identity in some form) resulted in a greater openness to new language practices. Abram was establishing a new nation; the old identity was no longer seen as useful and we may guess that this building of a new nation left the door open for a language (Canaanite), which, while still used for pagan worship, was not used for the specific paganism that Abram was leaving behind.

Language is next referred to, indirectly, in the episode of Joseph hiding his identity from his brothers by speaking through an interpreter (and therefore in Egyptian). In Egypt, our best guess is that the people of Israel, who lived as a separate people among the Egyptians, maintained Hebrew as their home language, though it is possible that they shifted to Egyptian (not a Semitic language) while in Egypt, and back to a Canaanite language or Hebrew after and during the conquest of Canaan. That Moses' name is Egyptian rather than Hebrew is not good evidence of a shift among the Israelites, as he was named by Egyptians rather than Hebrews. Other names seem to be Hebrew, which suggests that Hebrew was maintained during the four hundred years of exile in Egypt; the Israelites lived as a separate community, with a distinct identity and status; they effectively became slaves and separate from the Egyptians.

---

[2] Apart from personal names, that is.

Pre-exilic period

In the time of the Judges, we notice in the Shibboleth story (Judg 12:6) that the dialects of Hebrew had diversified to the extent of having different phoneme inventories—but this is a case of language evolution (or change) rather than shift.

We next get a clear picture of language use in the story of the siege of Jerusalem in 2 Kings 18. In verse 26 we read:

> Then Eliakim son of Hilkiah, and Shebna and Joah said to the field commander, "Please speak to your servants in Aramaic, since we understand it. Don't speak to us in Hebrew in the hearing of the people on the wall."

Here, it is clear that the common people of Jerusalem were monolingual in Hebrew (named in the text as *Yehudit*, literally "Judean"), and did not have a good understanding of Aramaic, while the more educated officials of the city were able to communicate in Aramaic. This looks like a pattern of elite multilingualism, perhaps similar to eighteenth century Europe, where the educated would be expected to be able to speak and read French alongside their national languages, or the Middle Ages where education would be mainly conducted in Latin. So we have a situation where the people of Israel were primarily monolingual in Hebrew, with certain members of the community being able to speak other languages based on their need for contact with outsiders and their level of education. Aramaic had become the lingua franca of the Near East by this time, despite not being the language of the founders of great empires.

The exile and beyond

The exile to Babylon constituted a great shock to the people of Israel, and at the very least would have meant a widespread acquisition of Aramaic (the interethnic imperial language). Whether and when the majority of the population shifted to Aramaic as their primary language is a matter of some debate, though there are some signs of incipient shift away from Hebrew in the book of Nehemiah. This debate has unfortunately been polemicized to some degree, with some seeming to embrace any evidence as supporting one position or another—whether it be the maintenance of Hebrew as the home language or a two-generation shift to Aramaic during the Babylonian exile (or even a later shift to Greek). This polemic complicates the question as it leads to people on both sides being prone to not weighing the evidence carefully. We will not take a strong position of when (and where) the shift of home language from Hebrew to Aramaic took place, though it seems certain that its seeds were at the very least sown by the exile in Babylon— our main interest remains in what value the Bible places on language shift and maintenance. Interestingly, this was the time that Hebrew started to be no longer written in what we now call paleo-Hebrew script, but in the square Aramaic script that we now often think of as Hebrew script. The use of the older script continued in some manuscripts up until the second century AD, and especially for writing the divine name. Examples of this can be found in some Dead Sea manuscripts—a marginal maintenance of the older form in a very specific context.

In the book of Ezra, recounting events in the fifth century BC, we find that the correspondence between officials in Judea and Artaxerxes, the Persian emperor, was written in Aramaic; the letter in Ezra 4:11–16 is given in Aramaic, and in 4:7 the text mentions that it was written in Aramaic, perhaps as preparation for the textual switch from Hebrew to Aramaic. However, the writing of a letter in Aramaic really does not tell us whether Hebrew was being used at home. In multilingual societies, different languages often serve different functions in different domains (Fasold 1984). A few years later, the reading of the Law by Ezra, which included "making it clear" (Neh 8:8), is sometimes quoted as demonstrating that a shift from Hebrew to Aramaic had occurred, as an interpretation would not have been needed if people spoke Hebrew. However, it is equally possible that the act was merely an explanation, so the verse cannot really serve as evidence of whether or not Hebrew was no longer understood.

However, by the end of the book of Nehemiah, we find direct evidence of some sort of language shift going on among at least some of the younger population of Jerusalem, and this seems to be the only time in the Bible where a specific case of language shift is viewed negatively.

> Moreover, in those days I saw men of Judah who had married women from Ashdod, Ammon and Moab. Half of their children spoke the language of Ashdod or the language of one of the other peoples, and did not know how to speak the language of Judah [*Yehudit*]. (Neh 13:23–24)

Nehemiah's action, however, is not to institute Hebrew classes for children of mixed couples; his focus is to stigmatize marriages with other peoples. The shifting language (Hebrew) in Jerusalem would seem to have been at EGIDS level 6b[3]: this means that not all children were learning the primary language of their parents, but were shifting to another language. This language shift was seen as a sign of how bad things had become with regard to the dilution of the Jewish identity that he was trying to restore.[4]

---

[3] EGIDS: Expanded Graded Intergenerational Disruption Scale. For an explanation, see Lewis and Simons (2010, 2016). Level 6b means the language is "threatened," not always being passed on to the children.

[4] See Tollefson and Williamson (1992) for an anthropological reading of the book of Nehemiah as a cultural revitalization process (p. 322). Venter (2018) sees that the underlying issue behind the concern about marriages is idolatry.

Exactly how to interpret Nehemiah's statement about the language practices of the children is unclear. He may be talking of an inability to speak Hebrew,[5] or that they were using another language at home. Moabite and Ammonite would be close enough to Hebrew to be mutually intelligible, unlike Ashdodite (which seems to indicate the language of the Philistines).

New Testament times

What the state of language shift or maintenance was in Judea and Jerusalem in the first century AD is a matter of some debate. Names of many locations are Aramaic rather than Hebrew, which might indicate language shift, but this could also be because Aramaic had been the language of power for many centuries. However, in Mark's Gospel in particular, we have verbatim reports of Jesus' very words, and the language is, when taken as a whole, unambiguously Aramaic rather than Hebrew. Some instances could be Hebrew, but there are no cases where it could not be Aramaic. So, by Occam's razor[6], we assume that it is all Aramaic. This is consistent with the wider view that the Jewish population of Galilee had shifted to Aramaic as their vernacular by this time. This does not preclude a knowledge of Hebrew through study, its use in the synagogue (where the Aramaic targum[7] may also have been used), and through contact with those in Judea who may perhaps have continued to use Hebrew as a vernacular. By this point there were two languages into which the Hebrew Bible had been translated—Greek and Aramaic. Judaism is a faith with a particular focus on observance of the law, and, therefore, instructions for how to keep it need to be comprehensible, which is an extra motivation for translation—the message needs to be understood.

The events of the day of Pentecost in Acts 2 give us a broad picture of what had happened in the Jewish diaspora, which formed a large part of the crowd present when the disciples began to speak in other languages. The crowd described hearing the apostles speaking "in our own language in which we were born" (Acts 2:8b, NKJV), which is most easily interpreted as the various vernaculars of their places of origin, presumably a number of languages including Persian, Aramaic, Greek, and Arabic. The most likely explanation for this is that the diaspora Jewish communities had shifted their home language to the language of the broader community, and then heard God's use of this vernacular at Pentecost as a sign to them. Their shift to various vernaculars is not portrayed in any way as a negative but as a means for God to show his power. Their vernacular was not a significant sign of their identity; their identity as faithful Israelites was secured through

---

[5] Or possibly Jewish Aramaic, but this seems an unlikely use of *Yehudit*, "Judean."

[6] The principle that the simplest explanation is the most likely to be accurate.

[7] Aramaic translations of the Hebrew Bible which would have been in use in at least some synagogues in the first century AD.

their obedience to the law. This picture of diasporic shift being the norm is further backed up by the portrayal of different groups of believers in Acts 6 as Hellenists (Greek-speaking) and Hebrews; we find many other examples of diasporic Jews settled in Judea (e.g., Simon of Cyrene, Barnabas, the men from Cyprus and Cyrene who spoke to Gentiles in Acts 11:20, and others, such as Paul). While both groups of Jewish believers in Acts 6 are viewed as true Jews, and believers in Christ, the language (and culture) issue does provide an opportunity for division and a split into two sub-groups.

In our final reflection on language shift and maintenance throughout the Bible, we note that the New Testament was written in Greek rather than Hebrew or Aramaic, the languages of the Hebrew Bible. This is consistent with the fact that the text was no longer being addressed just to those of a Jewish background, but to both Jews and Gentiles alike. We know that Paul was fluent in both Greek and Aramaic or Hebrew (most probably both) from passages like Acts 22 (see chapter 11). But he writes his letters to those in the Greek-speaking world in Greek. We do not have a letter to the church in Jerusalem, where he may perhaps have used another language. This remains, unfortunately, speculative.

A summary of language shift in biblical times

To summarize the key points then, we see three broad periods where language shift occurs, or was at risk of occurring.

1. The period of the patriarchs, which involves a shift of the language from what was spoken in Ur to what we now call the Hebrew language. It could be argued that this shift (very much in the background of the narrative) was consistent with a new identity as those devoted to the God of Israel, but more mundane explanations of it just being what people around them used are also possible. For example, in very early fragments of what could be Hebrew, it is sometimes impossible to distinguish it from what became Phoenician.
2. The initial post-exilic period, specifically the period of Nehemiah, where we see the one instance of resistance to incipient language shift. This was at a time of cultural renewal, when Jewish identity was at risk, and was being reinforced. The shift is seen as a consequence of a dilution of identity, rather than as its cause. Note that this was before any translation of the Scriptures, so those who knew no Hebrew would not have the direct information to know how to keep the law.
3. By New Testament times, the vernacular at least of Galilee had shifted to Aramaic, and the vernacular of many diasporic Jewish communities had also shifted to one of the languages spoken in the region. This is not seen in any way as diminishing their Jewish identity—it would seem that the close link between vernacular language and identity that existed at the time of Nehemiah had been weakened.

Implications of language shift for our missiology

How then should we see language shift? What are the implications of language shift for our missiology? An inevitable, and perhaps neutral, phenomenon which reflects the way things are? Or as a sign of marginalization, a loss of identity, which must be resisted at all costs in all cases? It seems that the biblical record is not consistent with a strong version of either of these positions. We see that the link between Jewish identity and the Hebrew language was originally strong, but weakened over time; language shift is often perceived as being linked to a weakening of identity, but in some cases this does not need to follow. The challenge here may be in discerning, with the affected community, the difference.

As has been noted by various writers (e.g., Roche 2019), language shift often occurs as a response to unequal power dynamics, which includes colonization. As such, it is a sign of injustice, and according to Roche, should be resisted as a matter of human rights (see chapter 17). In the case of the Tibetan minority that Gerald Roche investigates, there seem to be deliberate attempts to eradicate linguistic diversity. There is little doubt that this is often the case. We could characterize the neo-Babylonian empire's actions against the people of Judah, in sending them into exile, as one type of such colonization, which was at least a component in the eventual language shift away from Hebrew as a vernacular. However, the focus of Jewish resistance to Babylonian attempts at assimilation seems to have been more related to issues of faith and practice rather than language or revenge against the Babylonians (Jer 29:7).

While some cases of language shift are a result of deliberate language erasure, others occur more because of long-lasting power imbalances, such as the use of one language and not another in education or in the judicial system. Of course, it is up for argument whether this is a reflection of deliberate language erasure, depending on the context. When facing a minoritized position in a broader society, speakers of minority languages may see little perceived benefit (Karan 2011) in transmitting their own language to their children. This may seem to be a choice made freely, but reflects power imbalances stacked against the community, so it would seem that such decisions are both structural and communal.

However, what are we to make of cases of language shift in cities such as Lubumbashi in the Democratic Republic of Congo (DRC)? Here the powerful and the privileged have switched to Swahili and French (Ferrari et al. 2014, Gibson 2018), in many cases losing the ethnic languages of their forebears, due to the perceived lack of utility of these languages in the urban setting—a choice also supported by widespread intermarriage. While a decolonizing critique may see the direction of change as reflecting colonial patterns, new communities such as cities (or the surrounding mining settlements) need a language to serve as the medium of communication.

This means that newcomers need to learn the new communal language, reflecting urbanism rather than perhaps the rural connotations of the original vernaculars. It is also interesting to note that the urban choice of a non-local language levels the playing field; it does not favor one ethnic group over another.

In some cases, especially in settler colonial situations (such as Canada, the USA, or Australia), language shift among the Indigenous communities has been shown to correlate with other psychosocial problems, such as elevated suicide rates in Canada (Hallett et al. 2007). Here we can see a demonstrable correlation between language shift and what would appear to be continued psychosocial trauma after having adopted the language of the settler. Whether this level of trauma is associated with language shift in other cultural contexts has not been established. This raises the question of what constitutes flourishing for these communities? Evidently high suicide rates are an indicator of a problem. What should the missiological response be? It is unlikely that language development efforts on their own will be effective in reducing suicide rates—but it is possible that they could be part of a process of healing alongside other activities. It is hard to know the outcomes here, but an awareness of language shift possibly being a sign, a symptom, or a symbol of communal trauma may help inform our conversations (see also chapter 18 for a related discussion on identity poverty, aspirational poverty, and language death).

To summarise, losing a language can be a deeply traumatic experience for a community, or, conversely, the loss might reflect a loss of attachment to a previous identity (as was argued for the Nehemiah case). In addition, the loss of a language is a loss to science, specifically linguistics. But this is probably not the primary concern for the community itself.

On the other hand, all identities are somehow recent constructs (see, e.g., Lewis 2021). Yes, they may go back a very long way, but the construction of an identity is only meaningful if it has been passed on in the last generation or two. Many of us need not go back more than a few generations to find examples of language shift in our own families. In some cases this went with a change of identity, while in other cases it did not. An example of the latter is my wife's Welsh family where the switch from Welsh to English did not include a shift to an English identity. The Welsh language, however, still forms part of Welsh identity for both English and Welsh speakers in Wales. Identities and languages can both shift over the generations, sometimes at the same time, but not always. Identity is marked by different symbols at different times (Lewis 2021).

So where does this leave us as those who work with communities whose languages are generally minoritized in some way, and sometimes prone to shift? What are the implications for our missiology as we work with them? Do we work to preserve the languages whatever the cost, and try to persuade the community that their language is their unique treasure which they must keep if they are to stay their true selves? Or might we shrug our shoulders when seeing the language being lost, saying it is obviously the community's decision to move on? It would seem clear by now that I am not supporting either (perhaps extreme) characterization of position.

And I find myself in good company: presenting the *Sustainable Use Model*, Lewis and Simons (2016) propose an effective strategy for working with language communities, helping them see what might constitute realistic goals for language development. While the model is not directly presented within a missiological framework, the overall goal is the flourishing of the communities, so the missiological implications are clear.

While they lay out a theoretical model for decisions in language development, we find a practical "how-to" in tools based on the Sustainable Use Model, "A Guide for Planning the Future of our Language" (Hanawalt et al. 2016) and "The Language and Identity Journey" (Eberhard 2020). These publications outline methods for working with communities in a practical, feasible way. Overall, the Sustainable Use Model outlines three directions for a community to take in relation to its language:

1. Maintain the language at its current level (obviously not realistic where the language is currently shifting)
2. Move it to a more secure future by first ensuring continued oral transmission, and then developing literacy
3. Help prepare the community for a "soft landing" (Lewis and Simons 2016:213, 243), where the language shift is allowed to take its course, but the community will still be able to use some level of knowledge of the language in a way symbolic of their identity

It seems reasonable to suggest that these three approaches are all appropriate missiological responses to situations where communities are undergoing language shift, or feel a threat to their language (and therefore potentially to their identity). What is important to remember is that our response should be motivated by a desire for the people's (rather than the language's) flourishing. This may involve language-related activities, but the focus should remain on the people and what blesses them.

Conclusion

So what answer can be given to the Kenyan student with whom we introduced this chapter? In his case, it is probable that the Kikuyu language is an important part of a Kikuyu identity, but not necessarily an essential one. Really, this is up to Kikuyus to decide, and different communities (and different parts of those communities) will foreground language as part of their identity to different extents. Language is neither the be-all-and-end-all of identity, nor is it irrelevant. Therefore, the loss of a language—especially when forced—can be a deeply traumatic process for the community, or represent a scar from other wounds. However, in other cases it may leave little that is negative. It is not our role as outsiders to decide which is the case for the communities that we work alongside, but we may be able to be partners in a conversation on these topics with them.

The key in each of the three possible directions for language engagement above is that any activity should be an informed community decision rather than one dictated by an outsider's philosophy (which is unlikely to be effective, in any case). This approach seems to be consistent with what we have ascertained from the Bible: language is an important component of identity, but not necessarily an essential one. It is by recognizing this that we can respect the uniqueness of each community without prescribing what should be done, and enter into genuine conversations with the communities with whom we seek to partner. While this methodology cannot be directly deduced from our reading of the biblical narrative, it seems to be fully consistent with the traces we have noted within the Bible, and to be an appropriate missiological response.

References

Eberhard, David, ed. 2020. *The language and identity journey.* Dallas, TX: SIL International. https://sites.google.com/sil.org/thelanguageidentityjourney/the-journey.

Fasold, Ralph. 1984. *The sociolinguistics of society.* Oxford: Blackwell.

Ferrari, Auréllia, Marcel Kalunga, and Georges Mulumbwa. 2014. *Le swahili de Lubumbashi : Grammaire, textes, lexique.* Paris: Karthala.

Gibson, Maik. 2018. Report on operations research for ACCELERE! 1: Sociolinguistic mapping and teacher language ability. With Bagamba Bukpa Araali. U.S. Agency for International Development. https://pdf.usaid.gov/pdf_docs/PA00TRB3.pdf.

Hallett, Darcy, Michael J. Chandler, and Christopher E. Lalonde. 2007. Aboriginal language knowledge and youth suicide. *Cognitive Development* 22(3):392–399.

Hanawalt, Charlie, Bryan Varenkamp, Carletta Lahn, and Dave Eberhard. 2016. *A guide for planning the future of our language.* Dallas, TX: SIL International. https://www.sil.org/guide-planning-future-our-language.

Karan, Mark E. 2011. Understanding and forecasting ethnolinguistic vitality. *Journal of Multilingual and Multicultural Development.* 32(2):137–149.

Lewis, M. Paul. 2021. Remembering ethnicity: The role of language in the construction of identity. In J. Stephen Quakenbush and Gary F. Simons (eds.), *Language and identity in a multilingual, migrating world*, 35–53. Dallas, TX: SIL International.

Lewis, M. Paul, and Gary F. Simons. 2010. Assessing endangerment: Expanding Fishman's GIDS. *Revue Roumaine de Linguistique* 2:103–120. http://www.lingv.ro/RRL%202%202010%20art01Lewis.pdf.

Lewis, M. Paul, and Gary F. Simons. 2016. *Sustaining language use: Perspectives on community-based language development*. Publications in Ethnography 42. Dallas, TX: SIL International.

Roche, Gerald. 2019. Articulating language oppression: Colonialism, coloniality and the erasure of Tibet's minority languages. *Patterns of Prejudice* 53(5):487–514. https://www.tandfonline.com/doi/full/10.1080/0031322X.2019.1662074.

Tollefson, Kenneth D., and H. G. M. Williamson. 1992. Nehemiah as cultural revitalization: An anthropological perspective. In J. Cheryl Exum (ed.), *The historical books. A Sheffield reader*, 322–348. Sheffield, UK: Sheffield Academic.

Venter, Pieter M. 2018. The dissolving of marriages in Ezra 9–10 and Nehemiah 13 revisited. *HTS Teologiese Studies/Theological Studies* 74(4):a4854. https://doi.org/10.4102/hts.v74i4.4854.

Shin

*Seven times a day I praise you
for your righteous laws.
(Psalm 119:164)*

21

Linguistic Hospitality in the Mission of God

Based on papers by Grace Chou, John Ommani Luchivia, and J. Stephen Quakenbush

Introduction

Chapter 9 speaks of God's intentionality in creating language diversity. It asks whether language diversity is an "inconvenient barrier" and concludes that it is part of the beauty of God's design. However, there are times when it does seem like an inconvenient barrier, getting in the way of communication and relationships. Michael Pasquale and Nathan Bierma write, "Loving and welcoming the foreigner includes welcoming the foreigner's culture and language. In practicing linguistic hospitality, we are doing just that: making room for the languages of others, welcoming those languages, and acknowledging that language is a vital aspect of a speaker's identity" (2011:20–21). At the 2020 God and Language Forum hosted by SIL, the Kenyan missiologist John Ommani, the Taiwanese linguist Grace Chou, and the American sociolinguist Stephen Quakenbush all contributed works focusing on this concept of "linguistic hospitality". This chapter combines those contributions as an imagined conversation, with the extended quotes adapted from the authors' respective papers (Chou 2022; Ommani 2022; Quakenbush 2022).

After briefly exploring how individuals, communities, and societies can foster hospitality and inclusivity toward a diversity of language speakers, a case study of the Luhiya community in Kenya demonstrates linguistic hospitality in action. We then present a vision for how the Church can model linguistic hospitality for their communities.

Language diversity

John Ommani

> Language is both a means of communication for people who speak the same variety or dialect and a way of extending hospitality to outsiders. Similarly, diversity is a natural phenomenon and a reality which, if embraced, enables people to thrive. Yet, language diversity, when viewed through another lens, can divide individuals by magnifying their differences.
>
> Self-identity is inherent in all human beings. Hospitality is a human expression toward others, even those of different identities. Both aspects (self-identity and hospitality) are values that are treasured by humans and are conveyed consciously or unconsciously through language. There are underlying values attached to the language choices of multilingual speakers in different contexts. While this may not easily be noticeable in written domains, it is a common phenomenon in oral communication.
>
> How can individuals and communities promote tolerance and accommodation of others? This chapter maintains that linguistic diversity does not have to lead to language conflict but, through linguistic hospitality, can promote the living-out of the mission of God in community.

Linguistic unity in diversity in the Kingdom of God

In chapter 9 of this volume, Gary Simons presented the view that language diversity, reinstated at Babel, was a blessing from God, and in chapter 11 Mamy Raharimanantsoa discussed the events of the day of Pentecost (Acts 2) and the worship before the throne in heaven recorded in Revelation 7:9–12, where different nations, peoples, and tribes praise God each in their own language.

21 Linguistic Hospitality in the Mission of God (Chou, Ommani, Quakenbush)

Grace Chou

When the Holy Spirit descended on the believers gathered in Acts 2, the first thing that happened was that the apostles were enabled to speak people's native languages, thus acknowledging people's linguistic identities. In these diverse languages, the apostles spoke about "the wonderful works of God" (Acts 2:11b). The song in Revelation 7:9–12 expands this picture. Those who worship before the throne have two layers of identity: firstly, they belong to the Lamb of God (Rev 7:14); secondly, they belong to their nation, tribe, people group, and language (Rev 7:9).

These Scripture passages are important as we explore the picture of linguistic diversity in the Kingdom of God. The theme of language use (how we speak and listen) occurs in many other places in the Scriptures, including the book of Ephesians. Ephesians describes how the Body of Christ, although diverse, can be united. This is primarily demonstrated in the Church, in which the different parts of the Body of Christ are connected. Linguistic diversity, intentionally designed by God, is part of this picture of unity in diversity.

In a linguistically diverse environment, many different languages are spoken by people with different identities. However, they are interconnected with each other by appreciation and mutual shaping. It is not a matter of individual languages standing separately, side by side, but rather a dynamic process wherein many languages have different levels and layers of interaction and connectedness, as language communities interact with one another. Linguistic diversity is a characteristic of God's kingdom, affirmed at Pentecost when the Holy Spirit descended to the world.

I like to think about it like this: are languages separate entities in which only a few similar individuals interact? Or do languages create a hospitable space in which a diversity of people can interact with one another? A metaphor might be helpful here. Is linguistic diversity a picture of different valuable ingredients such as spices, vegetables, meat, flowers, etc. in the market? Or is it a picture of a feast offering many delicious and distinct dishes so that the host and the guests can enjoy their time together with love, joy, and peace?

Hospitality

Hospitality in missiology

Steve Quakenbush

From a missiological perspective, hospitality is based on love for the stranger and is ultimately grounded in God's love for and redemption of his creation. God's love for his (now estranged) creation and his invitation into communion with himself is evident from Genesis 1 onward. The hospitality of God in his mission is most clearly seen in Christ's supreme sacrifice on the cross. The theologian Hans Boersma (2006) declares that "the cross should be understood, first and foremost, as an act of hospitality" that "represents an opening up of God's very self to a world that has closed itself off from the divine embrace" (quoted in Kaemingk 2018:182). The hospitality of God is highlighted again in Revelation 19, where all of Christ's beloved are invited to the wedding feast of the Lamb.

Christine Pohl claims that "hospitality as a framework provides a bridge which connects our theology with daily life and concerns" (1999:8). Describing hospitality as "a lens through which we can read and understand much of the gospel," she adds that it is "a practice by which we can welcome Jesus himself" (1999:8).

Christ himself is, of course, the ultimate model for both guest and host. Christ came as a guest and foreigner, born in a manger in Bethlehem, remarkably dependent on the hospitality of others for the span of his earthly life. At the same time, Christ served as the ultimate host, welcoming the poor and needy, calling out to all who were hungry and thirsty, bidding all who were tired and weary to come to him and find their true home.

How has the theme of hospitality been applied to language-related issues?

Hospitality in translation studies and Bible translation

The earliest published use of the phrase "linguistic hospitality" that this author can find is from an address delivered in 1997 by the French philosopher Paul Ricoeur entitled "Translation as Challenge and Source of Happiness" (2006).

Ricoeur concludes his address with the claim that a translator's only happiness can come in accepting the notion of correspondence without total adequacy. Linguistic hospitality, he says, characterizes this realm "where the pleasure of dwelling in the other's language is balanced by the pleasure of receiving the foreign word at home, in one's own welcoming house" (Ricoeur 2006:10). The accomplishment of a happy translation, then, models linguistic hospitality and provides an ethical model for human interaction on a larger scale based on the same components—recognizing, respecting, and welcoming the other without insisting that the other completely assimilate or integrate into one's own language, culture, and world.

Linguistic hospitality

Linguistic hospitality creates a third space

In sociology, the term "third space" is often used to refer to a sphere of interaction in a community that functions differently from the typical spheres of home (private life) and work, school, or marketplace (public life).

Grace Chou

> Linguistic hospitality is the key to making linguistic diversity interconnected and inclusive. It involves both an acknowledgement of each language's existence (with appreciation for it), and also a willingness to enter into a dynamic process to find a comfortable hybrid of multilingualism.
>
> In this dynamic process, people from two or more language communities negotiate how they use languages with mutual respect, and maximize each individual's linguistic capacity with humility, love, and kindness. We accept and honor each one's linguistic identity, ability, and capacity, as well as each other's language attitudes and assumptions. We then interact in appropriate languages, following appropriate social norms. Through this process, a third space is opened up where two or more languages interconnect and may create something new.

John Ommani

> Fostering this kind of third space through the practice of linguistic hospitality is part of participating in the mission of God. Linguistic hospitality demands tolerance of linguistic differences. This act of acceptance and love is an enabler in

drawing people towards God. It helps people focus on the value and humanness of others rather than on their differences. It is hospitality within a language, in using language, and toward other languages. It brings one language alongside another language so that they both exist to serve the people involved. Pasquale and Bierma write, "What linguistic hospitality should involve is tolerance of, interest in, and celebration of other dialects as legitimate linguistic expression, and as part of a large tapestry of a language" (2011:64).

The acceptance, the belonging, matters a lot to people's self-worth and identity and, as a result, promotes the mission of God which enables people to know him and be known as his own. Michel Kenmogne says, "We need, in this world, to be exercising a bit more of what I have called 'linguistic hospitality,' where we learn to create room for all the languages that people actually use" (2020). This is accomplished as we take time to listen, and understand what God is speaking through his word to others. Translators know that no one language is sufficient to express the message of God fully; yet each language brings with it some aspects that help the hearers understand better. As others listen to our narrative and we listen to theirs, we build into the story of God, providing an opportunity to learn from one another and grow together.

Practicing linguistic hospitality

Linguistic hospitality can be practiced in overlapping ways by individuals, communities, and societies at large.

Steve Quakenbush

Individual

On the individual level, one can practice linguistic hospitality by attending to the linguistic repertoire of others in ways that make them feel welcome and help lead to mutual, effective communication. This begins by acknowledging the linguistic repertoire of the other. When the language repertoire of the person or people with whom one is conversing differs from one's own, exercising linguistic hospitality may be as simple as speaking slowly, enunciating carefully, using basic vocabulary, and avoiding figures of speech that require insider knowledge to interpret. These are all things any speaker can do with minimal effort, once aware of the need or benefit.

Community

Communities practice linguistic hospitality in much the same way as individuals. They attend to the linguistic repertoire of their members in ways that respect their identity and seek to meet their basic communicative needs. Figure 21.1 shows a striking expression of linguistic hospitality from this author's own physical neighborhood. Written in the languages of three major sectors of the population in our city and community, it is an explicit statement directed at those who do not use the majority language of English as their first or only language, as well as to those who do.

Figure 21.1. Sign in front of a private home in Grand Rapids, Michigan. (© 2024, J. Stephen Quakenbush. Used by permission.)

Societal

Linguistic hospitality on a societal level is practiced not only by individuals and communities but is also reflected (or not) in the practices and policies of larger governing bodies (including denominational offices, for instance, in the case of the church) and in the laws of the land. Educational policies that welcome and build on experience in the languages of the learner are examples of linguistic hospitality. Language learning classrooms in particular can be special places where hospitality is practiced, where others are valued. Attitudes and methods that model such attitudes build on respect and lead toward greater understanding, seeking to bless while being blessed. Efforts to provide critical information to all citizens and residents of a country in a language they can understand, as well as providing interpretation for legal, medical, and other services, are practices of linguistic hospitality that contribute to the common good of the whole society. On a national scale, official recognition of languages is also an act of linguistic hospitality.

The Luhyia: A case study in linguistic hospitality

The Luhyia of Kenya provide a model for the kind of societal-level linguistic hospitality we are envisioning.

John Ommani

The Luhyia speech community in Kenya comprises seventeen different dialects under the same language name tag. According to the 2019 Kenya census report, they number almost seven million. Like other communities, the Luhyia are proud of their language and culture. Besides their own language, most of them also speak English and Kiswahili, the official and national languages of Kenya, respectively. The community is diverse in both language and culture. The intelligibility level for the two most diverse Luhyia dialects is about 40 percent. Each group identifies most closely with their own smaller unit, yet the community prides itself in being hospitable toward outsiders and has welcomed many people from other languages who have bought land and settled among them.

The Luhyia church community is faced with migration, urbanization, and globalization issues like any other church today. This poses critical tension between sustaining a pure cultural and linguistic identity on the one hand, and on the other hand, obeying a divine call to accept and accommodate others who come with different cultures and languages.

The Luhyias are referred to as the *mlembe* people. *Mlembe* means 'peace'. Their social greeting is a wish of peace for one another. As a people who love their own language, culture, and peace, how do they relate to outsiders and make them feel welcome without compromising their own identity?

In Luhyia, God is referred to as *Nyasaye wooMulembe* or "God of peace". This is a term borrowed from the neighboring Luo language. Despite the Luhyia having their own word for God, *Were*, they took on the new term as one way of sharing in linguistic hospitality. When the Luhyia greet one another, they are wishing each other that aspect of God which is peace. From this cultural understanding, the goal of the mission of God is a people who are at peace with one another and with the environment in which they live. It is the *shalom* that God intended, as it was in the garden before the fall (Gen 1).

The Luhyia community has a saying: "*Omundu yemungwa obusumu. Likhuva tawe.*" 'A person may be denied food, but not a word'. Why is this so? It is based on the principle that through words we show the best of our community to others and, therefore, welcome them to be part of us. We offer them skills to survive and help them know how to participate in caring for the community. The stranger needs to feel at home in order to fully participate in the new community life and aspirations. Pasquale and Bierma write, "The stranger not only [will] be greeted, but also will be given loving attention. The stranger not only will be fed and given a drink, his or her voice will be granted space" (2011:21).

The Luhyia, being a community of many different dialects, realized that, for them to achieve their aspirations as a community, sharing knowledge with foreigners of different speech communities is central, thereby putting linguistic hospitality into action.

Linguistic hospitality in church life

Using English as an example of a dominant language, Pasquale and Bierma pose a question that all God's mission-minded believers should ask: "Should churches compel or even encourage the development of monolingual English congregations? Is language the basis of our unity?" (2011:36). Ommani observes that the manner in which a community of believers responds to this question points them to the core of their unity, which should be faith in one Lord, not one cultural, ethnic, linguistic, or any other identity. He proceeds by discussing linguistic hospitality: language is not the basis of our unity; Jesus is.

In his book *Multilingual Church*, the interpreter Jonathan Downie observes that while every modern city is multilingual, not many churches are (2024:19). Yet, the explicit vision of Scripture is one of all peoples speaking all languages worshipping before the throne (see, for example, Isa 66:18, Rev 7:9). Downie proceeds to quote Mario Wahnschaffe, senior pastor of a multilingual church in Bonn, Germany. Pastor Wahnschaffe says, "We have left behind the paradigm of being here to help the poor internationals. Instead we tell them they are needed, as only they can fulfill the international vision" (2024:94).

Downie unpacks this statement.

> A church must move from accommodating speakers and users of other languages to viewing them as people whose perspectives, talents, and voices are needed. This reinforces the idea that multilingual church is not about something we do as a program or ministry, but something we become. It means learning to share power and decision making. It means dedicating time, space, and thought to how best we can integrate the gifts of those who use different languages in our church. (2024:99)

There are a variety of ways of including two or more languages in a church service. However, without a vision for multilingual church, efforts will falter. How it will look depends on the style of the church. Downie gives two examples.

> [A] church that God has called to carry the torch of tradition, ceremony, and ancient modes of worship into a new generation might find that using translated liturgies, adopting some formalisms from other countries, or hiring leaders who speak different languages might suit them well.
>
> Conversely, a church that is called to "sing a new song of praise" to the Lord (Ps 33:3) by innovative forms of presentation, teaching, and even service structure will tend to find it more useful to look for agile forms of language provision, such as live subtitling, or interpreting provided by humans. (2024:109)

As the Scriptures are translated into an increasing number of languages, John Ommani points out that the church leadership can promote the reading of Scripture in as many languages as are available.

There are issues that need to be addressed, including the role (if any) of prestige languages, the pastor's natural preference for using the language in which he or she has been trained, the fact that using different languages may create a new awareness of ethnic identities which then highlight differences, and the sheer practical question of how many languages can be comfortably included in one church service. Additionally, the language of "host" and "guest" may not be useful, since it carries with it the danger of linguistic paternalism. Linguistic hospitality is not something the powerful offer to the powerless, or the static church members to the "poor internationals," but is something that everyone values because through it no one is barred from participation because of language. In God's paradigm "there are different languages, but there are no language barriers" (Downie 2024:31). The speakers of each language are not looking to their own interests but to the interests of one another (Phil 2:4). When this is done at a church, everyone, no matter what their language, can, as John Ommani describes it, "feel loved and accepted, they will be better able to benefit from the message, and the beauty of diversity will be on display."

It is also possible for a church to show linguistic hospitality while still using only one language, as in the following example.

Steve Quakenbush

> A church in Michigan, USA, provides a model for how showing linguistic hospitality can enhance the worship experience and resulting Christian community. ... Having been involved in refugee ministry for more than forty years, the refugee support team noted that very few of the refugees [coming from more than a dozen countries] with whom the church developed close relationships ever worshipped with them, even though a number of the refugees were Christians. They considered the possibility that the level of English and the complicated liturgy made participating in worship more difficult for English learners than it needed to be. So a second worship service in Basic English was introduced. The leaders for this service made efforts to speak slowly in simple English. They chose music with simple lyrics, and projected images on a screen to help with comprehension. The Basic English service has grown over the last ten years from a group of about twenty people to a gathering of more than 150 people.

Linguistic hospitality and spiritual growth

As we are hospitable to one another in our choice of language and demonstrate a willingness to learn from one another, our collective understanding of God is broadened and our worship deepened.

John Ommani

Most first-generation Luhyia believers were converted during the East Africa revival movement (Stanley 1978:8). Among the many teachings, love and care for neighbours were central messages[1] of the movement. The education system that came alongside Christian teaching transformed cultural worldviews; therefore, communities started embracing outsiders (Anderson 1977:113–114).

God created humanity to have a spiritual relationship with him. He communicates with them through his word. People experience transformation as they understand his message. In turn, they share their understanding of God's word with other people of the same or different speech communities. Each contributes to the collective understanding of who God is and his ultimate plan for humanity. Christopher Wright says, "Christian mission is not a matter of inviting or compelling people to become Westerners ... It is inviting people to become more fully human through the transforming power of the gospel that fits all because it answers to the most basic need of all and restores the common glory of what it is to be truly human—a man or woman made in the image of God" (2006:424). Linguistic diversity is a gift God has allowed us to have as a pre-taste of what heaven will be (Rev 7:9). Extending linguistic hospitality to people is not only a principle of inclusivity and cultural sensitivity, but is also a principle of seeking to worship God in our diversity as we share in his image and message (Ommani 2012:84).

When people use their language to share their understanding of God, it helps others to see God from a different perspective, and modifies their knowledge of who God is. Melchizedek, coming from a different location and culture, introduced God to Abraham as "the God Most High" (El Elyon) (Gen 14:19–22). From there on, God is seen by Abraham as the Most High God. We need to encourage

---

[1] Told to me, Ommani, and recorded in 1998 by my grandmother, Doris Lwimbo Luchivia who was born in 1888, became a believer in 1924, but was very much influenced by the revival.

people to speak of God and to use Scripture in the various languages available.

Spiritual leaders should see value in linguistic diversity and promote multilingual language use in the church. Scripture reading and worship can be done in different languages and cultures to display the beauty of diversity.

When people begin to appreciate the uniqueness of each language and the flavor they bring to worship, then linguistic hospitality becomes a virtue in society, and diversity is never seen as a bad thing. As we affirm every language in worship, God is glorified and he delights in his people as they pray, sing, praise, dance, and rejoice together.

Conclusion

Grace Chou

Heaven is a rich and complex multilingual and multicultural context; people are singing the same theme to glorify the Creator—in different languages. There are interactions between language groups as well. With these multiple layers of interconnection, we will live with linguistic hospitality toward brothers and sisters from all kinds of languages. To prepare ourselves, we should humbly practice linguistic hospitality now, as we await the realization of God's kingdom. This is a key characteristic of those who are in Christ, and it manifests God's beauty, peace, reconciliation, and abundance in the Body of Christ. It is that interconnectedness that attracts others to join the Body of Christ.

A prayer for linguistic hospitality

Steve Quakenbush

O God,
    who through inestimable love and sacrifice welcomes and invites us in,
    who transforms us from strangers and aliens into daughters and sons,
    who speaks life and light to us through the Living Word,
    who by your Spirit dwells with us and in us:
We praise you!
    Help us to open our hearts to others as you open your heart to us.
    Thank you for speaking to us in language we can understand.

We treasure and marvel at the beauty and diversity of languages in your creation, and how each one can be used to praise your name.

We pledge to listen well, to speak graciously, to honor and welcome others. As communicators in your image, we long to reflect your heart to those you love.

Help us, in the name of our Lord and Savior Jesus. Amen.

References

Anderson, William B. 1977. *The church in East Africa 1840–1974*. Nairobi, Kenya: Uzima Press Limited.

Boersma, Hans. 2006. *Violence, hospitality, and the cross: Reappropriating the atonement tradition*. Grand Rapids MI: Baker Academic.

Chou, Grace. 2022. Towards linguistic diversity with linguistic hospitality. In Greed and Kruger, 302–313

Downie, Jonathan. 2024. *Multilingual church: Strategies for making disciples in all languages*. Littleton, CO: William Carey Publishing.

Kaemingk, Matthew. 2018. *Christian hospitality and Muslim immigration in an age of fear*. Grand Rapids, MI: Eerdmans.

Kenmogne, Michel. 2020. Multilingualism, urbanisation and Scripture engagement. 5–6 May 2020. Unpublished video.

Ommani Luchivia, John. 2012. Contextualized language choice in the church in Kenya. PhD dissertation. Fuller Theological Seminary, Pasadena, CA.

Ommani Luchivia, John. 2022. Linguistic diversity and linguistic hospitality in the mission of God. In Greed and Kruger, 314–329.

Pasquale, Michael, and Nathan L. K. Bierma. 2011. *Every tribe and tongue: A biblical vision for language in society*. Eugene, OR: Pickwick Publications.

Pohl, Christine D. 1999. *Making room: Recovering hospitality as a Christian tradition*. Grand Rapids MI: Eerdmans.

Quakenbush, J. Stephen. 2022. Linguistic hospitality and the mission of God. In Greed and Kruger, 285–301.

Ricoeur, Paul. 2006. *On translation*. Translated by Eileen Brennan. London: Routledge.

Stanley, Brian. 1978. The East African revival: African initiative within a European tradition. Theology on the Web. https://biblicalstudies.org.uk/pdf/churchman/092-01_006.pdf. Original publication *Churchman* 92(1):6–22.

Wright, Christopher J. H. 2006. *The mission of God: Unlocking the Bible's grand narrative*. Downers Grove, IL: InterVarsity Academic.

Taw

May my cry come before you, LORD;
give me understanding according to your word.
(Psalm 119:169)

22

Conclusion: SIL, Language, and God's Mission

Michel Kenmogne
SIL Executive Director, 2016–2025

Introduction

Language has played a strategic role in extending the frontiers of the Kingdom of God and changing the demographics of the worldwide Church in the twenty-first century. God's kingdom grows each time the good news enters new cultural and linguistic spheres. While this truth is evident on instrumental and pragmatic grounds, the theological and missiological nature and value of language has not received sufficient and consistent attention.

This book has sought to fill that gap in the overall mission context. Various authors have argued that language is a theological category because the triune God of Christianity is a God who speaks (see chs. 2 and 15); his word creates and orders the world. Language is also a missiological category, because it is indispensable to the enacting of God's plans and intentions in the world. It is also one of the main manifestations of the creation of humanity in the image and likeness of God. Language allows us to express our thoughts and emotions, to order events in a logical sequence, and to bring human beings together into a community that provides them with a sense of corporate identity. In the words of Noam Chomsky, language is about the "human essence", what is unique to humanity and "inseparable from any critical phase of human existence, personal and social" (2006:88). For these reasons, the way that we handle language is foundational to issues of justice (chapter 17), fairness (chs. 18 and 19), dignity (chapter 3), and hospitality (chapter 21).

The various contributors to this book have sought to fill the gap of knowledge regarding the role that language plays in the enactment of God's mission to reconcile the whole world with himself through making himself known (see chapter 2). In this concluding chapter, I will briefly review SIL's quest to harness the potential of language to extend the bounds of God's kingdom. Also, looking forward, I acknowledge the changed context that globalization, urbanization, migration, and a digital age have brought, especially in minority language communities in the twenty-first century. This shift has important implications for the pursuit of God's plans and purposes for all the peoples of the earth and the role that language may play in it.

SIL and the discovery of a new frontier in world mission

In a classic article on the history of the modern mission movement, Ralph Winter (1981) identified three waves of mission in the last two centuries: mission to the coastlands (with William Carey as the main figure), mission to the interior (spearheaded by Hudson Taylor), and mission focusing on ethnic groupings rather than nation states. This third wave was prompted by SIL's founder, William Cameron Townsend, and others who reappraised the concept of nations (*ethne*) as ethnolinguistic communities. Language was identified as one of the main barriers that prevented members of smaller ethnolinguistic communities from enjoying God's plans and purposes for them (Steven 1995:40, Dahlquist 1995:2). According to the account of Cameron Townsend, a casual conversation with Francisco Diaz, a native Kaqchikel in Guatemala, revealed to him the plight of the Indigenous communities. Diaz expressed it in the following terms.

> There are three kinds of oppressors who keep the Indians down. The witch doctors teach superstitions, telling the Indians that the sun is their father and the moon their grandmother, and that every hill and volcano has its spirit-owner who demands worship and sacrifices. The clergy try to impose the Spanish religion upon us ... They only come when there are children to baptize or someone to marry or bury. Even then they use a language the people do not understand. And for these services they expect to be well paid ... They go to the Spanish speakers. No one evangelizes

the Indian in his own tongue ... And the saloon keepers ... cooperate with the finca [estate] owners who let the Indians drink on credit enough to keep them in the forced labor systems. My people have little hope. (Steven 1995:39)

In the words of Diaz, Christianity was a foreign or "Spanish religion" as long as it was not conveyed to the Indians in their own tongues. A foreign language was inadequate to engage the deep-seated beliefs in superstitions and root the people in the Christian faith. The failure to understand the foreign language naturally led to shallow experiences of faith. This realization prompted Townsend to turn away from his original calling to sell Spanish Bibles and instead to start working in language development and Scripture translation among the Kaqchikel people.

Besides the spiritual and linguistic issue, Townsend discovered that Indigenous people were denied the identity of human beings, equal in dignity with the people in the higher social classes of their society. He observed that it was "considered a disgrace for a Spanish-speaking person to be seen talking with an Indian as man-to-man, they being considered only an animal" (Steven 1984:198). The restoration of the dignity of Indigenous people, as people created in God's image, became Townsend's deepest motivation. Townsend's strategy was to use the mother tongue as the platform to allow them to recover their self-worth, find peace with their Creator, and relate with others within their societies (see chapter 3).

In chapter 3, I outlined how language is like a treasure chest, storing a community's experiences and memories. Edwin Smith writes, "Every language is a temple in which the soul of the people who speak it is enshrined. If it is sinful to exterminate them bodily, it is no less sinful to destroy their individuality" (quoted in Sanneh 2008:179). Lamin Sanneh concurs that "the speech that comes to people in their mother's milk is the most precious thing they have" (2008:179).

In light of the importance of each language for those who identify with it, language represents the most effective means to engage with people in a way that is genuine and respectful of who they truly are. It is also the way to lay a solid foundation upon which they can flourish spiritually, economically, individually, and socially (see chapter 3) without having to forsake their own identity as people. Therefore, behind Townsend's strategic focus on language, there was a clear vision to serve a broad range of issues. Townsend caught this vision around the same time that linguistics was developing as a modern science. This coincidence was certainly no accident in God's economy.

SIL and the rise of modern linguistics

At the dawn of the twentieth century, the Swiss linguist and philosopher Ferdinand de Saussure posited that language is a logical, structured system of elements that can be analyzed (see chapter 2). Linguistics continued to develop, both as an academic domain and as a key component and enabler in the development of the twentieth century mission movement, each contributing to the other. In fact, many missionaries were linguists.

The missional motivation of SIL hence allowed it to significantly contribute to the development of modern linguistics from the mid 1930s onward. These contributions include the following:

The collection, documentation, and dissemination of data on languages around the world

This data went a long way to facilitate the recognition that parts of speech, such as verbs and nouns, could be identified in all the languages of the world. Therefore, all languages, irrespective of their families, are worthy of respect and capable of serving as vehicles of any message, including God's word. In his review of the missionary impact on culture, Sanneh notes that, "whatever their motives … missionaries empowered mother-tongue speakers by undertaking the systematic documentation of the relevant languages" (2009:163).

Means of describing languages

Kenneth Pike (1947) argued that while on the one hand only native speakers are competent judges of their language, on the other hand researchers from outside the linguistic group can apply scientific methods in the analysis of language, producing verifiable and reproducible descriptions of the language. This distinction significantly helped linguists recognize the different perspectives that insiders and outsiders bring to linguistics (phonetics, phonology, tone, etc.), and cultural issues.

The discovery of text linguistics

The sentence had been considered the largest unit that could be studied to discover the rules that govern the way a language functions. But Robert Longacre (1976, 1983, 1996), in the context of Scripture translation, pioneered the study of text linguistics (discourse analysis and pragmatics) demonstrating that there are rules that govern the creation of a text beyond the sentence level.

Advocacy for vernacular/Indigenous languages rights

In the quest to create a more positive context for the speakers of minority languages to thrive, SIL has worked alongside governments, non-governmental organizations, and multilateral agencies to promote the rights of the speakers of all languages. Around most of the world today, the rights of languages have been acknowledged. Many countries' fundamental laws and constitutions proudly claim language diversity as a wealth and blessing rather than a problem to be solved. In the nation of Mexico, for example, where SIL formally began its work, the government has come a long way to acknowledge the rights of speakers of Indigenous languages and establish institutions to protect and promote them.

Scripture translation and applied linguistics

In an era marked by colonialism and Western hegemony around the world, it took Scripture translation to subvert the Westernization agenda of colonialists and enable the local appropriation of the Christian faith by local populations. As Sanneh (2007) observed,

> One thing that is absolutely clear is that the Christian impact overlapped almost exactly with the incidence of translation of Scripture into vernacular languages, almost everywhere. In other words, there were very few places, if any, where Christian awakening had taken root where people didn't have scriptures in their mother tongue.

Alongside Scripture translation, SIL used applied linguistics to further the empowerment of people. Mother tongue literacy and education became the primary means to address people's marginalization, affirm their dignity, and facilitate their integration within their wider national community (see chapter 3).

Three activities that went a long way to nurturing a positive context for what we observe as the rising church of the twenty-first century from the Global South and East are:

- acknowledgement of the adequacy of all languages to convey God's truth,
- description and preservation of languages, and
- advocacy for and promotion of languages through literacy and education.

Moreover, all around the world, we have seen the empowerment of people through the recognition and use of their languages. When the Nawuri people of Ghana received the New Testament in their language in 2012, the Chief of Kpandai Wura tearfully described the marginalization of his people: "When we go to the politicians, they don't know us. But now God knows us. Now we are counted among the children of God."

In this regard, Scripture translation and the empowerment it brings become a critical organizing principle and a practical tool for transformation. For a vulnerable and marginalized group like the Nawuris, being "counted among the children of God" is more than spiritual transformation. It is a key to transforming their perception of themselves (see chapter 18) and unleashing their potential to flourish in all aspects of life.

SIL and minority languages today

At the 2016 SIL International Conference, SIL delegates set out to reappraise and recapture the identity and purpose of SIL in the twenty-first century. The SIL International Board then took the work of the Conference, which expressed the deepest longing of SIL, and translated it into vision and mission statements, which were published in 2019. The mission statement reads:

> Inspired by God's love, we advocate, build capacity, and work with local communities to apply language expertise that advances meaningful development, education, and engagement with Scripture.[1]

SIL staff have overcome natural, cultural, linguistic, and other barriers, to work towards a future where speakers of every language can find reconciliation with God, with themselves, with their fellow human beings, and with their environment. All SIL's work is firmly anchored in the application of language expertise that, in turn, SIL keenly develops.

Today, SIL's mission statement is implemented in three ways:

- foundational research and tools,
- Scripture translation and engagement, and
- literacy, education, and development.

These three do not stand in isolation from one another but are complementary and mutually reinforcing. The next three paragraphs show how this threefold stream of SIL causes the one organization to be seen in three different ways.

Foundational research and tools

Through these programs, SIL provides a service to the academic, development, and Scripture engagement communities through research and increasing knowledge. SIL cares for those who speak non-dominant languages and contributes to building positive contexts and processes that will assist them in developing and using their languages effectively to meet their various needs. Those who relate with SIL primarily in this domain, i.e., research institutions and universities, would easily characterize SIL as an academic and research organization.

Scripture translation and engagement

SIL has been and remains a key player in Scripture translation globally. For many decades, SIL has provided direct leadership to Scripture translation projects. However, with the advent of a partner-rich environment in Scripture work,

---
[1] See the conclusion of chapter 2 for the vision statement.

SIL is responding by embracing two types of contribution: direct facilitation of Scripture translation, and supporting others who are implementing Scripture translation programs, including churches, language communities, and other partners. Nowadays there is a growing trend of local leadership in these programs. Another way that SIL contributes to Scripture translation is through tools and programs that help people engage with the translated Scriptures. Within the Forum of Bible Agencies International (see chapter 7) and in the church context, SIL is recognized as a bona fide Bible agency.

Literacy, education, and development

In this domain SIL collaborates with language communities and a variety of partners and agencies to address the language components of development, education, health improvement, creation care, and other aspects of God's mission. Undergirding this engagement is SIL's strong belief that the effective transformation of minority communities is holistic in nature. The use of local languages builds the bridge for access to God's word but also to other essential information needed for social and economic well-being. In this, SIL follows the pattern of Jesus' ministry which was uncompromisingly focused on the poor and needy, and those who were marginalized and disempowered in their society. He integrated his teaching about God's truth with his work of feeding the hungry, healing the sick, opening the eyes of the blind, and ministering to those who were looked down on by the spiritual leaders of his day. While SIL does not build health, education, or other infrastructure that address human needs, SIL is uncompromisingly committed to working with all to break down the language barriers that hinder their effectiveness in providing such services. Those who have known SIL primarily in this space would easily see SIL as a development agency.

As we move deeper into the fast-changing context of the twenty-first century, SIL upholds its commitment to enable language to advance all the facets of God's mission.

Into the future with God and language

Looking ahead, the trends of globalization, urbanization, migration, and the digital age that define the twenty-first century create more complexity in the ways that language is used to advance God's mission. Table 22.1[2] summarizes some of the main factors that will continue to inform and influence God's mission in marginalized language communities.

---

[2] Based on Harmelink et al. (2016).

Table 22.1 God's mission in marginalized language communities

Factors informing and influencing God's mission	Pre-20th Century	20th Century	21st Century
Language and Identity	Prescribed and corrected	Described and preserved	Interconnected
Minority Language Context	Isolated and ignored	Unreached and marginalized	Coexistence and interaction between dominant and minority languages
Linguistics	Prescribed and comparative philology	Descriptive with foreign-led experts	Contextual responses where local citizens and expatriates work together
Response to Language Diversity and Minority Identity	Colonial policy of elite language and culture	Rise of language and culture rights	Multicultural policy, multilingual education, multiple identities, linguistic citizenship
Language in Mission	Elite languages ONLY	Orthographies, grammars and written NTs for all	Contextual responses
Response to Language and Identity in Mission	"Your language is inadequate"	"Your language is adequate"	Contextual responses which serve holistic mission
Bible Translation Approach	Only into elite languages	Meaning-based translation by foreign experts with focus on NT	Contextual responses to complex multilingual situations based on community engagement

As table 22.1 shows, the realities that inform the understanding of language in mission are increasingly complex. For example, a direct equation between language and identity can no longer be established, as multilingualism leads people to attribute different uses and purposes to their repertoire of languages. A variety of factors, including the status of the actors (native speakers or cross-cultural workers) and the realities and needs of the church will influence the planning, the process, and the types of language activities. In such a delicate context, I suggest that the following four points guide our response:

- A diverse multicultural and multilingual community remains God's overarching pursuit (Rev 5:9, 7:9–10 [see chapter 1]).
- Minority language communities of the world remain among the 20 percent of the world's population who are least served economically, medically, politically, socially, educationally, and in terms of access to justice and Scripture (Watters 2019 [see chapter 3]). The vulnerable have a special place in God's agenda.
- Declining church attendance in the West and the growth of Indigenous churches elsewhere is a reality that will increase both the assertiveness of the church in the Global South and the need to take the demands of the context into account in all mission and development endeavors.
- The growing trends of language loss, multilingualism, and translanguaging (where the same speakers use multiple languages within the same context and events) will call for the reappraisal of the intrinsic value of language for human identity and flourishing, the functions of Scripture translation, the discernment of Scripture translation needs, and forms of Scripture engagement.

Language and Bible translation

As the Bible translation movement becomes more and more indigenous, the majority of translators nowadays are local speakers. This emerging reality raises the question of what the role of linguistics is in translation when it is carried out by native speakers. This is an important question for the contemporary Bible translation movement. There has been a naive assumption that local speakers do not need linguistics for Bible translation. It was also assumed that they are aware of how their language functions so that they can make more informed language decisions. However, local speakers involved in Bible translation have themselves expressed the desire for good orthographies and an ability to understand how their languages work. Therefore, in context, those involved in Scripture translation (expatriates and locals) need to explore appropriate ways to provide the necessary linguistic input into Bible translation.

Language beyond Bible translation

Two decades ago, I was stunned when the leader of another faith community approached a Bible agency in Cameroon to request a Bible translation in their language. I sought to understand the deeper motivation of this leader.

It turned out that it was not that he was keen to engage with God's word, but that he saw Bible translation and its related language development activities as a way to preserve his language from decline and eventual death. The fast rate of globalization, urbanization, and multilingualism is raising serious concerns among minority language communities. They feel the threat of losing their voice and identity in the global community if their languages are left out. This indicates that language remains a critical component of a people's identity and allows them to affirm their dignity and uniqueness as a people. Moreover, preserving languages goes a long way to maintaining the diversity of God's creation, thereby revealing his glory (see chs. 1 and 4).

The affirmation of people's dignity goes beyond language preservation. It also gives access to all the benefits of using one's own language. All around the world, minority language speakers, when empowered through literacy in their languages, become better citizens within their countries, exercising their rights and duties. Also, deep-seated issues such as poverty, healthcare, and injustice, all of which can mar the condition of these communities, will not be overcome without making use of their languages.

In light of these realities and the disconnect that has often existed between the study of languages (linguistics) and the people who use those languages, Felix Ameka (2022) recently advocated for the need for linguists to "articulate the social implications of languages for people, life and nature". He goes on to suggest redefining linguistics as the "humanistic and scientific study of languages," in other words, looking at the people behind the languages. At the beginning of this book, in chapter 2, we described the mission of God as one of self-revelation, so that, knowing God, human beings would experience life—flourishing life. Our quest for the role of language in God's mission, then, explicitly considers how language bridges the various gaps to the flourishing of people.

The role of language in mission in the twenty-first century

In view of the realities that inform language and mission in the twenty-first century, the role of language in God's mission should include the following:

- **Recognition of language issues:** The role of language is now central in mission strategy, and increasingly also in education and development programs. The inclusion of language in such programs requires close collaboration with all the actors, including churches and other missions and institutions. This will be done in a multilingual, multicultural, multifaceted environment.
- **Diverse global church:** Partnership within the body of Christ is not just a strategic issue. It is a key biblical principle, a moral issue. This requires us to examine our assumptions and address power imbalances that may be preventing some in the body of Christ from full participation in the mission of God because of language.

- **Integral mission:** Integral Mission recognises that "there is no biblical dichotomy between evangelistic and social responsibility in bringing Christ's peace to the poor and oppressed" (Lausanne Movement 2024). This perspective, which has been adopted by a significant proportion of the Global Church, significantly widens the potential roles that language plays in God's mission.
- **Contextualization:** Rather than seeing cultural diversity as a communication problem to overcome, it brings opportunities to counterbalance Western cultural biases and celebrate local identity and alternative insights.
- **Identity challenges:** As language communities become more connected with wider society, they face the challenge of adapting to change while appropriately maintaining their identity and culture.
- **Connectedness and multilingualism:** The way minority language communities use different languages is changing. As such, the medium or technology—written, oral, signed—needs to be appropriate for and relevant to the needs of diverse communities. Multilingualism also gives rise to the phenomenon of translanguaging, where the same speakers use multiple languages within the same context and events.

Conclusion

Given the trends of people movement, urbanization, globalization, digitalization, multilingualism, and translanguaging, the role of language in God's mission in the twenty-first century is increasingly complex. Our ability to continue to pursue this mission will be a matter of how painstakingly we build our efforts upon the solid foundation of the great commandment to love God and neighbor (Mark 12:29–31) and the great commission to go and make disciples (Matt 28:19–20).

The Mosaic law that was summed up in love for God and neighbor needs to undergird our commitment to serve the linguistic minorities in the twenty-first century. The ethics of love—and especially a deep compassion for those whose possibilities of flourishing are hindered because of language—are required to purposefully address the issues of language for the advance of God's kingdom.

Jesus' commission to go and make disciples and teach them all that he has commanded is about proclaiming the good news and making disciples, but it is also about teaching them to keep all that Jesus has commanded, and what Jesus commands is love (Mark 12:29–31, John 15:17). This takes us back to the justice and compassion that pervade the Gospels and the entire biblical narrative.

Finally, then, it will take a deep and costly commitment to continue to meet the needs of diverse language communities in the pursuit of God's mission this century. But we can remain confident for two reasons. Firstly, as we look back over the past century we can see the significant impact that results from the use of language to break down barriers for the spread of God's kingdom. This clearly reminds us of the enduring faithfulness of God. Secondly, despite shifting and challenging realities, we can press on into the future, confident that God remains the one who leads his mission. We know that his heart is always moved by those who are left at the margins of society and church life.

References

Ameka, Felix. 2022. Turning the tide from language endangerment to ethnolinguistic vitality. Paper presented at the University of Leiden, 30 September 2022. https://ciplnet.com/wp-content/uploads/2023/04/2022_Oratie-Ameka.pdf.

Chomsky, Noam. 2006. *Language and mind*. Third edition. Cambridge: Cambridge University Press.

Dahlquist, Anna Marie. 1995. *Trailblazers for translators: The Chichicastenango Twelve*. Pasadena, CA: William Carey Library.

Harmelink, Bryan, Francis Viscount, Andy Clark, Woza Olla Woyita, Grace Chou, Phil Smith, Larry Jones, David Ross, and Manna Mondal. 2016. How does God use language in what he's doing in the world? SIL International. https://drive.google.com/file/d/1u67XAAtdFjeEgt9xNPjsrcRtBU7ZDv5X/view?usp=sharing.

Lausanne Movement. 2024. Integral mission. https://lausanne.org/network/integral-mission#:~:text=Integral%20mission%20is%20defined%20as,to%20the%20poor%20and%20oppressed.

Longacre, Robert E. 1976. *An anatomy of speech notions*. PdR Press Publications in Tagmemics 3. Lisse, Netherlands: Peter de Ridder Press.

Longacre, Robert E. 1983. *The grammar of discourse*. New York, NY: Plenum Press.

Longacre, Robert E. 1996. *The grammar of discourse*. Topics in Language and Linguistics. Second edition. New York, NY: Plenum Press.

Pike, Kenneth L. 1947. *Phonemics: A technique for reducing languages to writing*. Ann Arbor, MI: University of Michigan Press.

Sanneh, Lamin. 2007. Bible translation and the birth of Christianity as a world religion. Paper presented at Andrew Walls Lectures, Wycliffe International European Training Programme, Horsleys Green, UK, 14 June 2007.

Sanneh, Lamin. 2008. *Disciples of all nations: Pillars of world Christianity*. Oxford: Oxford University Press.

Sanneh, Lamin. 2009. *Translating the message: The missionary impact on culture*. Revised and expanded edition. MaryKnoll, NY: Orbis Books.

Steven, Hugh. 1984. *A thousand trails: The personal journal of William Cameron Townsend, 1917–1919 Founder of Wycliffe Bible Translators*. White Rock, British Columbia: Credo Publishing.

Steven, Hugh. 1995. *Wycliffe in the making: The memoirs of W. Cameron Townsend 1920–1933*. Wheaton, IL: Harold Shaw Publishers.

Watters, John R. 2019. The state of minority languages in the twenty-first century. In Christopher L. Flanders (ed.), *Devoted to Christ: Missiological reflections in honor of Sherwood G. Lingenfelter*, 30–49. Eugene, OR: Pickwick Publications.

Winter, Ralph D. 1981. Three men, three eras: The flow of missions history. *Mission Frontiers*, February 1981. https://www.missionfrontiers.org/issue/article/three-men-three-eras. See also https://s3.amazonaws.com/files.frontierventures.org/pdf/Four-Men-Three-Eras.pdf.

Afterword

Evan Falk

People on the Margins of Language

God is God of the margins. God's care for the people on the fringes of society echoes throughout the Old and New Testaments. In Genesis 16, when Hagar the slave-turned-concubine runs away from an abusive situation, it is she who encounters God, and names him "the God who sees me" (Gen 16:13). This story of Hagar's meeting with God stands as an indictment not only of the others in the story who treated her so poorly, but of us as well. Yet in our reading of Abram and Sarai's story today, Hagar is often a mere footnote.

Hagar is no footnote to God.

Nor are the marginalized people of this world. As Michel Kenmogne relates in chapter 22, SIL's founder, Cameron Townsend, was strongly motivated by the plight of marginalized language groups like those of his friend Francisco Diaz. SIL has remained committed to working alongside those who are marginalized because of their languages, as we can see represented throughout this book.[1]

On every topic broached in this volume, though, there is much more to be said. We can never exhaust all that there is to say about language and the mission of God, and the last thing we would want is to marginalize people further by suggesting that we have now "seen" their experiences fully. Even more so, we recognize that there are people whose experiences are not described in this book. Here there are both "known unknowns" and "unknown unknowns", and we want to take this opportunity to acknowledge both, insofar as we are able.

---

[1] See in particular chapters 3, 17, 19, and 22, where authors explicitly engage with the issue of marginalization.

SIL has stated unequivocally that people's languages matter because people matter. What we have not always articulated as clearly is that people's *relationships* to language matter. It is often relatively straightforward to identify a group of people who have been pushed to the edges of society because of the language or languages they speak. What is more complex—and likely to fall through the cracks—is recognizing the individuals within a society whose experience of language does not fit our understanding.

"The great tragedy of my life is that I am not fluent in any language." This came from an intelligent young man with a university education and a good job. He had a complex linguistic heritage, with parents of two different language backgrounds, living in a multilingual cultural context. He was, in fact, fluent in the regional form of English, which was his internal language. But this language was seen globally as a "lesser" form of English, and locally as an imported language, lacking the dignity of the region's own heritage languages, even though those heritage languages were barely spoken. How might he have responded to the encouragement, "your language matters"?

This is just one example of someone whose experience of language is not well represented, either in this book or elsewhere. In chapter 20, Maik Gibson writes of another, where he notes a "demonstrable correlation between language shift and what would appear to be continued psychosocial trauma", extending well after Indigenous communities in Canada adopted the language of the settlers. Chapters 3 and 17 both touch on a similar finding among the Breton people of France. Further, what are the implications for language use when a language has been used as a tool of oppression or subjugation? These examples are touched on, but much remains to be explored if we are to better understand how these people's experiences with language can help us see them as God sees them, and inform our missional praxis.

In chapter 6, Stuart Thiessen identifies language deprivation syndrome in the context of deaf children who are not exposed to sign language early enough.[2] For these children, the language centers of the brain do not develop adequately in early life, and despite later exposure, the individual will experience language quite differently than the rest of us. Further exploration of how others' experiences of language differ from our own is needed and would be of great benefit.

Among those with different experiences are also the many who identify as neurodivergent—a description that encompasses many unique ways in which people experience life in ways that are not always understood or embraced by the neurotypical majority. SIL is enriched by the contributions

---

[2] While the vast majority of people with language deprivation syndrome are deaf, it can occur in any case where a person, for whatever reason, is not sufficiently exposed to language at a young age.

of our staff who live in this reality and add to our understanding of the diverse ways in which people experience God's gift of language.

We recognize that many people—whose experiences with language already place them at the margins—may not see their concerns, experiences, and lives represented in these pages. While the conversation within SIL is ongoing in all of the cases noted above, limitations of time and material prevented us from including in-depth explorations in this volume.

As people passionate about both language and mission, SIL's staff are always exploring the ways that these topics intersect with other aspects of life. Among the conversations that were not ready for this volume were explorations of:

- global issues such as ecological action and creation care,
- theological issues such as God's role as judge, or the voice of God in creation,
- ethical issues as they relate to language,
- cognitive issues such as how our lexemes—the meaning-based building blocks that form our linguistic repertoire—shape our experience,
- philosophical issues such as the role of language in thought, conscience, and our conceptualization of God.

Those conversations continue, and new ones take shape regularly as we discover more of the countless ways that language shapes our experiences, our relationships, and our faith.

This volume represents much of SIL's current thought and research on the role of language in the mission of God, but it is not exhaustive, either in expressing the ongoing conversations or the conversations we have yet to start about things we may not yet know that we don't know. The invitation to mission is an invitation to join God in what he is doing. He invites us to open our eyes to see those like Hagar whose experiences push them to the margins. And so we entrust ourselves and our future work to the God who sees, praying he will help us see as he does.

Scripture Index

Old Testament

Genesis (Gen)

1 20, 28, 44, 97, 101, 104, 121, 167, 248, 253
1:1–5 96
1:1–31 176
1:2 20, 101
1:3 19, 20, 22, 101, 102
1:3–5 102
1:6 19, 97
1:9 19, 97
1–11 111
1:11 97
1:14 19
1:14–15 97
1:20 19, 97
1:24 19, 97
1:26 19, 20, 28, 44, 97, 111
1:26–27 110
1:27 98, 167, 176
1:28 19, 44, 110, 112, 116, 168
1:29 19
1:31 75
2 110, 121, 204
2:9 109
2:17 75
2:19 21, 110, 116, 204
3 28, 91, 168
3:8 44, 211
3:8–13 33, 54
3:12 75
3:14 109
3:16–19 75
3:17 109
4 75
4:11 109
6 168
8:17 112
8:21 109
9:1 44, 112, 168
9:7 112
10 111, 112, 114, 115, 121, 124, 132, 168, 204
10:1 121
10:5 111, 114, 121, 168
10:8–11 108
10:8–12 114
10:20 111, 114, 122, 168
10:31 111, 114, 122, 168
11 109, 110, 112, 114, 121, 132, 139, 170

Genesis (Gen), continued

11:1 114, 169
11:1–9 107, 108, 109, 111, 112, 114, 115
11:2 115
11:3 114
11:4 108, 112, 114
11:7 111, 169
11:8 112
11:9 112, 132
12 132, 168
13:16 140
13–20 132
14 132
14:13 234
14:19–20 34
14:19–22 256
15:1 60
15:5 140
16 132, 273
16:13 273
17 168
17:4–5 168
17:4–6 141
17:16 141
18 92
20 132
21:22 34
21:22–23 34
23 132
24 133
24:35 34
26 133
26:18–29 34
26:22 34
30:27 34
30:30 34
31 133
31:47 132, 133, 235
32:12 141
34 133
38 133
42:23 133, 234

Exodus (Exod)

1 114
1:10 114
1:14 114
3:1–6 54
4 76
4:11 71, 75
16:10 42
19:4 45
19:4–6 45
19:17–20 42
22:21 xx
23:28 112
25:22 42n
26 41
29:42–43 42
29:45–46 42
33:11 44
33:16 46
34:6 14
36 42
40 42
40:34–38 42

Leviticus (Lev)

9:23–24 42
19:14 72
19:33–34 xx
23:40, 43 141
26:4–13 45

Numbers (Num)

9:15–22 42
13–14 78

Deuteronomy (Deut)

5:24 44
6:4 55
6:20–21 55
24:17–22 xx

Joshua (Josh)

2 133

Scripture Index

Judges (Judg)

12   134

12:5–6   134, 138

12:6   236

1 Samuel (1 Sam)

12:22   44

14:37   92

1 Kings

5:18   133

8:10–13   42

10   133

2 Kings

18   134, 234, 236

18:26   133, 236

2 Chronicles

32   134

Ezra

4   134
4:7   134, 237
4:11–16   237

4:18   134
6:18   134
7   134

7:12–26   134
7:27   134

Nehemiah (Neh)

1:1–4   230
8:8   134, 157, 237

8:15   141

13:23–24   136, 237

Job

3:9   103n

33:14–18   59

Psalm (Ps)

2:8   168
11:7   193
19:1   19, 44
19:1–2   44
22:27   14
22:30–31   14
27:1   103n
33:3   254
33:6   20
44:3   103n
78:14   103n
79:9   43

85:9   43
89:14   193
90:8   103n
97:2   193
103:6   193
106:8   44
119   57
119:1   7
119:11   11
119:18   25
119:32   41
119:33   53

119:48   65
119:52   81
119:58   95
119:72   107
119:74   121
119:88   131
119:92   145
119:101   155
119:105   167
119:114   175
119:124   181
119:135   195

Psalm (Ps), continued

119:144 211	119:164 245	139:11 103n
119:147 221	119:169 259	140:12 193
119:156 233	139 75, 76	

Proverbs (Prov)

1:8 55   3:19 20

Isaiah (Isa)

1:2 54	29:18 72	52:7 150
1:11 178	35:5 72	55:8–9 21
6:3 13	41:8–10 44	55:12 44
7:7 98	43:25 44	59:21 44
11:9 13, 103	48:11 44	66:18 254

Jeremiah (Jer)

1:8 98   29:7 240   33:3 92

Ezekiel

36 44   37:27–28 45

Daniel (Dan)

2:4 135   4:1 135   7:13–14 135–136

Micah (Mic)

4:4 15

Habakkuk (Hab)

2:14 13, 22, 43, 44, 103, 150   2:18–20 19   3:17–18 13

Zechariah (Zech)

3:10 15

New Testament

Matthew (Matt)

1:18–25 92	5:17 74	9:35–38 34
3:17 91	5:28–29 74	9:36 34
5–7 147	6:10 9	11:2–6 73

Matthew (Matt), continued

11:5 73
13:23 172
23:24 148
24:14 204

26:69 138
26:71 138
26:73 138
28:18 188

28:18–20 82
28:19–20 269

Mark

1:15 145
1:21 151
1:25 98
1:41 98, 99
2:5, 11 98
2:11 99
3:5 98
3:17 151
4:39 98
5 104

5:41 98, 148, 159
7 56, 99
7:31–37 73
7:34 98, 148
9:14–29 74
9:43 151
10:46 151
10:46–52 149
12:29–31 269
14:1 151

14:13 149
14:32–65 148
14:36 98, 148, 151
14:51–52 149
15:7 151
15:21 149
15:34 98, 148, 151, 160
16:15 48

Luke

1:26–38 92
2 172
2:41–50 146
4:16–30 147

4:18 211
4:22 146
6:20–21 217
6:20–49 147

7:14 99
7:18–23 73
7:22 73
12:18–19 15

John

1 137, 175
1:1 xxi, 19, 46, 176
1:1–2 176
1:3 176
1:4 47
1:9–12 47
1:11 48
1:14 42, 47, 48, 177
1:38 137
1:41 137
1:42 137
3:16 22
5:39–40 178

7 147
7:35 148
8:6–8 53
9:1–3 75
10:10 15, 22, 35
10:27 54
11:43 99
12:28 43
14:16 46
15:17 269
15:26 178
16:14 43
17 161

17:1 43
17:1–2 188
17:2–3 15
17:4–5 43
18:33–38 148
19:8–11 148
20:16 137
20:21 163, 176
20:22 42
20:24 137
21:1 137

Acts

1:5 42	2:7–8 9	17:16–34 19
1:8 42, 170	2:8 138, 142, 238	17:24 111
2 28, 33, 138, 139, 155n, 160, 170, 172, 238, 246, 247	2:9 139	17:26 111
	2:10 139	17:26–27 8
	2:11 138, 139, 247	21:27–31 140
	2:12 139	21:37 139
2:4 138, 139, 170	2:36 189	21:37–22:29 139
2:4–8 xx	6 239	21:40–22:2 140
2:6 138, 139	6:1 162	22 234, 239
2:7 138	11:20 239	

Romans (Rom)

1:20 19	5:21 16	9:15–23 75
1:23 126	6:23 16	10:17 70
5:12–19 75	8:11 16	

1 Corinthians (1 Cor)

6:19 42	13:1 177	13:12 150

2 Corinthians (2 Cor)

4 103, 104	4:7–10 103	12:7–10 75
4:1 104	4:14 104	12:9 49, 76
4:4 103	4:16 104	
4:6 101–103, 150	5:19 87	

Ephesians (Eph)

2:14 161	4:3 161	5:21–6:9 162

Philippians (Phil)

2 162	2:9, 11 43	4:13 49
2:4 255		

Colossians (Col)

1:19 47	1:20 21, 36

1 Thessalonians (1 Thess)

1:1 189

1 Timothy (1 Tim)

2:5–6 189
3:16 91

Hebrews (Heb)

1:1 19
1:1–3 1
1:2 47
9:1–11 42
13:5 42

1 John

1:1 xxi
4:16 14

Revelation (Rev)

1:1 140
5:9 8, 267
6:11 140
7:1–17 140
7:9 xx, 34, 116, 140, 141, 142, 170, 179, 247, 254, 256
7:9–10 xviii, 7, 267
7:9–12 246, 247
7:9–17 140
7:13–14 140, 141
7:14 247
7:15–16 140
7:15–17 140
19 248
21:3 42, 46
21:4 33
21:26 109, 116
22 109
22:2 109
22:3 109

Authors Cited

Ager, Dennis Ernest 224
Ahaligah, Kwame Aidan 128
Aldridge, Fredrick A. 183
Alexander, T. D. 56, 146, 157
Alim, H. Samy 199
Allison, Dale C., Jr. 138
Altbach, Philip G. 197
Altmann, Gerry T. M. 108
Ambrus, Gárbon 49
Ameka, Felix 268
Anderson, Bernhard W. 113n, 116
Anderson, Stephen R. 28
Anderson, William B. 256
Andiñach, Pablo R. 116n4
Aram I. 205
Aristotle 69–70
Arthur, Eddie xi, 155, 161
Arutz Sheva 108
Aune, David. E. 140
Austin, John 95, 100

Babalola, E. O. 171
Baker, Colin 224
Ball, Jessica 215
Banks, Robert 189
Barram, Michael D. 196
Barr, James 100, 146, 148
Barry, William A. 14–15, 41
Barth, Karl 177
Bauckham, Richard 149
Beale, G. K. 44–45
Beckner, W. Benjamin 122
Bediako, Kwam 128
Benner, Jeff A. 132
Benson, Carol 196n, 226
Berardinelli, Paula 229
Beti, Mongo 32
Bickerton, Derek 28
Bierma, Nathan L. K. 245, 250, 253
Birkeland, Harris 100
Blanchard, Yves-Marie 138
Blough, Neal 204

Boersma, Hans 125, 248
Bosch, David J. 12, 82–84, 161, 171, 204
Bruce, F. F. 139
Brueggemann, Walter 228
Bucholtz, Mary 199
Burke, Fintan 199
Burrow, Jim 229
Bushe, Gervase R. 212
Buth, Randall 99, 100, 147, 151
Butler, Phill 229

Carey, William 82
Carson, D. A. 20, 133
Carvill, Barbara 114
Chambers, Robert 212
Chandler, Michael J. 215
Chenoweth, Ben 149
Chester, Timothy 225
Chomsky, Noam 18, 260
Chou, Grace 245–246, 247, 249, 257
Christian, Jayakumar 228
Chua, How Chuang 14–15
Church, Jeffrey 200
Churchman, C. West 77
Clark, Robert P. 199
Cleaver, Bronwen xi, 53, 57, 61–62
Cleve, Van 74
Clines, D. J. A. 167
Coleson, Joseph 113
Collier, Virginia 31n
Collins, Francis S. 110
Coutand-Marin, Sophie 205
Cowan, George M. 122
Croasmun, Matthew 193
Croatto 116n4
Crosland, Matthew 17
Crossan, John Dominic 147
Crouch, Andy 110
Crouch, Barry 74
Crystal, David 16, 226
Dahlquist, Anna Marie 260

Daila Baba, Eliazar 56
Davies, W. D. 138
De Cuéllar, Javier Pérez 30
Delgado Gómez, Alfredo 99, 149
Denison, Norman 215
De Swaan, Abram 197, 198, 200
De Villiers, Pieter G. R. 157
De Witt, Dale S. 115
Dillon, Anna 170
Doll, Margaret 205
Dorren, Gaston 108
Downie, Jonathan 254–255
Duncan, Malcolm 193, 212–215

Eberhard, David 202, 211, 242
Edwards, John 141
Ehrensperger, Kathy 156, 159
Eyezo'o, Salvador 31
Eyre, Roy 31
Ezigbo, Victor I. 184

Falk, Evan xii, 3, 6, 273
Fasold, Ralph 237
Ferguson, Gibson 223–224
Fernandez, Miguel Pérez 132
Ferrari, Auréllia 240
Flett, John G. 83
Footitt, Hilary 226
Fox, Margalit 111
Frank, Paul xii, 5, 131–135, 141
Fretheim, Terence E. 113

Gallagher, Sarita D. 34
Gazzola, Michele 198
Gerner, Matthias 122
Gesenius, Wilhelm 13n
Gibson, Maik xii, 137, 233, 240, 274
Givón, Talmy 123
Glaser, Ida 45, 46
Gnanakan, Ken 82, 83

Authors Cited

Goheen, Michael 12, 45, 46
Gordon, Cyrus H. 115
Gorman, Michael J. 15, 195
Gousmett, Chris 115
Greed, Michael 170, 204
Greed, Teija 100
Greeley, Andrew M. 110, 116
Green, Joel B. 113n3, 116n
Grenoble, Lenore A. 216
Grieb, A. Katherine 195, 204
Grin, François 198
Guder, Darrell L. 83
Guilbert, Kieran 199

Hahn, Roger L. 12
Hallett, Darcy 215, 241
Hall, Matthew L. 67–68n4
Hall, Wyatte C. 67–68n4
Halpern, Gilad 108
Hamilton, Victor P. 115
Hanawalt, Charlie 242
Harmelink, Bryan 168, 184, 214, 265n
Harris, Roy 111
Haugen, Einar 116, 223–224
Hawthorne, Stephen C. 34
Hayashi, Larry S. 117, 203
Hefley, James 203
Hefley, Marti 203
Hiebert, Paul 35
Hiebert, Theodore 108–109, 113n, 114
Hill, Philip D. 109
Hornberger, Nancy H. 224, 226

IBT *See* Institute for Bible Translation
Idowu, E. Bolaji 185
Ingersoll, Clayton 112
Institute for Bible Translation (IBT) 152
Ireland, Jerry M. 185

Jeffrey, David L. 122, 128
Jiang, Wenying 17
Jobes, Karen H. 136
Johnson, David Cassels 226
Johnson, Todd M. 226
Joseph, John E. 202, 203
Jowett, Benjamin 69

Kabasélé, François 186, 187n3
Kaemingk, Matthew 248
Kane, Cheikh Hamidou 32
Karan, Mark E. 240
Kass, Leon R. 113n, 117
Kendrick. Graham 104
Kenmogne, Michel xii, xviii, 5, 25, 26n, 50, 250, 259, 273
Kerr, Glen J. 123n2
Kikama, Kividi xii, xiii, 181, 184–185, 189, 190–191
Kim, Daewoong 116n3
Kim, Mitchell 44–45
Kimbi, Paul xiii, 167
King, Ian 200
Klingler, Al 116n3
Knoors, Harry 67n2
Kosonen, Kimmo 196n, 201
Köstenberger, Andreas J. 45
Kreider, Alan 82
Kreider, Eleanor 82
Kroneman, Dick 62, 181–182
Kwon, Sung Chan xiii, 48, 175
Kyoungah White, Sara 85

Ladefoged, Peter 201–202
Laing, Mark T. B. 83–84
Lalonde, Christopher 215
Lausanne Movement 85, 117, 222, 227, 269
Leveen, Steve 116
Levinson, Stephen C. 123n1
Lewis, C. S. 127

Lewis, M. Paul 19, 214, 237n3, 241, 242
Longacre, Robert E. 28, 36, 262

Macfarlane, Roger T. 137–138
Makanzu, Mavulimusa Jean-Perce 188
Malembé, Paul 187n3
Mangano, Mark J. 45
Marlowe, W. Creighton 115, 116n3
Marmor, Thomas W. 212
Marschark, Marc 67n2
Martin-Achard, Robert 46
Martin, Ryan 59
McComiskey, Thomas E. 13n
McElhanon, Kenneth A. 124
McGrath, Alister E. 124
McIvor, Onowa 215
McWhorter, John 108, 111, 201
Miguez-Bonino, José 116n4
Milambiling, Joyce 200
Moore, T. C. 44
Morales, Erwin T. 140
Moreau, A. Scott 35
Morris, Leon 138
Mott, John 82
Mott, Stephen 198
Mounce, Robert. H. 141
Mukuka, Tarcisius 82
Myers, Bryant L. 212, 225

Nahir, Moshe 223
Neill, Stephen 84
Newbigin, Lesslie 83–84
Ngindu Mushete, Alphonse 185, 188
Nida, Eugene A. 123n2
Niebuhr, Ursala M. 43
Niemandt, Nelus 12
Nikolakopolous, Konstantine 159
Noll, Mark 184
Noonan, Benjamin J. 18–19

Nordquist, Richard 96
Notley, R. Steven 147
Nouwen, Henri 212, 217

O'Brien, Peter T. 45
Ommani Luchivia, John 245–246, 249, 252, 254, 255, 256
O'Neill, Daniel 225, 227–228
Ong, Hughson T. 147, 148, 156n, 157, 159

Padilla, C. René 37
Pasquale, Michael 245, 250, 253
Patterson, Paige 140
Paul, Ian 140
Paulston, Christina Bratt 200
Pennycook, Alastair 205
Peterson, Eugene H. 204
Pike, Kenneth L. 262
Pinker, Steven 123n1
Pittman, Richard S. 214
Plaut, W. Gunther 113
Pohl, Christine D. 248
Poirier, John C. 140, 146, 147
Pool, Jonathan 198
Porter, Stanley E. 147, 148n1
Prill, Thorsten 169, 170
Pym, Anthony 124

Quakenbush, J. Stephen xiv, 245, 246, 248, 250–251, 255, 257

Raharimanantsoa, Mamy 131, 137–141, 246
Razafinjatoniary, Olivia xiv, 91
Reddy, Michael J. 123, 125
Reimer, Johannes 229
Reynolds, Chase 62
Ricoeur, Paul 248, 249

Authors Cited

Rittel, Horst W. J. 77n
Robins, Robert Henry 16
Robinson, Stuart 60
Roche, Gerald 214, 240
Romaine, Suzanne 201
Ron, Zvi 113
Rosenblit, Moran 43
Ruíz, Richard 199, 200, 201, 205
Rydbeck, Lars 157

Sacks, Oliver 69, 70
Sama, Abou xiv, 3, 5, 53
Samuel, Vinay 212
Sanders, Chip xiv, xxv, 1, 2, 3, 88
Sanneh, Lamin 122, 128, 149, 150, 152, 158, 177, 178, 179, 183, 184, 190, 261, 262, 263
Sarna, Nahum M. 113
Scheppers, Emmanuel 198
Schirrmacher, Thomas 12, 15, 84
Schmidt, Ronald 117
Schor, Esther 108
Schreiter, Robert J. 185–186
Seager, Greg 228
Shank Lauwo, Monica 202
Sherman, Phillip Michael 114
Sider, Ronald J. 198
Silva, Moisés 136n
Simons, Gary 170, 214, 217, 237n3, 242, 246
Skandar, Nabila 31
Slageren, Jaap van 171
Slobin, Dan I. 123n1
Smith, David I. 113n, 114, 115
Smith, Edwin 261
Smith, Phil 228
Smuts, Jan Christiaan 202
Spolsky, Bernard 158
Stanley, Brian 256
Steiner, George 126, 202
Steven, Hugh 260–261
Stott, John 85
Strong, John T. 111

Stroope, Michael W. 83
Svelmoe, William Lawrence 214
Swarr, David 55, 57
Swartley, Willard M. 195

Takei, Wataru 68
Taylor-Leech, Kerry 225, 226
Tennent, Timothy C 161
Théry, David 54
Thiessen, Stuart xv, 2, 5, 65, 274
Thomas, Wayne P. 31n
Tiénou, Tite 184
Tinker, George E. 82
Titre Ande, Georges 12
Tizon, Al 82
Tofibam, Alfred Fuka 170
Tollefson, Kenneth D. 237n4
Torigoe, Takashi 68
Townsend, William Cameron 183, 203, 214, 260–261, 273
Tresham, Aaron 137, 138
Truth and Reconciliation Commission of Canada 82, 199
Tshibangu Tshishiku, Tharcisse 187

Uehlinger, Christoph 115
Ulfgard, Håkan 141
UNESCO 30, 200
UNICEF 229n3

Van Parijs, Philippe 200–202, 204
Veditz, George 76
Vella, Jane 229
Venter, Pieter M. 237n4
Véronique, Georges Daniel 169
Volf, Miroslav 20n, 193
Von Rad, Gerhard 109

Wallace, Lane 31, 202
Walls, Andrew 191
Walter, Stephen L. 31n
Ware, Bruce A. 167
Watters, David E. 126, 128
Watters, John R. 29–30, 86, 87, 267
Watters, Stephen (Steve) xv, 117, 121
Watters, Zachary J. 117, 121
Wenham, Gordon John 109
Whiston, William 112, 114
Whitecloud, Simone S. 216
Wiles, Jerry 58
Williams, Peter J. 148n1
Williamson, H. G. M. 237n4
Winter, Ralph D. 260
Wisbey, Matthew 228
Witherington, Ben III. 139

Woll, Bencie 68
Wolterstorff, Nicholas 195
Wright, Christopher J. H. 12–14, 44–46, 84, 109, 168, 226, 229, 256
Wright, N. T. 99
Wright, Paul. H 138
WSJ [Wall Street Journal] 108
Wycliffe Global Alliance 85–86, 122, 183

Yeh, Allen 86–87
Yoder, John H. 204
Young, Catherine M. B. 50, 222n
Yule, George 17

Zurlo, Gina A. 226

SIL Publications
Publications in Scripture Engagement Series
ISSN 2994-7286

2. **Language in the Mission of God,** edited by Michael Greed. 2025, 290 pp., ISBN 978-1-55671-580-8 (pbk), ISBN 978-1-55671-581-5 (ePub).
1. **Translating the Bible into Media,** by Andreas Ernst. 2023, 94 pp., ISBN 978-1-55671-546-4 (pbk), ISBN 978-1-55671-547-1 (ePub).

SIL Global Publishing Services
7500 W Camp Wisdom Road
Dallas, TX 75236-5629 USA
publications@sil.org

www.ingramcontent.com/pod-product-compliance
Lightning Source LLC
Chambersburg PA
CBHW050621300426
44112CB00012B/1596